Beyond the Keynesian Endpoint:

Crushed by Credit and Deceived by Debt—
How to Revive the Global Economy

Tony Crescenzi

Vice President, Publisher: Tim Moore
Associate Publisher and Director of Marketing: Amy Neidlinger
Acquisitions Editor: Jeanne Glasser
Editorial Assistant: Pamela Boland
Senior Marketing Manager: Julie Phifer
Assistant Marketing Manager: Megan Graue
Cover Designer: Chuti Prasertsith
Managing Editor: Kristy Hart
Senior Project Editor: Lori Lyons
Copy Editor: Language Logistics, LLC
Proofreader: Apostrophe Editing Services
Indexer: Lisa Stumpf
Senior Compositor: Gloria Schurick
Manufacturing Buyer: Dan Uhrig

Pearson Education, Inc.
Publishing as FT Press
Upper Saddle River, New Jersey 07458

FT Press offers excellent discounts on this book when ordered in quantity for bulk purchases or special sales. For more information, please contact U.S. Corporate and Government Sales, 1-800-382-3419, corpsales@pearsontechgroup.com. For sales outside the U.S., please contact International Sales at

international@pearson.com.

First Printing October 2011

Pearson Education LTD.
Pearson Education Australia PTY, Limited.
Pearson Education Singapore, Pte. Ltd.
Pearson Education Asia, Ltd.
Pearson Education Canada, Ltd.
Pearson Educatión de Mexico, S.A. de C.V.
Pearson Education—Japan
Pearson Education Malaysia, Pte. Ltd.

ISBN-10: 0-13-259521-4
ISBN-13: 978-0-13-259521-6

To my enchanting daughters, Brittany, Victoria, and Isabella.
Each of you adds immeasurable joy and happiness to my life.
I love each of you so much and dedicate my life to you.

To my brother and sisters and to my nurturing parents,
Anita and Joseph, for their unconditional love and for the freedoms
I was given in youth to explore, to dream, and to have fun—lots of it!

To Jeffrey Tabak and Jeffrey Miller for their friendship and for giving
me the freedom to probe all boundaries of the financial markets,
the economy, and the investment world.

To Bill Gross and Mohamed El-Erian, for whom I have deep respect,
for the opportunity of a lifetime to work for them and contribute to
PIMCO, an organization I am honored to be a part of.

To friends we gain in the many stages of our lives,
for the great comfort, joy, and enduring memories they give us.
Thank you to my old and new friends,
Jackie Rubino, Neil Visoki, Tommy Scott, Jeanine Ognibene,
John Barone, Diana Mangano, John Vito Pietanza,
Ray and Debbie Candido, Dave Bochicchio, Phil Neugebauer,
Mark Shorr, and Mark Porterfield.

To all who, in one way or another, are survivors, and who, despite the
many obstacles and challenges they face in their daily lives,
each day find the inner strength to endure and indeed to excel.

Table of Contents

About the Author

Tony Crescenzi is an Executive Vice President, Market Strategist, and Portfolio Manager at PIMCO in its Newport Beach office. Prior to joining PIMCO in 2009, he was Chief Bond Market Strategist at Miller Tabak, where he worked for 23 years. Mr. Crescenzi has written four other books, including a 1,200-page revision to Marcia Stigum's classic, *The Money Market*, in 2007. He regularly appears on CNBC and Bloomberg television and in financial news media.

Mr. Crescenzi taught in the executive MBA program at Baruch College from 1999-2009. He has 28 years of investment experience and holds an MBA from St. John's University and an undergraduate degree from the City University of New York.

Introduction

Reaching the Keynesian Endpoint

After the fall of Lehman Brothers in September 2008, the scope of the financial crisis became so great that the fiscal and monetary authorities of the developed world possessed the only balance sheets large enough to resolve the crisis and thereby restore stability to the world's financial markets and the global economy. In essence, the ills of the private sector were set to shift to the public sector. The sense at the time was that it would work; after all, the borrowing abilities of the United States and the rest of the developed world were proven, and the ability of central banks to print money was and remains indisputable. Moreover, Keynesian economics had "succeeded" at restoring stability to ailing economies before through the elixir of government borrowing and spending ever since John Maynard Keynes pioneered the concept during the Great Depression. Nevertheless, there was a sense of discomfort in the supposed solution.

After Lehman fell, I posed a question, calling it the question of our age: If the Unites States is backing its financial system, who is backing the United States? The basic premise rested on the idea that efforts to stabilize economies and markets were likely to work if investors tolerated the additional debt the efforts required. If not, there would be financial Armageddon. The direst outcome was of course avoided, but dark days have smitten many nations, including Portugal, Ireland, and Greece, and the gloom is threatening to spread to the world at large, where sovereign debt threatens financial calamity for nations whose actions over many decades have left them teetering on the edge of a cliff, clinging by their nails, pulling ever-downward toward an unforgiving and impervious landing below. The grim fate of the indebted, once viewed as unfathomable, is increasingly seen as possible because the magic elixir of Keynesian economics has morphed into poison.

Nations have reached, in other words, the Keynesian Endpoint, where there are no private sector or public sector balance sheets left to fuel economic activity and rescue the world's financial system. This is not literally true but true in practice because investors at the present time have no tolerance for fiscal profligacy or any form of government borrowing geared toward reviving weakness in private sector demand, especially if the lapses in demand are the result of the private sector's effort to reduce its own indebtedness. There is also little appetite for the monetization of deficits by the world's central banks.

Nations are left with old playbooks and few choices to revive the global economy and stabilize the world's financial system. This means that time, devaluations, and debt restructurings will be the only way out for many nations. It also means the citizenry will need politicians who think outside of the box and act with greater determination and resolve than ever before. This is a time for leadership to emerge in local towns, cities, and states, and in the capitols of nations throughout the world. Today's political leaders are behooved to solve their nations' problems by being realistic about them. Most importantly, they must put ideology aside and subordinate their self-interests to those of the people they serve, something they are not accustomed to. There can be no more fiscal illusions, consumption binges, or Ponzi schemes. The Keynesian Endpoint has revealed what lies behind the curtain of those who say that the answer to every economic ill is debt. The transformation of a century is upon us, and the folly of many decades is over.

Not Enough Jam to Fit the Size of the Pill

In his classic book *The General Theory of Employment*, John Maynard Keynes theorizes that the marginal propensity to consume, which measures the proportion of increased spending that is expected to result from each unit of change in income, is far closer to 100 percent than it is to zero. Keynes believed that with people more likely to spend new income rather than save it, the multiplier effect resulting from government spending will be large enough to justify spending initiatives geared toward reviving lapses in aggregate demand. In other words, government spending is justified if it boosts national income by an amount greater than the amount of the spending and if it increases the total level of employment.

In the excerpt from *The General Theory* that follows, Keynes describes this dynamic, providing a qualification that can be applied to the current situation, chiefly the possibility that the employment gains will be smaller if the "community" holds back its spending, as is presently occurring in the United States, where the savings rate is on the rise. Keynes recognizes that there are times such as today when the psychology of spending will foil efforts to revive consumption no matter how far the fiscal authority puts its pedal to the metal:

> It follows, therefore, that, if the consumption psychology of the community is such that they will choose to consume, e.g. nine-tenths of an increment of income, then the multiplier k is 10; and the total employment caused by (e.g.) increased public works will be ten times the primary employment provided by the public works themselves, assuming no reduction of investment in other directions. Only in the event of the community maintaining their consumption unchanged in spite of the increase in employment and hence in real income, will the increase of employment be restricted to the primary employment provided by the public works.[1]

The impact that the current deleveraging process might have on the marginal propensity to consume begs the question: Can the world's fiscal authorities, having reached a point where the private sector's want, need, and in many cases only choice is to reduce debt and hence the desire to consume, rationally expect that by ever-increasing the amount of public borrowing they can increase the total amount of employment in any manner that even remotely resembles the way they were able to in the past? Is it possible to boost aggregate demand when both the ability and the impulse to spend have become relics of an era now past? Suppose as policymakers might, this scenario seems implausible. Although the desire to consume to impress, to fulfill primal needs, and to display power is everlasting, the psychology of spending has been altered and won't return with the same verve for at least a generation. The psychological desire is gone, as are the social cues and the money—there is no balance sheet to finance consumption willy-nilly any more.

Today's policymakers must recognize that when Keynes speaks to the idea of a multiplier, he does so with a very important qualification that unequivocally applies today and in any other period of deleveraging. Specifically, although Keynes surmises that the marginal propensity to consume is close to 100 percent, there are exceptions:

> If saving is the pill and consumption is the jam, the extra jam has to be proportioned to the size of the additional pill. Unless the psychological propensities of the public are different from what we are supposing, we have here established the law that increased employment for investment must necessarily stimulate the industries producing for consumption and thus lead to a total increase of employment which is a multiple of the primary employment required by the investment itself.[2]

Today's Keynesians are failing to realize this notion, that the psychological propensities of the public are indeed dramatically changed. Keynesians continue to believe that government spending will ignite aggregate spending and employment. This is a very difficult view to reconcile against the post-crisis experience. Is it not apparent in Figure I-1 that consumers either can't or won't borrow to consume like they used to?

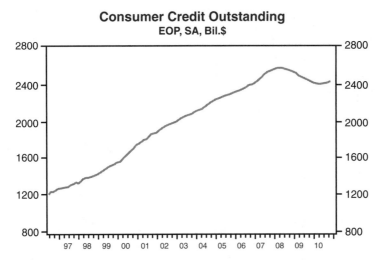

Figure I-1 In the past, consumers borrowed through thick or thin. Not this time.

Source: Federal Reserve Board/Haver Analytics

The bottom line is that nations must recognize that the economic agents upon which they rely to boost consumption and eventually employment are impaired and are now on a path of deleveraging that will limit the effectiveness of new fiscal stimulus. The decrease in the marginal propensity to consume, which is evidenced in the extraordinary decline in consumer credit, as well as the rising U.S. savings rate shown in Figure I-2, weaken the multiplier effect. It is extraordinarily unreasonable to assume that fiscal stimulus in an age of deleveraging will boost private spending in the same fashion as it has in the past, especially with debt now associated with pain rather than pleasure—a major psychological barrier to reviving the growth rates in aggregate spending to pre-crisis levels. Consumers simply do not have the stomach to engage in an activity that resulted in their getting kicked out of their homes and losing their jobs. This is in addition to the idea that there are no more balance sheets to fund the stimulus.

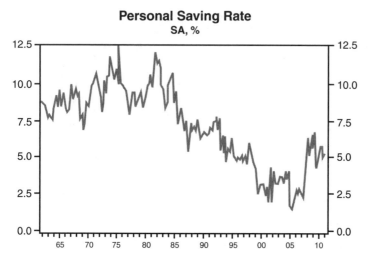

Personal Saving Rate
SA, %

Figure I-2 Following a 30-year spending binge, it's back to basics and saving for a rainy day.

Source: Bureau of Economic Analysis/Haver Analytics

The harsh realities of the Keynesian Endpoint put academicians, politicians, and opinion writers in a cloister, where others who recognize the existence of the Endpoint will engulf their collective voice and influence. Intransigent Keynesians will be significantly outnumbered by the masses of people having the good sense to know that to avoid the societal harm that can come from excessive indebtedness, they must choose fiscal austerity and other remedies over further indebtedness. Sometimes the masses will stand in the way of structural changes needed to repair a damaged society. Greece exemplifies this more complicated and challenging condition. When in cases such as this the masses stand in the way of change, politicians must in the face of enormous pressure be bold and take the lead and act against the will of the people like a sick child who resists taking his medicine.

The Keynesian Endpoint has been reached because investors have decided sovereign debts are too large relative to the balance sheets available to support them, posing risk of eventual sovereign debt defaults. In today's era of deleveraging, investors are intolerant of fiscal profligacy and will choose to invest in nations with improving balance sheets over those that are worsening or are mired in a protracted steady state where debt hamstrings economic activity. Having tapped the last balance sheet, nations at the Endpoint will place burdens on many, including their citizens, trading partners, savers, and bond holders. They will do so by inflicting their pain over time, taking as long as is necessary to liquidate their debts. In so doing they will be spared the worst of the sovereign debt dilemma and avoid technical default, but they will experience sub-par economic growth over the longer term, resulting in low inflation, low policy rates, steep yield curves, low investment returns, and a weakening domestic currency.

The lack of cohesion and policy coordination among troubled nations will result in a sharp divergence between winners and losers. It is notable, for example, that whenever stress levels have reached a fever pitch—as judged by periods of weakening equity markets, widening credit spreads, and more volatile foreign exchange rates—capital flows into traditional safe havens has increased, including into the United States, Germany, and Switzerland in particular.

Some nations will find the Holy Grail and look beyond Keynesianism and find new means of stimulating economic growth. Others will be intransigent, clinging to their Keynesian ways and in the process fail to take measures that restore fiscal stability. These nations will be forced to devalue their currencies, restructure their debts, or eventually adopt more severe austerity measures that lead to a muddle-through economic growth path that perpetuates stagnation for the sake of liquidating debt, all of which put at risk a nation's productivity, the essential element that defines a nation's standard of living and the quality of life of its citizens.

1

Beware the Keynesian Mirage

Those who refer to historical examples where fiscal stimulus worked and where despite increased indebtedness there was no corresponding increase in market interest rates do so with contempt toward the financial crisis and its profound message about overleveraged societies and the extended period by which the deleveraging process tends to last and leave destruction in its wake. Reinhart and Rogoff,[1] for example, suggest that the deleveraging process that follows a financial crisis tends to last about ten years. McKinsey & Company find similar results, as shown in the summary in Table 1-1:[2]

TABLE 1-1 Duration and Extent of Deleveraging Following a Financial Crisis

Archetype	Number of Episodes	Duration[1] (Year)s	Extent of Deleveraging (Debt/GDP Change)		Debt CAGR[4] (Trend vs. Episode[3)]
			%	pp	
"Belt-tightening"	16	6–7	-29	-40	21 vs. 2
	Median	*5*	*-24*	*-34*	*21 vs. 3*
"High inflation"	8	7	-53	-93	50 vs. 46
	Median	*8*	*-62*	*-34*	*36 vs. 27*
"Massive default"	7	6	-36	-46	41 vs. 10
	Median	*8*	*-55*	*-72*	*28 vs. 9*
"Growing out of debt"	1	6	-25	-44	0 vs. 12
Total²	**32**	**6–7**	**-37**	**-54pp**	**32 vs. 14**

[1]Duration is defined as the period during which debt/GDP levels decrease.

[2]Two outliers have been removed from the averages: Turkey '87-'03, Poland '87-'95.

[3]Historic trend defined as the 10 years or longest time series available before the start of the deleveraging episode.

[4]Compound annual growth rate

Note: Averages remain similar when including episodes of deleveraging not induced by financial crisis.

Source: IMF, McKinsey Global Institute

The source of this contempt almost certainly is rooted in the behavior of the interest rate markets amid the buildup of government debt over the past three decades and especially in the aftermath of the financial crisis, which has been marked by a plunge in market interest rates despite a massive increase in sovereign debt outstanding relative to the increase in economic activity in sovereign nations. In other words, although debt-to-GDP ratios for nations in the developed world have increased, there has been no corresponding increase in market interest rates. In fact, market interest rates have fallen for 30 years, as shown in Figure 1-1.

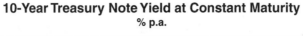

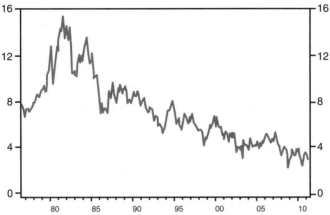

Figure 1-1 The "Duration Tailwind"

Consider Figure 1-2, which reflects the deterioration in the U.S. fiscal situation, as illustrated by a sharp increase in its debt-to-GDP ratios.

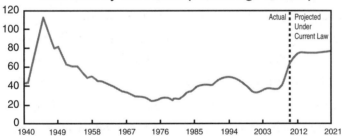

Figure 1-2 Sovereign debts are becoming mountainous.

Source: Congressional Budget Office; http://cbo.gov/ftpdocs/120xx/doc12039/01-26_ FY2011Outlook.pdf

When looking at Figure 1-2, it is important to keep in mind that in addition to the historical perspective, there is widespread expectation for further deterioration in the years to come, owing in no small part to expected increases in entitlement spending, such as health care and retirement benefits, particularly in developed nations (see Figure 1-3). This is especially true in the United States where in 2011 the so-called Baby Boomers (those born in the years 1946 through 1964) began turning 65.[3] I discuss the very important implications of this and the powerful concept known as gerontocracy in Chapter 6, "Age Warfare: Gerontocracy." Investors are familiar with the implications and as such their expectation for further deterioration in public sector balance sheets will be a major driver of cash flows for many years to come, which is to say that many investment decisions will be made on the belief that the developed world will be saddled by debt and be a relatively risky place to invest.

Figure 1-4 shows more closely the behavior of interest rates over the past decade in the United States, the United Kingdom, France, and Germany, as reflected by the ten-year yield for government securities in each of the respective countries.

Keynesians would say that the combined message from these charts is that they illustrate the very small extent to which bond investors worry about the buildup of sovereign debt and the deterioration of public sector balance sheets. After all, Keynesians will tell you, interest rates on sovereign debt decreased substantially during a period when public sector balance sheets deteriorated substantially. Keynesians also stress that this is how it has been for decades, with interest rates tending to fall during periods when public deficits increased.

Keynesians in fact believe that recessions are a good time to increase government borrowing. They seize upon the idea that during periods of economic weakness it is much easier for the public sector to issue debt and to do so at interest rates lower than those that prevailed prior to the weakness because during such times private demands for credit tend to be weak, resulting in a redirection of investment flows toward government debt. This has certainly been true historically: During periods of economic weakness, the creation of bank loans, the origination of mortgage credit, and issuance of company bonds slows or declines, and during such times money flows to government bonds because it's the only game in town—money must find a home.

Under Pressure

Public health care spending is projected to rise by 3 percent of GDP in advanced economies, and by 1 percent of GDP in emerging economies, with regional variations.

Advanced Economies

(change in public health spending, percent of GDP, 2011-30)

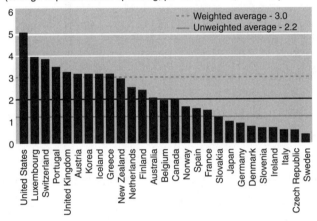

Emerging Economies

(change in public health spending, percent of GDP, 2011-30)

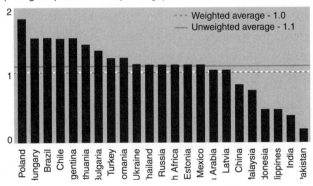

Figure 1-3 Projected global health care spending—the U.S. tops them all.

Source: http://www.imf.org/external/pubs/ft/fandd/2011/03/Clements.htm

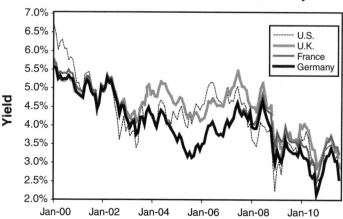

Figure 1-4   Don't be fooled by these falling rates.

Another source of contempt relates to the way investors are using the credit histories of developed nations to rationalize assigning low levels of market interest rates to sovereign debt in the developed world. Investors believe that because these nations have favorable long-standing credit histories that they remain "risk free." Take the United Kingdom, for example. It has not defaulted on its debts since the Stop of the Exchequer in 1672.[4] So why should anyone question adding on still-more debt to try to bring down unemployment? It is rational, in fact, to believe that nearly 350 years of pristine credit is a formidable defense for continuing Keynesian economics and to believe there is no such thing as a Keynesian Endpoint where nations reach their limits for gainful borrowing.

It is a fallacy to believe that the ability of nations to issue ever-increasing amounts of new debt at the Keynesian Endpoint will be the same as it was in the past, and it is lunacy to believe that in the immediate aftermath of the financial crisis that bond investors will turn a blind eye to a continuation of fiscal profligacy. Investors have evolved and now have distaste for fiscal irresponsibility, as has the public, especially after the disappointing results of the massive fiscal stimulus deployed in 2009 by many countries in the developed, in particular in the United States, to counteract the financial crisis. Evidence of evolving views toward government indebtedness is illustrated by the behavior of bond markets toward nations at the lower end of the wrung in terms of their fiscal situations, particularly toward Europe's periphery, especially Portugal, Ireland, and Greece, and to a lesser extent Spain (commonly referred to by the acronym, PIGS), which has thus far been spared the worst outcome by successful attempts by Europe to ring-fence its problems to Portugal, Ireland, and Greece. Europe has done this by building many "bridges to nowhere" that have bought Spain as well as Italy time for Europe's banks to derisk their portfolios and rebuild their capital before any defaults occur.

Figure 1-5 shows the behavior of government bond yields for PIGS relative to German and French bond yields, which have been suppressed by capital flows both globally and from money previously invested in Europe's periphery that has in recent times been directed toward "core" Europe – Germany and France, whose debt problems are more manageable and where economic growth has been substantially better than for PIGS, as shown in Figure 1-6, which shows the unemployment rate for nations in Europe.

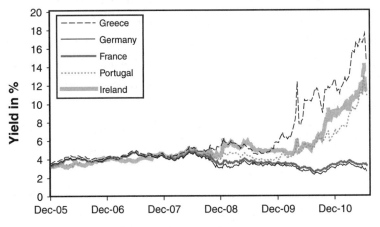

Figure 1-5 Oh, what debt can do to rates!

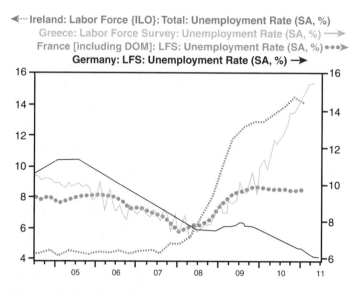

◀··· Ireland: Labor Force {ILO}: Total: Unemployment Rate (SA, %)
Greece: Labor Force Survey: Unemployment Rate (SA, %) —▶
France [including DOM]: LFS: Unemployment Rate (SA, %) ●●●▶
Germany: LFS: Unemployment Rate (SA, %) —▶

Figure 1-6 Oh, what debt can do to an economy!

Rather than consider the potential for contamination and contagion from Europe's periphery to its core, Keynesians prefer the notion that past is prologue and believe that global bond investors will continue to be attracted to debt markets in nations with strong credit histories despite the significant deterioration in their underlying credit fundamentals. This is unwise thinking. The move toward joining the least worst in the league of heavily indebted nations and the clan that in the immediate aftermath of the financial crisis has seemingly stabilized is merely a pit stop—the move by investors away from the core is likely to be nonlinear, which is to say that it will most likely occur gradually, as a process, not an event, when investors begin to believe the periphery is rotting the core. And deterioration in core Europe has the potential to occur faster than investors expect because more than ever the deterioration in underlying credit fundamentals put developed nations at a tipping point and make them vulnerable to a breakdown in confidence.

Investors tend in general to underestimate the risks of a sudden stop, and they tend not to position themselves for tail events—the big, unexpected events that make news only after they have happened, not while they are developing. These events tend to occur much more often than many expect when they consider normal distribution curves, as illustrated by Table 1-2. In other words, tail risks in the investment world have proven to be far larger than models would predict. Investors therefore need to think and position their portfolios in terms of tail risks and be leery of normal distribution curves. At the Keynesian Endpoint, this means investors should position for the possibility of sovereign defaults and their vast ripple effects in the global economic and financial system.

TABLE 1-2 Big Things Happen More Often Than Most People Expect.

Daily Change in DJIA 1916 – 2003 (21,924 Trading Days)

Daily Change (+/-)	Normal Distribution Approximation	Actual	Ratio of Actual to Normal
> 3.4%	58 days	1001 days	17x
> 4.5%	6 days	366 days	61x
> 7%	1 in 300,000 years	48 days	Very large

Source: PIMCO, Benoit Mandelbrôt: *The (Mis)behavior of Markets, Basic Books, March 2006*

Investors in developed markets must also stay attentive to attempts by indebted nations to repress them for the sake of liquidating public debts. These nations will attempt to suppress market interest rates to levels that are close to or below the rate of inflation, hoping that their economies will grow at a rate that exceeds the interest rates they pay on their debts, a combination that enables nations to reduce their debt-to-GDP ratios. In these cases, investors will experience a loss of purchasing power on two fronts. First, they will be put behind the eight ball by lagging inflation and thereby losing domestic purchasing power. Second, low or negative real interest rates will reduce the attractiveness of their home currency, which is apt to depreciate and thereby result in a loss of purchasing power internationally. Investors must recognize also that policymakers intend to carry out their repression in a way that makes them akin to frogs that stay in slowly boiling pots only to die. Investors instead should be like frogs that are placed in pots already boiling and jump out.

A paradox to some, the Keynesian Endpoint means that Austrian economics, which is predicated on the idea of a laissez-faire style of governmental involvement, will regain popularity and will therefore become more influential in shaping policymaking in the time ahead. Mind you, I do not mean to say that the Austrian style of economics that dominated the later part of the twentieth century will return— long live Reaganism and Thatcherism. Instead, Keynesians will be forced to let Austrian economists shape the heavy hand of government involvement and control that has dominated the post-crisis policy-making landscape. For example, taxpayers will demand that tax receipts be directed more efficiently than they have in the past, such that every unit of currency taken in is spent in ways that they believe are most likely to benefit society. One example is the doling out of benefits to public sector unions, which continue to receive health and pension benefits that far exceed those received by the private sector.

This means that government will attempt to stimulate economic activity not by increasing its spending, but by changing the composition of its spending. Policymakers will also seek changes in taxation and regulations that encourage businesses and households to spend and invest. The goal from here on will be to ignite multiplier effects that debt spending can no longer ignite. A major challenge in this regard will be the ability of developed nations to muster sufficient political support for changing their mix of government spending at a time when their populations are aging. These nations are predisposed to spending more on health care and retirement benefits, which will make it difficult to direct money away from these areas toward areas that tend to promote strong, sustainable economic growth, including infrastructure, research and development, and education.

The integration of the Keynesian and Austrian schools of thinking will be necessary because Keynesians have no more balance sheets to spend from, and followers of the Austrian school of thinking are not yet in control of balance sheets (nor do they want to be in control). This transformation could take quite a bit of time, but not all that long because the populace will provide a mandate for change, the same as it did in the early 1980s and then again in the early 1990s when supply-side economics was tweaked. How will this happen? High levels of unemployment or general economic discontent always lead citizens to rise up, either in arms or with their votes. Economic stress has a way of crystallizing the sorts of policies that are both the least and most desirable for a given time. The result of the November 2010 U.S. election is an example of this. Voters picked candidates that seek reduced government activism, rebuking Keynesian economics. The November 2012 general election will be the next big opportunity for voters to express their views on Keynesian economics, the dominant policy tool at the onset of the financial crisis. Indications are that voters will reject the philosophy and oust incumbents that have supported it because in the U.S. as well as throughout the world, the fiscal authorities have failed to reduce unemployment to desirable levels in spite of massive fiscal stimulus efforts.

More than at any time since the 1980s, citizens throughout the voting world will vote to eject "leaders" who favor a continuation of fiscal policies that yield little in terms of economic growth and in fact create conditions that could actually erode economic activity because of both an inefficient use of public money and a decrease in confidence tied to concerns about the long-term risks and implications of government activism. Confidence in the ability of policymakers to adopt policies that bear fruit has diminished in today's world for many reasons, not the least of which is the fear that taxpayers have about the future confiscation of their income to pay for the run-up in government debts. Moreover, the loss of the Keynesian security blanket—the now apparent inability of government to increase employment by waving their magic debt wand—has shaken the foundation by which investors and consumers take risks, and this uncertainty is causing them to disengage. Policymakers must find new ways to boost confidence, and these days many believe the best way is for them to get out of the way.

At the Keynesian Endpoint, the ability of nations to pursue expansionary fiscal policies is curtailed, leaving nations with few options other than to run expansionary monetary policies that lift asset prices and power economic growth in the short-run. Many long-run options exist; in particular a redirection of fiscal spending toward investments that address the structural challenges that nations face rather than the cyclical ones. Unfortunately, it's a long slog, and it will therefore be some time before the deeply indebted see a return to "old normal" levels of economic growth. Nations seen as the worst offenders in the debt crisis will be forced to hasten the repair of their balance sheets, and they will have to reduce their spending, crimping their economic growth rates—materially in some cases, especially relative to nations in the emerging markets, many of which are now creditor nations.

With the ability of the fiscal authority curtailed, the monetary authority—the central bank—is left to do the heavy lifting. Mind you, there are limits to what central banks in the developed world can do because they risk losing hard-won inflation-fighting credibility they took decades to build. These include the Federal Reserve, the Bank of England, the Bank of Japan, and the European Central Bank (largely through the German Bundesbank, upon which the ECB's credibility was established). Neither of these banks is likely to succumb to their respective fiscal authorities and monetize profligate fiscal behavior. Instead, they will pursue only the most responsible irresponsible expansionary policies, which is to say they will use policy tools that in normal times would be deemed irresponsible but today are necessary to achieve a set of outcomes different from what is deemed normal for the central banker. In particular, the central banks of highly indebted nations (primarily those of developed nations) will implement policies designed to prevent deflation and restore their respective inflation rates to levels that reduce the risk of deflation, generally to around 2 percent. One of these responsible irresponsible policies is the attempt to reflate asset prices. This is accomplished by establishing a low policy rate and by indicating it will be kept there for an "extended extended" period that creates a virtual house of pain in shorter-term fixed-income assets, compelling investors to move out the risk spectrum, as shown in Figure 1-7. Responsible central banks will recognize their limits, preventing any meaningful acceleration in the inflation prices of goods and services and in the reflation of the prices of financial assets, carrying important investment implications.

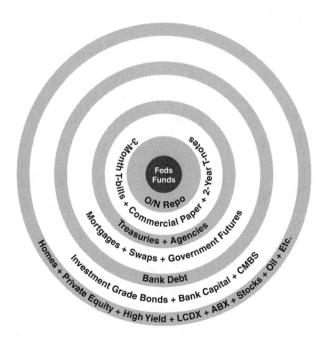

Figure 1-7 Low interest rates compel investors to move to the perimeter of the risk spectrum.

Source: PIMCO

The investment implications in conditions such as these where the fiscal authority is rendered powerless in the short-run and the monetary authority is constrained by the defense of its hard-won credibility are many, and they mainly relate to the likelihood of slower than historical rates of economic growth, low to negative real interest rates for shorter-term fixed-income securities, and an ever-present risk of tail events, which will persist until debt levels are reduced relative to incomes. These elements in particular should guide portfolio positioning.

Following are a few of the many conditions and investment implications of the Keynesian Endpoint, which are covered in greater detail in Chapter 9, "The Investment Implications of the Keynesian Endpoint."

Condition: Low Policy Rates Set by the World's Central Banks

To boost asset prices, liquidate government debts, reduce the debt burdens of the private sector, and stave off deflationary pressures that result from shortfalls in aggregate demand relative to supply, central banks will keep short-term interest rates low for the foreseeable future.

Investment Implications

Steep Yield Curves

Low policy rates engender steep yield curves in two ways in particular. First, they anchor rates at the short-end of the yield curve, pinning them lower. Second, low interest rates and accommodative monetary policies more generally enliven expectations for a strengthening of economic activity, boosting longer-term interest rates, where expectations for future inflationary pressures and eventual increases in short-term interest rates reside. Central bank rate cuts are a clarion call for investors to engage in strategies designed to benefit from a steep yield curve for many months forward because monetary policy regimes tend to be long lasting. One strategy is to speculate against the possibility of future interest rate hikes, which many investors implement by betting against any central bank rate hikes that might be embedded in Eurodollar or federal funds futures contracts. In Europe, investors bet against increases in EURIBOR and EONIA, two key short-term interest rates in Europe. Investors can also invest to benefit from the positive carry and "roll down" that can be earned by investing in short maturities. For example, a U.S. 2-year Treasury yielding 0.80 percent will "roll down" the yield curve such that in a year's time, when it becomes a 1-year Treasury, its yield will reflect the yield on 1-year maturities, say at 0.40 percent, picking up more for a year's worth of "roll down" than is possible, say, from owing a 20-year maturity that becomes a 19-year maturity in a year's time. (If a 40-basis-point yield difference existed for all securities on a yield curve spanning 20 years, the 20-year maturity would yield over 8 percent!)

Lower Rates Across the Yield Curve

Low short-term interest rates anchor interest rates across the entire yield curve, and in an environment such as today's where vast amounts of excess capacity are keeping a lid on wage inflation, inflation and hence interest rates are likely to stay under downward pressure for some time to come. The strategy therefore is to maintain a higher level of duration, or interest rate sensitivity in fixed-income portfolios than normal, at least until evidence begins to mount that the world's central banks are becoming successful in reflating asset prices. In 2011, signs emerged in this regard, and a pickup in inflation is reducing the attractiveness of duration—credit is more likely to be the better source of value in a case where economic growth is sustained and inflation pressures are building.

In the early stages of monetary easing, "soft" duration is preferred over "hard" duration, which is to say it is better to increase the duration of a portfolio by increasing the amount of exposure to short-term maturities, such as Eurodollar contracts, or 2-year notes, which are likely to outperform long-term maturities on a duration-weighted basis. (An investor must purchase many more 2-year notes than, say, 10-year notes, in order to equate the interest rate sensitivity of 2-year notes to 10-year notes.) Eventually, investors should shift to "hard" duration and choose longer-term instruments when it appears likely that the Federal Reserve is set to begin its sequence of policy steps that will lead to a hike in short-term rates. When this happens the yield curve will flatten, and long-term maturities will outperform shorter maturities.

Low Interest Rate Volatility

When policy rates are kept steady for an extended period, interest rate volatility tends to be lower than it is during periods when the central bank is either raising or lowering rates. The reason is because of the anchoring principle mentioned earlier. It is notable, for example, that at no time in the past 40 years has the 10-year Treasury note yielded more than four percentage points more than the federal funds rate—now *that's* an anchor! When a central bank is expected to hold its short-term rate steady, an investment strategy that has worked well historically is to bet against volatility, through yield enhancement strategies such as selling option premiums, either by selling listed options or over-the-counter options, in the swaptions market, the options market for the giant interest rate swaps market. It's not a strategy suitable for all investors but one often deployed by institutional investors.

Tighter Credit Spreads

When interest rates are kept low for an extended period, investors tend to become increasingly compelled to seek out higher returns, pushing them out the risk spectrum. In doing so, widespread purchases of so-called "spread" products, which include corporate bonds, asset-backed securities, mortgage-backed securities, and emerging markets bonds, cause these instruments to tend to perform well relative to assets deemed less risky, in particular government securities such as U.S. Treasuries. The strategy in this case therefore is to purchase spread products. Importantly, however, today's risky credit environment means investors need proceed cautiously. This means staying high in the capital structure—choosing bonds over equities and choosing bonds that are more senior in terms of rank in the event of a company's liquidation. It also means investing in bonds of high quality and of those whose cash flows will be less vulnerable in an economic recovery. Moreover, it sometimes means choosing companies with hard assets to sell because in the aftermath of a financial crisis, the recovery rates for bondholders of any liquidation is likely to be lower than in other times. Bonds that tend to make sense under these conditions include pipelines, utilities, and those of companies in energy and energy-related industries, as well as in the metals and mining arena. Each of these industries will retain some degree of pricing power, and their cash flows will be less vulnerable to cyclical forces than industries such as housing, gaming, lodging, retail, and those related to consumer discretionary spending.

Condition: Reduced Use of Financial Leverage

Banks are unwilling to lend, and borrowers are unwilling to borrow; both parties wish to derisk their balance sheets, having learned lessons about risk the hard way during the financial crisis.

Investment implications

Lowered Investment Returns

A nation that can no longer turbo-charge its economy through the use of financial leverage will experience some degree of slowing in the nominal growth rate of its economy. In other words, the actual level of spending the country experiences will be constrained by a lack of credit availability and a reduced willingness to spend, along with a higher personal savings rate. Moreover, having reached the last balance sheet, government spending will be restrained, too. In response to these realities, businesses will spend cautiously. Combined, these behaviors will translate into a lower rate of growth in overall spending and in many cases an outright decline when austerity measures by necessity are large. Slower growth rates in overall spending result in slow growth in revenue, the lifeline for corporate profits, weakening the prospect for investment returns in corporate equities. It also puts some corporate bonds at risk because cash flow is what is needed to meet payment obligations. Investment returns are damped also by a lack of corporate pricing power, which thins profit margins.

Condition: An Altered Global Economic Landscape

It's an upside-down world: Developed countries now dominate the list of highly indebted countries, and developing countries top the list of creditor nations.

Investment Implications

Home Biases Are Risk—Scour the Globe

The current era is a remarkable one, where the mighty have fallen and the meek have risen to the top. Developed nations such as the United States, Japan, and those in Europe are now at the bottom of the wrung in terms of fiscal health, and emerging nations, including China, Brazil, and India, as well as many of their regional brethren, which were once at the mercy of the developed world but now supply capital to the capital-starved developed world rather than vice versa. It is a topsy-turvy world where emerging countries have become creditor nations. China's $3 trillion in international reserves are a towering testament to the shifting global tide. In a world where investor confidence in any single nation can quickly evaporate and money can flee—call it *moneytourism*—keeping money invested in nation's whose poor balance sheets put their economies and financial markets at risk is an unattractive proposition. In contrast, countries that have built up reserves and have self-insured themselves against risk can self-finance their economic expansions and escape the worst of the Keynesian Endpoint. These nations, particularly those that entered the financial crisis with favorable initial conditions including demographics (relatively young populations and an increasing labor force), low budget deficits, low debt-to-GDP ratios, current account surpluses, high national savings rates, and high international reserves (relative to the size of their economies) are likely to have a strong ability to meet their payment obligations. For bond investors, this makes the high real interest rates of the developing world attractive, like blood to a vampire, yet many investors keep their money trapped in their home countries even though real interest rates there are either very low or in some cases negative. Assuming the emerging world has truly learned lessons from its past and will continue to behave as prudently as is has over the past decade or so, these real interest rates represent a glorious opportunity both outright and on a risk-adjusted basis. Investors need alter their old ways of thinking with respect to sovereign credit risk and broaden their opportunity set by exploring the many investment opportunities that exist in the emerging markets.

Intransigent Nations—Bad Places to Invest

In many countries, there will be little or no integration between the Keynesian and Austrian schools of thinking because the Keynesian camp will be intransigent. The implementation of austerity measures in these countries will be challenging and painful. For years these countries made social promises to their citizens that have become too burdensome to keep. Yet the citizens of these nations will be unwilling to wean themselves from the familiar and comforting hand of government for the free market's invisible hand. As a result, these countries will see their economies languish because the Keynesian Endpoint means it will be impossible for them to raise money to support their social contracts and efforts to use debt to stimulate economic activity. In these cases, social unrest, income inequality, currency devaluations, debt restructurings, high unemployment, accelerated inflation, high real interest rates, and low investment returns will be key features. In short, the standard of living in these countries will decline.

In addition to differentiating between intransigent and flexible nations, investors must also examine the nature of programs developed to battle the financial crisis. The Austrian school believes that temporary government programs can be viral, becoming permanent features of an economy and stifling the private sector. This is why investors must judge which countries might become victim to policies that could crowd out the private sector. Investors must examine not only the size of government programs, but their half-lives; in other words, the speed and extent to which the programs will be unwound. Investors must also closely examine the exit strategies of governments from the fiscal and monetary programs they implemented during the financial crisis.

When nations reach the Keynesian Endpoint they have no choice but to reverse course on many of the priorities that brought got them there because reaching the Endpoint means they have gone too far or at are at the risk of going too far, a verdict easily surmised through a variety of market-based indicators such as real interest rates, the shape of the yield curve, credit default swaps, credit spreads, bank deposits, capital flows, and so on. These indicators will reflect underlying trends in key gauges of fiscal health, including debt-to-GDP ratios, budget deficits, primary balances (a nation's budget deficit minus interest payments; see example forthcoming), savings rates (internal and external), reserve accumulation, and factors that influence these trends including budget rules, effectiveness in tax collecting, demographics, and the level of personal consumption relative to GDP (a gauge of the excess within an economy).

When reaching the Keynesian Endpoint, it is important for nations to ultimately achieve a zero primary balance because without it they cannot stabilize their debt-to-GDP ratios. When a nation achieves a zero primary balance, the amount of debt outstanding will tend to increase at the same rate as the nominal interest rate paid on the debt, leaving the debt-to-GDP ratio unchanged. For some nations, a stable primary balance fails to stabilize the debt-to-GDP ratio because the nominal interest rate paid on the national debt exceeds the growth rate of GDP. This will be the case for nations that are heavily indebted and that lack credibility in their fiscal affairs. Greece is an example. This presents an extra hurdle for many nations caught in today's sovereign debt dilemma: To stabilize their debt-to-GDP ratios, not only must these nations reduce their primary balances to zero, but they must gain sufficient credibility in the financial markets to keep their nominal interest rates at or below their growth rates in GDP. If they can't, they won't be able to alleviate their debt burdens. In a world of finite capital, serial defaulters and those with burdens deemed by investors as likely to be too difficult to fix with austerity measures alone will lose—the nominal interest rate will stay high, thus raising the risk of a default, which would be the only means of reducing their debt-to-GDP ratios.

Sharing the Burden

At the Keynesian Endpoint, a nation must engage in burden sharing and spread the pain among four groups in particular, as discussed next.

Citizens

Countries at the Endpoint have no choice but to re-examine and in most cases reduce their entitlement spending, which means cutting pension and health care benefits promised to their citizens. Politically, this is the most challenging element in the burden-sharing imperative, but without it nations at the Endpoint will be unable to put themselves on a sustainable fiscal path. Nations at the Endpoint, particularly those in Europe's periphery, are likely to see their entitlement policies converge with those of their neighbors; in other words, these nations will use as models for change the policies of their regional trading partners as well as their extended trading partners when proposing changes to their existing social contracts. For example, European countries that currently allow retirees to receive retirement benefits at ages that are below that of nations in relatively better fiscal health will probably raise their retirement ages, although not necessarily to the same level as these healthier nations, at least for while, owing to the large political difficulties of doing so. In addition to cuts in entitlement programs, citizens will likely have to bear the burden of targeted tax increases and other revenue generators, including those gained from consumption taxes and "sin" taxes that attempt to recoup costs associated with the poor habits the sin taxes are placed against. These habits of course include smoking, where associated medical costs are a direct hit to taxpayers. Citizens will likely also be forced to endure a reduction in services. Wise nations will target service cuts in areas where there will be little impact on the health and well-being of their people and that will minimize any impact on education, which is vital to the long-term vitality of a nation.

Trading Partners

A nation at the Keynesian Endpoint must allow its currency to depreciate in order to boost its economic growth rate and to attract capital. Those that do can effectively distribute some of their burden onto other nations. Nations that allow their currencies to depreciate will grab exports from other nations whose currencies are appreciating against their own, thus resulting in a positive in terms of trade shock. European nations that are part of the European Monetary Union are challenged in this respect because they do not possess the ability to devalue the euro. It is an internal dilemma. These nations will lack offsets to their fiscal austerity programs, rendering their economic growth rates low for a lengthy period of time.

Monetary Partners

Nations that reach the Keynesian Endpoint will borrow from their monetary brethren, which is to say relatively richer nations within a monetary union will transfer money to their brethren in need. This will boost the debts of the contributing nations. In Europe, this means Germany and France will increase their debt loads in order to save the periphery and keep them in the European Monetary Union. From another perspective, problems in states and cities in the United States will be shared by healthier states and cities.

Bond Holders

Via restructuring, investors holding bonds of countries that reach the Keynesian Endpoint will likely be forced to take "haircuts," or losses, on their bonds. In some cases nations will ask investors to voluntarily agree to roll their debt at terms attractive only from the standpoint being the least worst alternative—bond investors would rather have their bonds redeemed at par at the original maturity date.

Emphasize Investment, Not Consumption

Nations can boost their economies more over the long-run by channeling their funds toward investments rather than attempting to boost consumption. In other words, countries must recognize empirical evidence indicating that the multiplier effect from money channeled toward investments is greater over the long-run than the multiplier effect for money channeled toward consumption. At the Keynesian Endpoint it is imperative for nations to increase the multiplier effect of every unit of currency they deploy because they have no new money to deploy.

By emphasizing investment over consumption, nations can boost their productivity and in doing so raise their standard of living. Keynes himself, in an era of depression and at a time when long-range economic forecasting was, because of a lack of empirical data and economic theory, in its infancy, fully appreciated the importance of productivity:

> From the sixteenth century, with a cumulative crescendo after the eighteenth, the great age of science and technical inventions began...What is the result? In spite of an enormous growth in the population of the world...the average standard of life in Europe and the United States has been raised, I think, about fourfold...In our own lifetimes...we may be able to perform all the operations of agriculture, mining, and manufacture with a quarter of the human effort to which we have been accustomed.[5]

Emphasis on investment should include government support for research and development, as well as education, training and retraining for both the unemployed and the under-employed (discouraged workers who have dropped out of the workforce and those working part-time solely because they can't obtain a full-time job), and productivity-enhancing infrastructure projects, including those that create more efficiency with respect to energy consumption and immigration laws designed to boost intellectual capital.

Government Spending Must Be Redirected as Well as Cut

The term "fiscal multiplier" is the same conceptually as "bang for the buck." Government spending that boosts a nation's income by more than the amount it spends results in a fiscal multiplier of greater than 1.0. Here I highlight how at the Keynesian Endpoint, traditional concepts on the fiscal multiplier must be re-examined and reworked if government spending is to be a net positive for a nation's economy.

To begin our discussion, there is no better place to start then to turn to the shepherd of the fiscal multiplier, John Maynard Keynes. He discussed the fiscal multiplier at length in his book, *The General Theory of Employment*, and it is at the center of Keynesian economics. In his book, Keynes refers to the works of Richard Kahn, who, Keynes says, was the first to introduce the concept of the multiplier in 1931 in his article on "The Relation of Home Investment to Unemployment" (*Economic Journal*, June 1931). Keynes interpreted Kahn's theory as follows:

> His argument in this article depended on the fundamental notion that, if the propensity to consume in various hypothetical circumstances is (together with certain other conditions) taken as a given and we conceive the monetary or other public authority to take steps to stimulate or to retard investment, the change in the amount of employment will be a function of the net change in the amount of the investment; and it aimed at laying down general principles by which to estimate the actual quantitative relationship between an increment of net investment and the increment of aggregate employment which will be associated with it.[6]

Keynes goes on to introduce the concept of the marginal propensity to consume (MPC), which measures the proportion of disposable income that is spent. The difference between disposable income and the marginal propensity to consume is the marginal propensity to save. Keynes believes that as long as the MPC is high, increases in government spending result in a fiscal multiplier:

> If the marginal propensity to consume is not far short of unity, small fluctuations in investment will lead to wide fluctuations in employment.[7]

Keynes allowed for leakages, pointing to important factors "not to overlook" when calculating the multiplier, including the source of funds used for government spending and the impact that the use of these funds might have on interest rates and inflation; the "confused psychology which often prevails" from government spending and its effect on confidence and therefore liquidity preferences; and the likelihood that "in an open system with foreign-trade relations, some part of the increased investment will accrue to the benefit of employment in foreign countries." In other words, some of the spending will be on imported products, not domestically produced ones.

These leakages are major elements of the Keynesian Endpoint because the leakages reduce the effectiveness of continued fiscal profligacy and of traditional Keynesian-style efforts to stimulate economic activity through deficit spending.

Consider, for example, the impact of large budget deficits on liquidity preferences. Alan Greenspan (2011)[8] argues that the size of government affects investments in long-term assets, finding that as a share of corporate liquid cash flow, long-term fixed corporate investment "is now at levels, relative to cash flow, that we have not experienced since 1940." He explains it this way:

> I infer that a minimum of half and possibly as much as three-fourths of the effect can be explained by the shock of vastly greater uncertainties embedded in the competitive, regulatory and financial environments faced by businesses since the collapse of Lehman Brothers, deriving from the surge in government activism. This explanation is buttressed by comparison with similar conundrums experienced during the 1930s. I conclude that the current government activism is hampering what should be a broad-based economic recovery.[9]

Adding,

U.S. fixed private investment has fallen far short of the level that history suggests should have occurred given the recent dramatic surge in corporate profitability.[10]

Greenspan makes a vitally important point about how uncertainty affects human behavior, and he draws a link between the recent spreading of government activism and current uncertainties:

The inbred reaction of businessmen and householders to uncertainty of any type is to disengage from those activities that require confident predictions of how the future will unfold... While most in the business community attribute the massive rise in their fear and uncertainty to the collapse of economic activity, they judge its continuance since the recovery took hold in early 2009 to the widespread activism of government, in its all-embracing attempt to accelerate the path of economic recovery.[11]

If a nation is to be effective in optimizing the use of its taxpayer dollars, it must stop the leakages to which Keynes referred and get out of the way, so to speak. People will continue to fear confiscation of their income and cuts in benefits and services as long as their country is filled to the gills with debt and overly active. When these leakages are controlled or reduced, nations should focus on redirecting taxpayer money toward areas likely to provide lasting benefits, including infrastructure (why not retrofit buildings to make them more energy efficient?), research and development (spend to create new products that provide new sources of income), and education (or else the jobs will go elsewhere and the newly unemployed will have difficultly regaining employment).

It can be helpful for nations that have reached their borrowing limits to implement budget rules that investors will find credible. This is especially true for serial defaulters, who need to gain the credibility of investors. If they don't, the nominal interest rates on their debts will exceed the nominal growth rates of their economies. In this case, the debt-to-GDP ratio will rise in perpetuity unless the nation runs a budget surplus large enough to offset the interest payments. In other words, achieving a zero primary balance (discussed earlier) won't necessarily be enough to stave off continued deterioration in a nation's fiscal situation if investors lack confidence that the zero primary balance will be sustained. A recent study by the IMF ("Fiscal Rules Can Help Improve Fiscal Performance," December 2009)[12] supports this idea.

Nations at the Keynesian Endpoint are starved for sources of economic growth. One that has been dependable is the implementation of free trade agreements (FTAs). To illustrate, consider data from the United States. In 2001, the U.S. had forged three FTAs. By 2006, it had signed 14 of them. Data from the Census Bureau in 2006 show that the 14 FTAs accounted for over 42 percent of U.S. exports even though these countries accounted for only 6 percent of the world economy. Data from the White House show that after 5 years of signing FTAs, the average increase in trade between bilateral trading partners was 32 percent; after ten years it bolted to 73 percent; after 15 years the increase surged to 114 percent. These data and numerous other data clearly show the benefits of free trade in boosting economic activity, presenting an enormous source of growth for countries willing to put down their protectionist arms.

Suppose a nation's economy is growing at a 5% annualized pace overall and 2% minus inflation. Suppose also that the nation's budget deficit is 4% of GDP. The nation decides that in order to reduce its debt-to-GDP ratio it will inflate its way out. In doing so, it boosts its money supply growth to say 8%, thereby spurring an 8% overall increase in the economy, but at the expense of more inflation, which increases to a 5% annual pace. In five years, this nation will have seen its economy grow by 40% in nominal terms, and its debts will have increased by 20%, lowering the GDP ratio by 4% per year. This seems desirable, but it isn't; the nation's purchasing power declined as a result of the increase in the inflation rate. This lowers the nation's standard of living. The lesson is that nations must be careful about using this tempting math to lower its debt load because although it might solve the debt problem, it will create many unintended consequences.

Despite the risks, nations for centuries have turned to coinage and the printing of money as a means of shedding debt, in many cases with disastrous consequences. The many lessons learned from the debasement of currencies nevertheless are lost upon Keynesians, as they seeing through rose-colored glasses debt spending as the cure for all that ails a nation.

2

The 30-Year American Consumption Binge

As we begin this chapter, first consider the following pieces of wisdom:

"Money never made a man happy yet, nor will it. There is nothing in its nature to produce happiness. The more a man has, the more he wants. Instead of its filling a vacuum, it makes one. If it satisfies one want, it doubles and trebles that want another way. That was a true proverb of the wise man, rely upon it; "Better is little with the fear of the Lord, than great treasure, and trouble therewith."

—Benjamin Franklin

"Contentment is natural wealth; luxury, artificial poverty."

—Socrates

"In time we hate that which we fear."

—William Shakespeare

To understand why American consumers discarded prudence and embraced greed for a glutinous consumption binge that lasted 30 years, it is necessary to have an understanding of the social sciences—in particular sociology, anthropology, and psychology—and the many other influences that comingled in the post-industrial world to accommodate the primal urges associated with these social sciences, including the ability to mass produce goods and services; the proliferation of marketing facilitated by the Information Age; and financial innovation.

These collective influences infected not just the United States, but also many other nations in the developed world, contributing significantly to the buildup of their debts. The developing world will not be spared and will eventually be infected by this bug, albeit at some distance in the future, because no society can immunize itself from the trappings of human nature and the scourge associated with capitalist and political aggressors who, in their inevitable and constant pursuit of wealth and power, will subordinate the welfare of society to their own. These forces are so powerful that the developed world almost certainly will succumb to them again in the future because future generations will have none of the many scars that the current generation wears across its back from the many lessons it learned during the financial crisis.

How Consumerism Is Linked to Barbaric Times and Primal Needs

Stripping away the relative orderliness of modern societies and the knowledge that mankind has accumulated over the centuries, it can be persuasively argued that the inner workings of individuals and society as a whole have not changed much and that the primary motives that drive decision-making and the actions of mankind at large are the same as those that drove men to commit heinous acts in barbaric times. These primary, or primal motives represent the very basic and unlearned needs of human beings as well as animals and include: hunger, thirst, aggression, desire, and avoidance of pain. Individuals in one fashion or another express each of these primary motives in their consumption behavior.

Maslow (1943) depicts a hierarchy of man's basic needs, or goals, all of which substantially influence consumption behavior. His well-renowned pyramid is shown in Figure 2-1. The five needs are physiological (physical health), safety, love, esteem, and self-actualization.

Maslow believes that individuals constantly strive to meet these needs and are "motivated by the desire to achieve or maintain the various conditions upon which these basic satisfactions rest and by certain more intellectual desires."

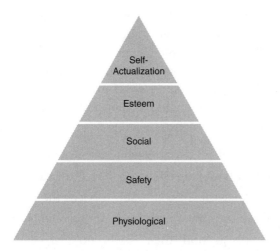

Figure 2-1 Maslow's Hierarchy of Needs

Source: Adapted from Maslow (1970)

Maslow also believes that as an individual works up each level of the pyramid, that level of the pyramid monopolizes his or her attention until the goal for that level is met. After it is, the individual then focuses on the next level, or goal, which again dominates the individual's consciousness and becomes the focal point of a his or her actions because, as Maslow says, "gratified needs are not active motivators," and therefore provide no benefit to motivation for the next set of goals. In other words, even though an individual will attain a certain degree of satisfaction when he or she fulfills a set of needs and goals, in and of itself that fulfillment provides no motivation for meeting the next set of needs and goals.

Keep in mind that an individual can be perceived as having met a goal even if it hasn't been met fully, which is to say that an individual might begin focusing on a new set of goals if, for example, 85 percent of a goal has been achieved. This has important implications for consumption patterns because most people, Maslow believes, fail to reach the top of the pyramid, leaving them with insatiable desires. In this context, consumers are always feeling unfulfilled, driving them to consume to excess, as can be inferred from this excerpt:

> Thus man is a perpetually wanting animal. Ordinarily the satisfaction of these wants is not altogether mutually exclusive, but only tends to be. The average member of our society is most often partially satisfied and partially unsatisfied in all of his wants. The hierarchy principle is usually empirically observed in terms of increasing percentages of non-satisfaction as we go up the hierarchy.[1]

It follows that the perpetual wanting to which Maslow speaks leaves a consumer feeling constantly dissatisfied and that this dissatisfaction will exist no matter how many goods and services the consumer acquires, driving them to pursue ever increasing amounts of goods and services in attempts to fulfill their needs and goals. This puts the consumer on a treadmill that takes them as all treadmills do: to nowhere.

It is very important to recognize that the basic needs of individuals across cultures are met in vastly different ways—for example, through the different types of food that people consume—but that the underlying motivations that drive individuals to meet these needs are the same. Recognizing these primal motives rather than the outward way in which the primal motives are met makes it possible to compare modern societies to more primitive societies, and to speculate on the outlook for economies in the now-thriving developing world, which, according to this theory, will be substantially driven by the motivations of individuals to meet basic needs. These basic needs themselves will evolve and leave individuals perpetually wanting to acquire more and more goods and services and always feeling dissatisfied, just as has occurred in the developed world.

The commonality that exists among people throughout the world therefore are important to recognize when analyzing the motivations that drive consumer behavior, speaking as they do to the primal motives that are sure to exist in perpetuity in all people. Maslow

(1943) speaks in this excerpt about the importance of these common-alities across cultures:

> Certainly in any particular culture an individual's conscious motivational content will usually be extremely different from the conscious motivational content of an individual in another society. However, it is the common experience of anthropologists that people, even in different societies, are much more alike than we would think from our first contact with them, and that as we know them better we seem to find more and more of this commonness, We then recognize the most startling differences to be superficial rather than basic, *e.g.*, differences in style of hairdress, clothes, tastes in food, etc, Our classification of basic needs is in part an attempt to account for this unity behind the apparent diversity from culture to culture. No claim is made that it is ultimate or universal for all cultures. The claim is made only that it is relatively *more* ultimate, more universal, more basic, than the superficial conscious desires from culture to culture, and makes a somewhat closer approach to common-human characteristics. Basic needs are *more* common-human than superficial desires or behaviors.[2]

Maslow makes a strong case for looking more deeply at the motivations that lie behind the way people behave and in so doing awakens our senses to a major driving force behind the consumer spending behavior.

The Pursuit of Leisure and the Roots of Consumerism Began in Barbaric Times

Thorstein Veblen, a Norwegian-American economist and sociologist, in 1899 wrote a controversial book titled, *The Theory of the Leisure Class*, which is one of the first to thoroughly examine consumerism. Veblen believes that the leisure class within societies, which can also include the middle class, can be found in the early stages of barbaric times; for example in feudal Europe and feudal Japan. The creation of the leisure class, Veblen believes, is rooted in the earliest forms of differentiation that occurred between occupations in the world's first societies. Efforts by the upper and middle class to sustain this differentiation has been a powerful motivational force behind the pursuit of wealth as well as the acquisition of goods and services among individuals. In this context it is important to gain an understanding of how the leisure class evolved in primitive societies because it can help us to understand the primal forces that influence the way people—and in particular, consumers—behave in today's societies.

According to Veblen, in barbaric times, the differentiation between labor was distinct, with four occupations in particular distinguishing the upper class from lower classes: government, warfare, religious or priestly service, and sports. Any occupation having to do directly with industry, manual labor, or the everyday work of earning a livelihood is considered an occupation of the "inferior" class. The middle class consists of employments Veblen characterizes as subsidiaries to occupations held by the upper class. For example, the production and servicing of arms and related accouterments; war canoes; the dressing and handling of animals owned by the upper class, including horses, dogs, and hawks; and the preparation of items used for religious worship. The lower classes are excluded from these "honorable" employments, except in cases where the employments are purely of an industrial nature.

It follows, then, Veblen believes, that the emergence of a leisure class coincides with the beginning of ownership because both are the result of the same economic forces. The early periods of differentiation between classes in the lower stages of barbarism included a division between the works performed by men and women. Similarly, the earliest form of ownership in the lower stages of early barbarism included ownership of women by "the able-bodied men of the community." Veblen points to an important element in this beastly form of ownership, which is that it begins apparently with the seizure of female captives, seemingly for their usefulness as "trophies." This barbaric practice evolved into marriages dictated by ownership, or ownership-marriages, which led to men becoming heads of households. Following that, men began to have other captives, which included men and women that by nature were an extension of slavery. Velbin connects the barbaric practices to ownership of other types of goods. He notes that ownership-marriages, which are premised on coercion, and the custom of ownership are indistinguishable in their initial stage of development because

> both arise from the desire of the successful men to put their prowess in evidence by exhibiting some durable result of their exploits. Both also minister to that propensity for mastery which pervades all predatory communities. From the ownership of women the concept of ownership extends itself to include the products of their industry, and so there arises the ownership of things as well as of persons.[3]

This therefore is the way in which the consumption of goods began, and it reveals the dastardly inner motives that underlie the pursuit of wealth and leisure. Veblen (1899) notes also that the motives extend to services as well as goods, underscoring the underlying forces behind consumption more generally:

> In this way a consistent system of property in goods is gradually installed. And although in the latest stages of the development, the serviceability of goods for consumption has come to be the most obtrusive element of their value, still, wealth has by no means yet lost its utility as a honorific evidence of the owner's prepotence. Wherever the institution of private property is found, even in a slightly developed form, the economic process bears the character of a struggle between men for the possession of goods.[4]

A further link between the actions of barbarians and consumers in today's society can be drawn from Veblen's view of status within the barbarian society and the way in which the barbarian man pursued and defined his status. Veblen's view is consistent with the relative income hypothesis developed by Dusenberry, who theorizes that personal consumption is dictated by an individual's assessment of his or her consumption relative to others.[5] The barbarian man also made such comparisons when seeking to infer upon himself a certain level of status:

> In order to stand well in the eyes of the community, it is necessary to come up to a certain, somewhat indefinite, conventional standard of wealth; just as in the earlier predatory stage it is necessary for the barbarian man to come up to the tribe's standard of physical endurance, cunning, and skill at arms. A certain standard of wealth in the one case, and of prowess in the other, is a necessary condition of reputability, and anything in excess of this normal amount is meritorious. The possession of wealth confers honor; it is an invidious distinction. Those members of the community who fall short of this, somewhat indefinite, normal degree of prowess or of property suffer in the esteem of their fellow men; and consequently they suffer also in their own esteem, since the usual basis of self-respect is the respect accorded by one's neighbors. Only individuals with an aberrant temperament can in the long run retain their self-esteem in the face of the disesteem of their fellows.[6]

Based on this it is necessary to further illuminate the notion that man has sought to accumulate wealth for motivations that have evolved beyond those for subsistence, making ownership a distinctly human trait.

The common thread between Maslow's hierarchy of needs and Veblen's theory of the leisure class is the insatiable desire of individuals to reach basic needs and goals, in particular those related to self-esteem. Perpetual dissatisfaction and unquenchable desires are seen as powerful motivators of behavior by both researchers. Veblen makes this clear and draws parallels to Maslow in his description of the insatiable nature of consumption behavior and the perpetual dissatisfaction that follows:

So soon as the possession of property becomes the basis of popular esteem, therefore, it becomes also a requisite to the complacency which we call self-respect. In any community where goods are held in severalty it is necessary, in order to his own peace of mind, that an individual should possess as large a portion of goods as others with whom he is accustomed to class himself; and it is extremely gratifying to possess something more than others. But as fast as a person makes new acquisitions, and becomes accustomed to the resulting new standard of wealth, the new standard forthwith ceases to afford appreciably greater satisfaction than the earlier standard did.

The tendency in any case is constantly to make the present pecuniary standard the point of departure for a fresh increase of wealth; and this in turn gives rise to a new standard of sufficiency and a new pecuniary classification of one's self as compared with one's neighbors. So far as concerns the present question, the end sought by accumulation is to rank high in comparison with the rest of the community in point of pecuniary strength. So long as the comparison is distinctly unfavorable to himself, the normal, average individual will live in chronic dissatisfaction with his present lot; and when he has reached what may be called the normal pecuniary standard of the community, or of his class in the community, this chronic dissatisfaction will give place to a restless straining to place a wider and ever-widening pecuniary interval between himself and this average standard. The invidious comparison can never become so favorable to the individual making it that he would not gladly rate himself still higher relatively to his competitors in the struggle for pecuniary reputability.

In the nature of the case, the desire for wealth can scarcely be satiated in any individual instance, and evidently a satiation of the average or general desire for wealth is out of the question. However widely, or equally, or "fairly", it may be distributed, no general increase of the community's wealth can make any approach to satiating this need, the ground of which approach to satiating this need, the ground of which is the desire of every one to excel every one else in the accumulation of goods."[7]

Seen through this lens, consumer behavior in the years leading up to the financial crisis that began to unfold in 2007 is better understood. It is obvious, for example, that a credit card is a conduit by which an individual can attempt to satisfy his inner cravings and project his outward image to the rest of society. The acquisition of physical goods and the use of debt to facilitate it is the modern means of a barbaric inclination to showcase one's exploits and prowess and to project power and status through the ownership of goods—the modern version of a despicable practice by barbaric men to own and showcase women and other captives as trophies. Beyond goods, the consumption of services is simply an extension of the barbarian's motivation for owning women and slaves as trophies, primarily for the utility of their services.

Who would have thunk: a link between Conan the Barbarian and the American consumer!

To Each His Own: The Influence of Personality Traits on Consumption

As just discussed, the driving force behind an individual's relentless and insatiable pursuit of wealth and consumption of goods and services is related largely to psychological and sociological factors. Individuals are motivated first and foremost to fulfill their most basic needs, eventually moving beyond subsistence to focus on the pursuit of wealth in order to differentiate themselves from the rest of society and to display their prowess and power. In both cases, dissatisfaction reigns; hence individuals relentlessly pursue goals that like a carrot on a stick are always beyond their reach no matter how far they travel. People on the whole are linked by the commonalities they share with respect to the psychological and sociological factors that lie behind the pursuit of wealth and the consumption of goods and services, but the cultural differences that exist between people of different societies result in far different outward expressions of the various goals that people pursue. I discussed this idea earlier when referencing Maslow's work.

In addition to cultural differences, personality traits also significantly influence the way in which individuals express themselves when attempting to meet their basic needs and achieve goals related to sociological factors. The American Psychiatric Association describes personality traits as "enduring patterns of perceiving, relating to, and thinking about the environment and oneself that are exhibited in a wide range of social and personal contexts."[8] Two of the most important traits are extroversion and introversion.

As an example, let's compare two famous characters from two very different but famous movies. Among the most introverted of famous movie characters is Adrian from *Rocky*. Certainly one of movie history's most extroverted and infamous characters is Scarlett O'Hara from *Gone With the Wind*. In considering how each is likely to seek fulfillment of her needs and goals, we of course have to put wealth aside, given that Adrian works in a pet store cleaning out bird cages and cat boxes while Scarlett, well, she doesn't work and lives on a plantation.

Casting wealth aside, let's think for a moment about what type of car Adrian and Scarlett would likely buy. From what we can gather from watching them on the silver screen, it seems Scarlett is the one most likely to purchase a Ferrari. Adrian would probably purchase a used car, if she were to buy a car at all (she'd probably rather walk alone or take a bus, keeping to herself in a seat at the front). Adrian's sociological impulse simply isn't as strong as Scarlett's, which is to say that her standards are low relative to the standard established by people within her social framework. Nevertheless, Adrian has a minimal standard that she would accept, which means she will pursue it in the same way that Scarlett will pursue her personally chosen standard. The major difference is in the consumption choices that Adrian and Scarlett make when seeking to meet their needs and goals.

Culture, it can be said, is what defines the personality of a nation, affecting the standards by which individuals compare themselves against others in the country or region that they live. This significantly influences their consumption behavior. In the United States, for instance, many people hold themselves to a standard that in an undeveloped country many people would consider either a very high standard or one that is unattainable altogether. This sociological construct affects the pattern of consumption in individual nations in terms of what people buy and the intensity at which they pursue the acquisition of goods and services, consistent with Duesenberry's relative income hypothesis.[9] This means that when a particular good or service is purchased in sufficient quantities it is apt to become even more desirable to individuals in a particular society because they will measure their place in society against the norm of society. Even if that particular item is not bought, it will set a standard by which an individual judges himself.

Although the personality traits differ greatly among people, these traits tend to be relatively stable among individuals throughout their lives. Think of yourself. You likely have a strong sense of what type of person you are, and although much has probably changed about you and your circumstance in your years, you probably feel as I do that the core of who you are has been relatively steady from your youngest days. The "who we are" influences our behavior, just as it does Adrian and Scarlett.

Freud (1933) believes that interaction between three distinct parts of our minds drive much of our personality: the id, the ego, and the superego. Freud's definition of these three parts leaves plenty of room to draw connections to the motivations behind consumer behavior and the causes of excessive spending and use of debt.

The id, according to Freud, represents the raw part of our personalities, the part that acts on a "pleasure principle," demanding immediate gratification with little regard for consequence. Sound familiar? Seems like the consumers who went in over the heads. Here is Freud's (1933) definition of the id:

> It is the dark, inaccessible part of our personality; what little we know of it we have learned from our study of the dream-work and of the construction of neurotic symptoms, and most of that is of a negative character and can be described only as a contrast to the ego. We approach the id with analogies: we call it a chaos, a cauldron full of seething excitations.... It is filled with energy reaching it from the instincts, but it has no organization, produces no collective will, but only a striving to bring about the satisfaction of the instinctual needs subject to the observance of the pleasure principle.[10]

The ego adheres to a reality principle, keeping the id in check, as Freud (1933) describes:

> The ego is that part of the id which has been modified by the direct influence of the external world.... The ego represents what may be called reason and common sense, in contrast to the id, which contains the passions.... in its relation to the id it is like a man on horseback, who has to hold in check the superior strength of the horse; with this difference, that the rider tries to do so with his own strength, while the ego uses borrowed forces.[11]

The ego has the additional burden of serving the superego, which represents our conscience, placing moral judgment and societal rules upon the ego. As Freud says, the ego "serves three masters: the external world, the superego, and the id." The ego is therefore heavily burdened and "breaks out in anxiety—realistic anxiety regarding the external world, moral anxiety regarding the superego, and neurotic anxiety regarding the strength of the passions in the id."[12]

Consumers over the past few decades have obviously had a great deal of difficulty controlling the pleasure-seeking side of their personalities, in part because the societal elements that shape development of the superego have broken down over the years, with excessive consumption and the use of debt seen as acceptable by large portions of society. Moreover, nothing in the construct of parenting—the other major force that shapes development of the superego—gave individuals either the guidance or the guilt to associate the use of debt as a negative. Similarly, government did little to inject any semblance of reason or moral guidance because it, too, was a debt user.

Henry Murray, who in 1938 wrote *Explorations in Personality*, a 742-page study of human nature and the differences in people's personalities that many consider the seminal work in psychology, identifies a wide variety of basic needs that tend to be expressed by people at varied levels of intensity based on differences in their personalities. Similar to Maslow, Murray defines a need as

> a hypothetical process the occurrence of which is imagined in order to account for certain objective and subjective facts. In starting with a consideration of behavior we suppose that we are focusing upon one of the most significant aspects of the organism, and hence of the personality. For upon behavior and its results depends everything which is generally regarded as important: physical well-being and survival, development and achievement, happiness and the perpetuation of the species.[13]

To this end, Murray compiles the five needs shown in Table 2-1, which are derived from primary needs and are linked to consumer behavior. I list a few examples of goods and services that consumers might desire, to meet each of the needs Murray describes:

TABLE 2-1 Human Needs and a Sampling of What They Buy or Acquire to Fulfill Them

Need	The Consumable Goods and Services and Venues Consumers Choose to Meet This Need
Acquisition (Acquisitive attitude): To gain possessions and property. To grasp, snatch or steal things. To bargain or gamble. To work for money or goods.	Real estate, casinos, flea markets, eBay, auctions, general employment and general purchases of goods and services
Conservance (Conserving attitude): To collect, repair, clean and preserve things. To protect against damage.	Car washes, plastic wrap, plastic containers, household cleaning agents, detergents, vacuums, washing machines, irons, ironing boards, steamers, furniture covers, window cleaners, carpet cleaners, tools, tool kits, warranties, stamp and coin collecting
Order (Orderly attitude): To arrange, organize, put away objects. To be tidy and clean. To be scrupulously precise.	Dry cleaning services, storage facilities, closet organizers, computer hard drives, cloud computing, electronic calendars, personal digital assistants (PDAs), wall calendars, desks, cabinets, wall shelves
Retention (Retentive attitude): To retain possession of things. To refuse to give or lend. To hoard. To be frugal, economical and miserly.	Cash, coins, savings deposits, time deposits, stocks, bonds, piggybanks, attics, basements, closets, scrapbooks
Construction (Constructive attitude): To organize and build.	Home extensions, kitchen remodeling, porches, patios, driveways, general contracting

Source: Murray, 1938

In addition to the above there surely are plenty of other types of needs that fit with the plethora of goods and services that consumers can't seem to get enough of.

Having looked closely at the psychological and sociological factors that influence the lives of human beings, the behavior of consumers over the past 30 years is more easily understood. In many ways, people simply can't help themselves because they, like all living creatures, are predisposed to meet their basic needs. Human beings, however, are unique, having a predisposition to pursue goals that reach well beyond subsistence and into the realm of social structures that act as extraordinarily powerful influences on the way in which people behave, including toward the pursuit of wealth and the consumption of goods and services.

Productivity and the Conspicuous Consumer

I never take modern conveniences for granted. I am fascinated by everything around me, from televisions (they're one-half-inch thick!), to airplanes (I can be in Italy in eight hours!), to computers (I can write a book on it!). It astounds me in particular to walk into a supermarket. Think about it. Walking in with my rickety cart, I am surrounded by an abundance of food representing every food group (and some questionable ones!) produced in all parts of the world. Walking through the aisles I find not only the food products I need for the savory meal I plan, I find many choices of that particular food, from the expensive brand label to the lower priced store brand and a few in-between. After picking up a few extra goodies I head to the checkout counter where I toss in a magazine and a pack of gum, swipe a plastic card, pack my bags and head to my motorized vehicle, where I press on that little rectangular rubber pedal, and I am quickly home.

If this were 200 years ago, I would have had to work all day to grow and prepare food for the meals I can today prepare in a tiny fraction of the time. This is the essence of productivity growth, which is the determinant of the growth rate in a nation's standard of living. It is also a magnificent facilitator of personal consumption.

Frederick Winslow Taylor in 1911 published *The Principles of Scientific Management*, to, as he said, "point out, through a series of simple illustrations, the great loss which the whole country is suffering through inefficiency in almost all of our daily acts. Second, to try to convince the reader that the remedy for this inefficiency lies in systematic management, rather than in searching for some unusual or extraordinary man."[14]

Taylor correctly saw that the nation's productivity could be significantly increased if more attention were put on its inefficiencies and the remedies available that could reduce or remove them. He therefore developed a system of management for improving efficiencies, targeting in particular engineers and managers of industrial and man-ufacturing establishments, as well as the working class. Taylor said that he hoped his principles would reach well beyond his targeted audi-ence and be applied in the management of homes, farms, churches, philanthropic institutions, schools, and government. (It looks like his hopes were met in all but the latter!)

Taylor summarizes scientific management as consisting of no sin-gle element but a combination of the following:

- Science, not rule of thumb.
- Harmony, not discord.
- Cooperation, not individualism.
- Maximum output in place of restricted output.
- The development of each man to his greatest efficiency and prosperity.

To test his theories, Taylor went to Bethlehem Steel Company, which needed to ship 80,000 tons of pig-iron for use in the Spanish War. Pig-iron was produced as far back as 1,100 BC by the Chinese. It has been used for centuries in industrial societies to produce iron and more recently, steel. Pig-iron is so called because when many of them are gathered together in a heap, the pig-iron appear as piglets feeding on a sow. Pig-iron is made relatively small for easy handling, weighing about 90 pounds. Hence, at the Bethlehem factory there were many individual pig-iron in those 80,000 tons that had to be moved—by hand, of course, because there were no machines that could handle the task in those days.

Taylor (1911) studied the 75 men who moved the pig-iron daily from large heaping piles to inclined wooden planks that leaned against the side of a rail car and then into the rail cars. He noticed that the most efficient men moved about 47 tons of pig-iron per day compared to an average of about 12.5 tons for all of the men combined. So he decided to select four men who he believed were capable of boosting their daily output to 47 tons per day, offering them a pay incentive to motivate them. One of these men Taylor called "Schmidt." He made $1.15 per day. Taylor figured him a good candidate for his experiment, noticing that he would trot home about a mile after work with the same vigor as he did at the start of the day. Schmidt was also known to be a bit tight with his money (who wouldn't be at $1.15 per *day*!). The combination of these factors made Schmidt an ideal candidate for Taylor's method, so he made Schmidt an offer. The conversation went like this:

"Schmidt, are you a high-priced man?"

"Vell, I don't know vat you mean."

"Oh yes, you do. What I want to know is whether you are a high-priced man or not."

"Vell, I don't know vat you mean."

"Oh, come now, you answer my questions. What I want to find out is whether you are a high-priced man or one of these cheap fellows here. What I want to find out is whether you want to earn $1.85 a day or whether you are satisfied with $1.15, just the same as all those cheap fellows are getting."

"Did I vant $1.85 a day? Vas dot a high-priced man? Vell, yes, I vas a high-priced man."[15]

Taylor agreed to pay Schmidt $1.85 per day on one condition—that he do all that his manager told him to do; to rest when his manager said rest and to work when his manager said work.

By the time Schmidt finished his first day of work under Taylor's program, he had moved 47.5 tons of pig-iron. Taylor then extended the program to all of the pig-iron workers, and before long all of the workers were moving pig-iron at a daily rate of 47.5 tons per day.

It would appear to the casual observer and certainly to labor advocates that Schmidt and his colleagues were shortchanged in the deal because Bethlehem Steel had achieved a productivity increase of about 360 percent, whereas the pig-iron handlers had received a pay increase of only 60 percent. Taylor (1911) recognizes this seeming unfairness but makes a very important claim with respect to consumers, claiming they in the final analysis are the biggest beneficiaries of systems such as his that are designed to produce worker productivity:

> It does seem grossly unjust when the bare statement is made that the competent pig-iron handler, for instance, who has been so trained that he piles 3 6/10 times as much iron as the incompetent man formerly did, should receive an increase of only 60 per cent in wages.

> It is not fair, however, to form any final judgment until all of the elements in the case have been considered. At the first glance we see only two parties to the transaction, the workmen and their employers. We overlook the third great party, the whole people, the consumers, who buy the product of the first two and who ultimately pay both the wages of the workmen and the profits of the employers.

> The rights of the people are therefore greater than those of either employer or employee. And this third great party should be given its proper share of any gain. In fact, a glance at industrial history shows that in the end the whole people receive the greater part of the benefit coming from industrial improvements. In the past hundred years, for example, the greatest factor tending toward increasing the output, and thereby the prosperity of the civilized world, has been the introduction of machinery to replace hand labor. And without doubt the greatest gain through this change has come to the whole people, the consumer....[16]

Taylor's point is critical because it speaks to the ability of consumers to purchase goods at affordable prices and to have an ample amount of goods to choose from. The availability of larger amounts of goods at lower prices facilitates *conspicuous consumption*, a concept created by Veblen (1899) to describe spending by the leisure class solely for the purpose of demonstrating the possession of wealth.[17] Velbin defined "leisure" in this context, saying that it connotes "a nonproductive consumption of time," where the amount of time spent is excessive relative output, and where the time spent showcases one's financial ability "to afford a life of idleness."[18] The increased availability of goods has facilitated this sort of behavior. Nystrom (1928) believes advances in society have caused individuals to depart from old-time standards of religion and philosophy

> ...and having failed to develop forceful views to take their places, hold to something that may be called, for want of a better name, a *philosophy of futility*.[19] This lack of purpose in life has an effect on consumption similar to that of having a narrow life interest, that is, in concentrating human attention on the more superficial things that comprise much of *fashionable* consumption.

Nystrom believes this attitude leads individuals to relentlessly seek instant gratification in frivolous things, such as fashionable apparel, leaving them with constant feelings of dissatisfaction.

The concept of conspicuous consumption is one of the most critical to understand when attempting to comprehend the behavior of consumers over the past century and the past 30 years in particular. Psychological and sociological factors are at the root of the behavior and are what have led people to upsize their homes; buy second homes, second cars, new furniture, expensive jewelry, fancy clothes; globetrot; even turn their homes into virtual ATMs—and oh, so much more. Consumption could not have been nearly as conspicuous as it has been if not for the more widespread availability of goods at prices that made it possible for the behaviors of the leisure, or upper class, to be emulated by the middle class. Indeed, as Veblen (1899) says

> The motive that lies at the root of ownership is emulation; and the same motive of emulation continues active in the further development of the institution to which it has given rise and in the development of all those features of the social structure which this institution of ownership touches. The possession of wealth confers honor; it is an invidious distinction.[20]

The ability of the middle class to emulate the upper class was entirely a twentieth-century phenomenon; it wasn't possible before the industrial evolution, except on a much smaller scale. There simply weren't enough proprietors selling to the masses, and there weren't enough products on store shelves to facilitate conspicuous consumption in the manner seen in the twentieth century. There are only so many items the tinsmith can make in a day, after all, and even though some items could be mass-produced (candles, for instance, by 1850 could be produced at a rate of over 500 per hour[21]), there isn't much to impress one's neighbor from the candle shop, but fancy yourself with a new car, and you will get everyone talking!

It takes more than a plentiful supply of goods and services to facilitate conspicuous consumption, however. Consumers have to make payment somehow. Moreover, consumers need standards by which to compare themselves to others in society so that they can set goals for wealth accumulation and consumption and thus ultimately fulfill their insatiable primal and sociological needs. To wit, let's now explore two additional contributors to conspicuous consumption: mass marketing and financial innovation.

Mass Marketing: The Serpent in the Garden of Eden

When Adam and Eve were tempted in the Garden of Eden to eat of the Tree of Knowledge, they had to be sold on the idea first. After all, their Creator had told them that if they ate from the tree they would die. That's a far worse consequence than getting a bad FICO score as a result of walking away from mortgage and credit card debt they could not afford to service! Nevertheless, the temptation to Adam and Eve was too great, and they ate of the tree, changing everything. They didn't die literally, just morally, and they had to suffer for years afterward in ways they wouldn't have otherwise. So in a way, it was like the modern household choosing to let their credit score get wrecked and having to deal with the consequences for years afterward.

The connection between both Adam and Eve and American households is that both were tempted into actions they might not have taken otherwise. The serpent that tempted Adam and Eve set the standard for marketers for every generation of marketers that followed, having tempted the garden dwellers to risk death for a chance to taste the succulence of an apple the serpent said would make them more like God. How can we blame them for giving in to the temptation? Who doesn't want to feel as if they are bigger and better than everyone else? By comparison it doesn't seem so bad that consumers would accumulate debt to taste the best of what the bourgeois could eat, drink, wear, drive, and live in.

Here are two striking stories highlighted by the Federal Reserve in a study by Reid (2010) on the social processes influencing the mortgage borrowing decision that illuminate the power of marketing in spurring conspicuous consumption:

> Cesario Gonzalez said he was encouraged to go for his first home last year by a mortgage broker handing out business cards in front of Pancho Villa Farmers Market on El Cajon Boulevard. Gonzalez said through a translator that he still is uncertain what kind of loans he signed up for on the $565,000 duplex he purchased in May 2007. With monthly mortgage payments of $4,200 and monthly income of $3,200, the purchase appeared dubious...He could see his neighbors being owners of houses. He trusted the Realtor and the loan officer. He wanted a home.

> Colvin Grannum, an African American who grew up in a black neighborhood in Brooklyn, explained that his father bought several properties in the 1950s and '60s, often without turning to banks. "I don't want to say it's in the cultural DNA, but a lot of us who are older than 30 have some memory of disappointment or humiliation related to banks," Mr. Grannum said. "The white guy in the suit with the same income

gets a loan and you don't? So you turn to local brokers, even if they don't offer the best rates."[22]

Reid believes the anecdotes suggest that "mortgage lending is as much a social process as it is an economic decision, and highlights the importance of local context in shaping what has been construed predominantly as an economic transaction."

Three themes related to social embeddedness emerge from the many interviews that Reid conducted for her study. First, the networks from which borrowers obtained information about mortgage transactions were very insular, and very few respondents had additional means of obtaining independent information about loan products and pricing, leaving them more susceptible to deceptive marketing. Second, borrowers relied heavily on social networks to help them to choose mortgage brokers and lenders. This tendency was especially heavy among immigrant and African-American respondents, resulting in a preference for brokers in their communities because they were perceived to be more likely to understand their needs and treat them fairly. This false sense of trust added to the susceptibility of borrowers to marketing efforts that were designed to be purely transaction oriented. Third, respondents identified themselves with the social norms that developed during the housing boom, raising their expectations about home ownership and its potential financial benefits. This let the id within people's personalities win over the ego and superego, which were operating on a poor construct and providing too little discipline, and thus they were unable to control people's desires for pleasure.

When faced with the decision on whether to buy a home and if so, the sort of mortgage to obtain, the social cues pointed very clearly in one direction. It is a major explanation for the many poor decisions that many people made during the housing bubble. Social cues in general can be viewed this way, and they are at the root of many speculative bubbles. Granovetter (1985) argues that behavior deemed nonrational might be deemed more reasonable when the social context of that decision is fully understood, including how the behavior fits with the decision-maker's goals, both financially and in terms of the person's social status and/or acceptance within society.[23]

Granovetter further argues that there are three ways in which social networks shape the economic decisions that people make and that make it more likely they will make seemingly irrational decisions. First, the networks impact the information that people receive and act on, sort of like a filter. Second, the networks influence people's motives. For example, the decision to buy a home can be influenced by a sense within a social network that doing so will be beneficial. Third, social networks influence the level of trust people place in others with whom they come into contact. Excessive trust by prospective homebuyers in people within their social networks made them vulnerable during the housing boom in the U.S. in the early 2000s.

A very important theory forwarded by Granovetter is his notion of the "strength of weak ties," a theory that suggests, according to Reid, that new and more diverse information flows through weak social networks—acquaintances—than through strong social networks such as family members and close friends. Weak ties are very important because they familiarize individuals with information outside of what they can garner from their immediate social circle. Granovetter believes that weak ties provide information, ideas, and contacts that are different than those that an individual can get from one's immediate network because people within a particular network have similar information available to share with each other that is less diverse than the combination of outside sources.

With the plethora of social cues pointing squarely in one direction and individuals predisposed to satisfying their primal needs and assuring their place in society, not much persuasion was necessary during the housing boom to get people to make decisions that turned out to be bad ones. Marketers nonetheless put on a full press, seeking to persuade perspective home buyers to buy more home than they could afford, as well as convince people to get credit cards—lots of them.

500 Million Credit Cards, but Who's Counting? Financial Innovation in Action

Data from the Federal Reserve show how rampant the use of credit cards was in the time leading up to the recent financial crisis, underscoring the substantial impact that financial innovation had on the growth in the use of debt. Frame and White (2009) define financial innovation as

> something new that reduces costs, reduces risks, or provides an improved product/service/instrument that better satisfies financial system participants' demands. Financial innovations can be grouped as new products (e.g., subprime mortgages) or services (e.g., Internet banking); new production processes (e.g., credit scoring); or new organizational forms (e.g., Internet-only banks).[24]

Figure 2-2 shows the number of credit cards outstanding, which peaked at 500 million in the second quarter of 2008, falling a whopping 120 million by the third quarter of 2010.

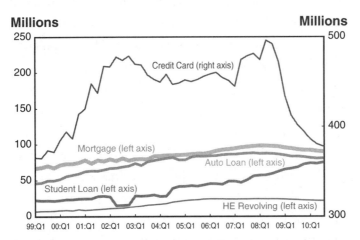

Figure 2-2 Number of credit cards and other forms of credit outstanding

Source: Federal Reserve Bank of New York Consumer Credit Panel; http://www.newyorkfed.org/research/staff_reports/sr480.pdf

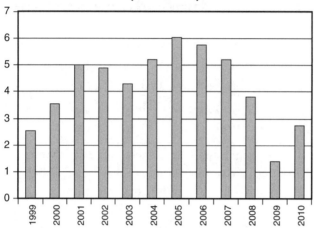

Figure 2-3 Take my credit, please!

Source: Synovate Mail Monitor

The proliferation of credit cards is attributable in no small part to the massive amount of mail solicitations that people received to apply for credit. Figure 2-3 shows the dramatic increase in the number of mailed credit card solicitations in the years leading up to the financial crisis. As the table shows, in 2005 over 5 billion mail solicitations were sent, which was twice as much as ten years earlier. The population during that period increased by about 30 million people, which means that the increase in mailings far outstripped the population growth, resulting in many more solicitations per household.

The increase in home ownership in the years leading up to the financial crisis can be attributed in part to financial innovation. Dynan and Kohn (2007) support this view, finding the increase in household indebtedness may be related to the increase in access to credit, noting that the share of households with some debt increased from 70 percent in 1983 to 77 percent in 2004.[25] Dynan and Kohn find the increase in debt associated with increased credit availability is attributable more to increased availability of credit for households already having access to credit than to increases in the share of households that could obtain credit (sometimes known as the *democratization of credit*). In addition to increased credit availability, a lowering in the cost of debt also contributed to household indebtedness.

A controversial subject among researchers is whether the securitization of mortgages might have lowered the yield spread between mortgage rates and "risk-free" rates. Kolari, Fraser, and Anari (1998) argue securitization lowered spreads,[26] while Todd (2000) sees a weaker connection between securitization and spreads.[27] Whatever researchers believe, it just seems common sense that the massive growth in securitization of mortgages increased the availability of mortgage credit to households, given the way in which it enabled banks to allay their risks onto investors.

Dynan and Kohn cite three reasons to believe household indebtedness may have been bolstered by interactions between financial innovation and the rise in home prices. First, rising home values gave households additional equity, or collateral, to take advantage of the reduced cost of liquefying home equity. Second, a reduction in financial hurdles for home ownership—for example, a reduction in required down payments relative to prices—may have boosted home prices. Third, financial innovation fed upon itself in the sense that it created the incentive for financial institutions to find new ways to increase the ability of home owners to liquefy their home equity, which itself was a source of profits for institutions and thus a strong motivational force in shaping innovation on top of innovation.

A powerful force in the housing boom was the combination of financial innovation, low interest rates, and capital inflows into the United States. Sa, Towbin, and Wieladek (2011) find that excessive financial innovation in countries with a high degree of mortgage development may act as a propagation mechanism, boosting the effects of low mortgage rates and capital inflows.[28] The researchers find that legislation facilitating the issuance of mortgage-backed securities increased the impact of the surge in capital flows to the United States and other countries by a factor of two on several fronts, including real house prices, real residential investment, and real credit to the private sector, mainly by the way mortgage securities transform illiquid mortgages into high-quality, publicly traded assets deemed attractive to foreign investors. This is the main way by which foreign money played a significant role in the housing boom in the United States and other countries with developed mortgage markets.

Technology almost certainly played a major role in innovation, enabling individuals to more easily apply for credit—gaining a response to their applications in under a minute in some cases. Moreover, technology made it easier to access credit by making it easier to withdraw home equity from a local ATM, for example. Frame and White (2009) support this idea, finding that technological changes relating to telecommunications and data processing spurred financial innovations that altered bank products and services and production processes.[29] An example is the use of credit scoring tools rather than human judgment when evaluating consumer loan applications. Such an approach creates the sort of transparency that facilitates securitization of debts, including credit card and mortgage debts.

Financial innovation probably contributed to the subprime debacle, doing so by creating a false sense of security among lenders that utilized the many new statistical analyses that were developed to measure risk and establish risk-based pricing. In other words, the statistical modeling created a comfort level that led financial institutions to underestimate the risks associated with subprime lending. This led to rapid growth in the subprime market, which grew substantially in the early 2000s, accounting for about 20 percent of all mortgages originated between 2004 and 2006, and increasing to $1.2 trillion all mortgages outstanding. These figures are astounding when put in the context of today's mortgage market, which is essentially shut to new lending. Lenders have learned that their risk models were faulty, to say the least.

The financial reforms that took place in the 1990s arguably were the most in terms of the numbers of regulations rolled back since the Great Depression, reflecting a rolling back of the Glass-Steagall Banking Act of 1933, which separated the activities of bank and non-bank financial intermediaries. Boz and Mendoza believe that the financial reforms led to many consequential financial innovations that contributed to the housing and credit booms while simultaneously leading to a "natural" underpricing of risk associated with the new financial environment, thus leading to a surge in credit and asset prices—and ultimately a collapse.[30] The researchers say that the underpricing was "natural" because there was no data on the default or performance records of the instruments because they were new. Makes sense! Moreover, there was a lack of understanding about the risks that existed in the new regulatory framework. This misunderstanding led to layering of risks on the belief that the new financial instruments that were being created were well diversified and practically risk-free. This view was reinforced by new portfolio models that combined top-rated tranches of assets with riskier asset tranches on the belief that the assets were priced correctly (which of course they weren't). Only a big left-tail event could bring the structure down, the modelers believed. Well, it did.

Boz and Mendozza believe that three reform Acts contributed most to the problem: The 1995 New Community Reinvestment Act, which strengthened the role of Fannie Mae and Freddie Mac in mortgage markets and facilitated mortgage securitization; the 1999 Gramm–Leach–Bliley Act, which removed the prohibition that prevented bank holding companies from owning other financial companies; and the 2000 Commodity Futures Modernization Act, which stipulated that financial derivatives such as credit default swaps (CDS) would not be regulated as futures contracts, securities, or lotteries under any federal law.

Underscoring the role of financial innovation in the financial crisis, Mendoza and Terrones (2008) find that 33 (22) percent of credit booms observed in the 1965–2006 period in developed (emerging) economies occurred after periods of large financial reforms.[31]

Saving for a Rainy Day: A Lost Art Returns, Sort Of

The consumer spending binge of the past 30 years is illuminated by numerous data, including the continuous increase in the square footage of new homes, the numbers of cars owned per licensed driver, debt metrics, and the personal savings rate, which is shown in Figure 2-4.

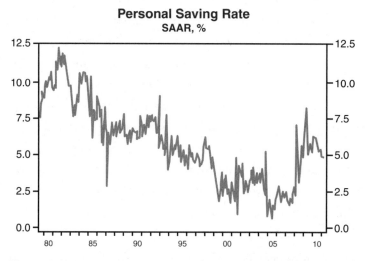

Figure 2-4 For 30 years, people preferred to spend rather than save.

Source: Burean of Economic Analysis/Haver Analytics

The decline in the personal savings rate is one of the more jarring statistics because it shows the extent to which consumers were willing to mortgage their futures, so to speak, believing they eventually would either be wealthier or realize income gains large enough to make it safe to let their savings run to the ground over the short-run. One of the most important reasons why households let their savings rates fall was because their net worth had increased. Figure 2-5 illustrates the strong correlation that has existed between wealth and savings over the past 50 years. Gains in household net worth began accelerating in the mid-1990s when nonfarm productivity climbed in response to advances in technology that led to a technology shock and boosted corporate incomes and thus share prices. The bursting of the financial bubble in 2000 temporarily disrupted the trend before share prices began recovering and, more importantly, home prices began to rise rapidly. Concomitant with the increase in net worth, households began feeling more comfortable with their financial situations, believing that their wealth gains were permanent. This created a wealth effect, which research from Muellbauer (2007) and many others indicate amounts to about 6 or 7 cents on the dollar.[32] In other words, for every $1 increase in the value of a home, a household increases its spending by 6 or 7 cents. This is more than the wealth effect for corporate equities, which many researchers estimate runs at about 3–5 cents on the dollar. Benjamin, Chinloy, and Jud (2004) believe that the wealth effect (or, put differently, the marginal propensity to consume) originating from home equity is 8 cents on the dollar, or four times larger than the marginal propensity to consume out of financial assets. The researchers also investigated the decline in the savings rate, concluding that

> ...about half of the decline in the fraction of income that Americans save, from 6.5 percent in 1995 to 1 percent by 2001, is attributable to increases in real estate and financial wealth. Virtually all of the decline in consumption occurring from the stock market decline of 2000–2001 is offset by rising consumption from real estate wealth. Real estate smooths and stabilizes consumption when other assets are performing poorly.[33]

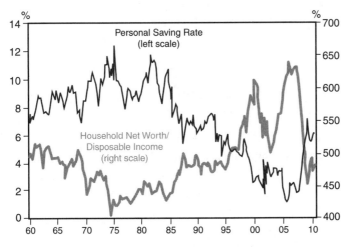

Figure 2-5 People save more when their net worth declines, and vice versa.

Source: http://www.frbsf.org/publications/economics/letter/2011/el2011-01.html

During the housing boom, consumer spending was significantly boosted by the rise in home prices with the extraction of equity through three channels in particular: sales of existing homes; home equity loans; and so-called cash-out refinancings, whereby homeowners increased the size of their existing mortgages. Greenspan and Kennedy (2007) estimate the amount of free cash resulting from the three types of equity extraction averaged about $530 billion annually during the period between 1991 and 2005.[34] About 67 percent of the extraction is attributable to sales of existing homes, and about 20 percent is attributable to home equity loans. The remainder is attributable to cash-out refinancing.

Greenspan and Kennedy estimate that during the period between 1991 and 2005, these extractions were used directly to finance an average of close to $66 billion per year of personal consumption expenditures (PCE), or about 1 percent of all PCE. Consistent with the rise in home prices, the attribution from housing to PCE was larger in the 2000s than in the 1990s, accounting for about 1.75 percent of PCE, compared to an average of 0.6 percent of in the 1990s. The attribution is even larger when making adjustments for nonmortgage debt repayments because the repayments tended to be for bridge loans households made within their balance sheets, with installment debts serving as bridge financing for PCE and mortgage debt as the ultimate source of funding. Following these adjustments, Greenspan and Kennedy estimate equity extraction financed 1.1 percent of PCE from 1991 to 2000 and a whopping 3 percent from 2001 to 2005. The numbers almost certainly increased further just prior to the onset of the financial crisis.

Greenspan and Kennedy's data help to substantially explain the decline in the savings rate, which resulted from the extraction of equity from people's homes.

Consistent with the focus placed earlier in the chapter on psychological and sociological influences, I focus now on behavioral influences that may have affected the savings rate. Benton, Meier, and

Sprenger (2007) provide compelling arguments that help explain the glaring inconsistency between an individual's stated long-term goals and their short-term decisions.[35] The researchers utilize behavioral economics to discuss how self-control problems could play a crucial role in determining financial outcomes such as borrowing and saving.

To explain the apparent disconnect between high levels of debt and low levels of savings, the researchers cite evidence to indicate that this condition is considered by individuals themselves to be far from ideal. The researchers believe that a plausible explanation is that individuals at times make suboptimal financial decisions and that a *lack of self-control* is sometimes to blame:

> That is, if asked beforehand to plan future financial decisions, an individual will respond in line with his or her long-run best interest. When the future actually arrives, however, and the decisions must be taken, the individual may no longer be able to stick to this plan. The resulting decisions are suboptimal with respect to long-run self-interest. Though such decisions appear to be optimal at the time they are made and are in line with the individual's immediate self-interest, they do not represent the individual's desired behavior over the long-run... The growing field of behavioral economics adds to the traditional understanding of individual financial decision making with insights from psychological research. One critical contribution from behavioral economics is the importance of self-control problems for personal financial decisions.[36]

Most of us can relate to this, having faced some degree of difficulty in self-control at one time or another, whether it was reaching for scrumptious snacks while on a diet, purchasing items that we really didn't need, or repeatedly choosing consumption over savings. The temptation of immediate gratification can be strong, and it causes us to overvalue the immediate benefits versus the long-term costs, even when our decisions run counter to our plans and our long-term goals. Individuals do not intend to destroy their long-term plans, but the wayward decisions they make accumulate and can be quite destructive over the long-run. Such has been the pattern in America over the past 30 years, with Americans spending too much and saving too little.

The Return of the Piggybank

Judging by the rebound in the savings rate shown in Figure 2-4, consumers apparently have learned that they were saving too little for a rainy day. Data from the Federal Reserve's triennial survey of consumer finances (SCF) provide very convincing evidence of this change in attitude. Table 2-2 contains the results, which indicate that nearly 30 percent of families who moved up by three or more percentile points and nearly a quarter of all other families reported desired precautionary savings that were at least 200 percent higher in 2009 than in 2007. Importantly, a substantial minority of families said that they had not increased their precautionary savings in 2009. Maybe another crisis will convince them to save more.

TABLE 2-2 Changes in Desired Precautionary Savings Level, Expected Retirement, and Attitude Toward Financial Risk

Change in wealth percentile	Percentiles of Change in Desired Precautionary Savings (Percent)			Unwilling to Take Financial Risk (Percent)		Change in Age at Which Stop Full-Time Work (Years)		
	Median	25th	75th	2007 level	2007–09 change	Median	25th	75th
Less than -10	24.4	-29.7	189.7	40.8	11.8	0	0	5
-10 – -3.1	18.6	-45.5	189.7	38.1	5.7	0	-1	4
.3 – 2.9	28.8	-35.6	189.7	35.2	4.9	0	0	3
3 – 9.9	54.5	-21.9	262.1	45.9	6.0	0	-1	5
10 of more	60.9	-3.4	286.3	45.8	-0.5	0	-2	3

°For household heads aged 63 or younger working full-time at the time of the 2007 and 2009 surveys who either reported a stopping age in both surveys or said they would never stop full-time work in both surveys.

Source: Federal Reserve; http://www.federalreserve.gov/pubs/feds/2011/201117/201117pap.pdf

With the savings rate running at a pace of about 5 to 6 percent and personal income running at a pace of about $13 trillion annual, precautionary savings will accumulate slowly but surely such that every two years the savings rate will produce a cushion of between $1.3 trillion to $1.6 trillion. This is a substantial firewall against future economic stress that will lessen the depth and duration of any economic downturn. Having lost trillions of dollars of wealth, households almost certainly wish they had consumed less and saved more in the years leading up to the financial crisis.

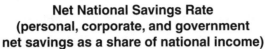

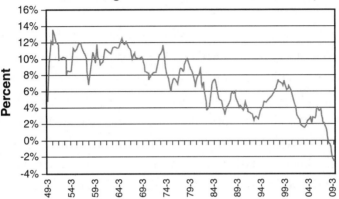

Figure 2-6 Without savings, investment will flounder and harm the U.S. economy.

Source: Reuters, http://blogs.reuters.com/felix-salmon/2010/01/04/chart-of-the-day-negative-net-national-savings/

Although it is good news to see households saving again, it is extremely important to recognize that the United States as a whole is not; the net national savings rate turned negative in 2008 for the first time since the Great Depression, owing to the vast amount of money that the United States borrows from domestic and foreign investors (Figure 2-6). Put another way, the money that households are saving is money that was essentially transferred to them by the government using money it raised by issuing U.S. Treasury securities. The net national savings rate is equal to the combined savings of the personal, business, and government sectors divided by national income. When it is negative it puts a nation at risk of borrowing economic growth from the future that must be paid back at some point. A negative national savings rate impairs a nation's ability to invest, as is illustrated by the following equation:

$$I = S + (T{-}G) + (M{-}X)$$

The equation shows the important link between savings and investment: Total investment is equal to the sum of private saving (S) and public saving (T–G), where T=taxes and G=government spending, and the net inflow of capital from abroad (M–X), where M=imports and X=exports. Depreciation of capital goods is often deducted from net national savings to reflect the reduction in economic value associated with the aging of capital goods.

The negative national savings rate is one of many signs indicating that the United States has reached the Keynesian Endpoint because any attempt to stimulate economic growth with Keynesian-style debt spending will reduce the nation's economic growth potential by curtailing investments. This supports the idea that sovereign debt will be a major driver of cash flows for many years to come, affecting economic growth, financial market performance, and global capital flows. Debt crushes the ability to invest and hence grow an economy.

Give Me My Space and a New Car, Too

"If thou art rich, thou art poor, for like an ass whose back with ingots bows, thou bearest thy heavy riches but a journey, and death unloads thee."

—William Shakespeare, *Measure for Measure*

It's a great feeling to close on a new home or to get the keys to a new car. Few purchases bring more satisfaction on both a psychological and sociological basis. It's no wonder, then, that people went over their heads to make these and other purchases. Little did people know that their riches would make them poor.

It wasn't enough to achieve the American Dream of owning a new home. The home also had to be *large*. Figure 2-7 shows the substantial increase that occurred in the size of new homes from the 1980s onward. As the chart shows, the square footage of single-family homes increased about 50 percent from 1983 through the peak in 2007. Mind you, this increase occurred even as the number of people per U.S. household was *decreasing*, to 2.6 from 2.76 in 1980, 3.14 in 1970, and 3.35 in 1960.

Median and Average Square Feet of Floor Area in New Single-Family Houses Completed by Location[1]
(Medians and averages computed from unrounded figures)

	Median square feet							Average square feet						
				Region							Region			
Year	United States	Inside MSAs	Outside MSAs	North-east	Midwest	South	West	United States	Inside MSAs	Outside MSAs	North-east	Midwest	South	West
1973	1,525	1,625	1,380	1,450	1,445	1,555	1,575	1,660	1,760	1,490	1,595	1,615	1,670	1,715
1974	1,560	1,665	1,405	1,465	1,490	1,640	1,540	1,695	1,785	1,545	1,600	1,660	1,760	1,660
1975	1,535	1,630	1,365	1,405	1,460	1,605	1,510	1,645	1,735	1,490	1,575	1,580	1,705	1,635
1976	1,590	1,675	1,425	1,505	1,495	1,660	1,565	1,700	1,775	1,560	1,630	1,655	1,755	1,685
1977	1,610	1,705	1,440	1,540	1,540	1,660	1,615	1,720	1,795	1,565	1,650	1,650	1,770	1,730
1978	1,655	1,735	1,490	1,640	1,615	1,685	1,630	1,755	1,830	1,610	1,730	1,730	1,785	1,740
1979	1,645	1,735	1,485	1,690	1,605	1,675	1,625	1,760	1,845	1,605	1,795	1,720	1,795	1,730
1980	1,595	1,670	1,450	1,660	1,520	1,615	1,570	1,740	1,825	1,575	1,770	1,685	1,750	1,735
1981	1,550	1,650	1,415	1,655	1,480	1,540	1,580	1,720	1,820	1,535	1,805	1,670	1,715	1,735
1982	1,520	1,600	1,355	1,605	1,405	1,500	1,595	1,710	1,795	1,545	1,755	1,655	1,700	1,740
1983	1,565	1,610	1,445	1,650	1,515	1,565	1,545	1,725	1,785	1,570	1,795	1,735	1,720	1,695
1984	1,605	1,645	1,495	1,665	1,600	1,590	1,610	1,780	1,840	1,600	1,860	1,800	1,750	1,785
1985	1,605	1,655	1,445	1,655	1,625	1,590	1,595	1,785	1,830	1,610	1,830	1,820	1,765	1,770
1986	1,660	1,700	1,470	1,695	1,685	1,655	1,635	1,825	1,865	1,640	1,850	1,855	1,825	1,800
1987	1,755	1,800	1,565	1,840	1,740	1,755	1,730	1,905	1,950	1,700	1,955	1,890	1,915	1,870
1988	1,810	1,880	1,570	1,810	1,840	1,790	1,845	1,995	2,055	1,750	2,005	2,015	1,985	1,995
1989	1,850	1,920	1,570	1,870	1,800	1,815	1,910	2,035	2,105	1,750	2,075	1,970	2,030	2,065
1990	1,905	1,985	1,630	1,955	1,850	1,855	1,985	2,080	2,155	1,800	2,105	2,005	2,055	2,160
1991	1,890	1,970	1,635	1,950	1,800	1,870	1,980	2,075	2,155	1,815	2,105	1,990	2,065	2,155
1992	1,920	1,990	1,700	2,000	1,870	1,945	1,890	2,095	2,160	1,870	2,115	2,020	2,130	2,090
1993	1,945	2,000	1,700	2,050	1,855	2,000	1,845	2,095	2,160	1,860	2,160	2,025	2,150	2,050
1994	1,940	1,995	1,700	2,035	1,850	2,000	1,835	2,100	2,160	1,865	2,195	2,025	2,165	2,025
1995	1,920	1,975	1,720	2,095	1,850	1,945	1,835	2,095	2,150	1,870	2,240	2,020	2,125	2,045
1996	1,950	2,000	1,735	2,100	1,900	1,995	1,890	2,120	2,170	1,915	2,280	2,025	2,160	2,070
1997	1,975	2,015	1,765	2,130	1,900	2,000	1,930	2,150	2,200	1,955	2,265	2,065	2,175	2,135
1998	2,000	2,050	1,750	2,100	1,945	2,000	1,985	2,190	2,250	1,930	2,270	2,125	2,200	2,200
1999	2,028	2,089	1,811	2,175	1,937	2,044	2,001	2,223	2,274	1,991	2,298	2,135	2,244	2,234
2000	2,057	2,121	1,824	2,266	1,971	2,075	2,014	2,266	2,321	2,024	2,435	2,170	2,287	2,244
2001	2,103	2,152	1,905	2,305	1,965	2,128	2,080	2,324	2,361	2,162	2,466	2,209	2,351	2,317
2002	2,114	2,171	1,884	2,330	1,979	2,120	2,127	2,320	2,379	2,068	2,516	2,209	2,317	2,350
2003	2,137	2,177	1,941	2,288	1,998	2,142	2,166	2,330	2,382	2,113	2,443	2,198	2,335	2,387
2004	2,140	2,207	1,933	2,361	1,993	2,164	2,149	2,349	2,402	2,122	2,543	2,222	2,368	2,352
2005	2,227	2,273	1,952	2,339	2,054	2,259	2,236	2,434	2,479	2,137	2,556	2,310	2,463	2,434
2006	2,248	2,305	1,909	2,395	2,035	2,286	2,275	2,469	2,519	2,120	2,612	2,290	2,499	2,488
2007	2,277	2,319	1,956	2,281	2,064	2,325	2,286	2,521	2,581	2,133	2,550	2,328	2,573	2,524
2008	2,215	2,270	1,963	2,312	2,019	2,266	2,216	2,519	2,582	2,203	2,651	2,331	2,564	2,508
2009	2,135	2,185	1,909	2,211	1,931	2,198	2,140	2,438	2,490	2,156	2,594	2,216	2,488	2,434
2010	2,169	2,203	1,877	2,336	2,001	2,184	2,143	2,392	2,443	2,091	2,613	2,265	2,393	2,386
RSE	2	2	4	6	3	4	3	2	2	4	6	2	3	4

A Represents an RSE that is greater than or equal to 100 or could not be computed.
NA Not available. RSE Relative Standard Error.
S Withheld because estimate did not meet publication standards on the basis of response rate, associated standard error, or a consistency review.

[1] Includes houses built for rent (not shown separately).

Figure 2-7 Give me my space! Home sizes have grown.

Source: U.S. Census Bureau; http://www.census.gov/const/C25Ann/sftotalmedavgsqft.pdf

What's more American than owning a new car? Owning two of them. In the years leading up to the financial crisis, the easy availability of credit and social cues compelled Americans to purchase cars in large numbers, despite the fact that cars were lasting longer than ever. Figure 2-8 highlights the sharp increase in the number of cars per licensed driver. As the chart shows, the upward climb began in the early 1980s, coinciding with the decline in the U.S. savings rate, underscoring the notion that Americans were overborrowing and undersaving.

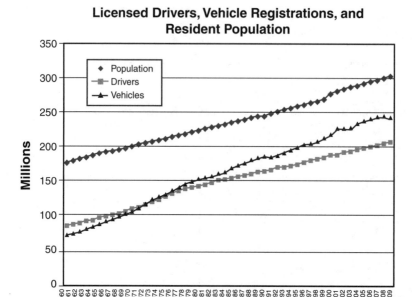

Figure 2-8 More people, yes, but even more cars

Source: U.S. Department of Transportation; http://www.fhwa.dot.gov/policyinformation/statistics/2009/dv1c.cfm

I can go on and on with a litany of illustrations showing the excesses in consumer spending that occurred over the past 30 years, but it is better to understand the many driving forces that led to the binge, as was described earlier in the chapter. It is useful nonetheless to summarize the analysis by adding to the powerful message inherent in Figure 2-6 by showing the household sector's debt binge, as reflected in a wide variety of indicators. One of the most important of these is the ratio of household debt to disposable income, shown in Figure 2-9. It has been upward trending since the early 1980s, and it catapulted higher in the 2000s. The near hyperbolic surge is attributable primarily to a surge in mortgage debt, which from 1999 to 2007 increased from $4.4 trillion to $10.6 trillion, a whopping 140 percent! Consumer credit, which consists of credit card debt as well as loans for automobiles, boats, educations, vacations, and mobile homes, surged as well, increasing by $1 trillion to $2.5 trillion.

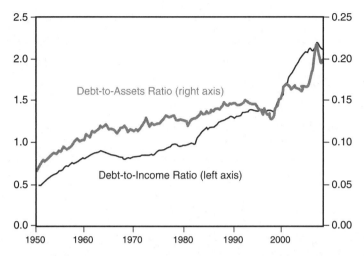

Figure 2-9 Household debt compared to wages and compensation

Source: Federal Reserve Bank of San Francisco; http://www.frbsf.org/publications/economics/letter/2011/el2011-02.html

Consistent with the increase in the debt-to-income ratio, the debt-to-asset ratio also increased, particularly after asset prices fell during the financial crisis, also shown in Figure 2-9. The increase in the debt-to-asset ratio resulting from the decline in asset prices is akin to exposing a naked person in the water when the tide goes down.

A very important characteristic of the debt binge is that it coincided with the decline in the savings rate, as shown in Figure 2-10. The trend speaks to the idea that consumption and savings trends were driven not only by gains in household net worth, but by increases in credit availability, as supported by work from Ludvigson (1999), whose findings support the intuitive belief that credit growth boosts consumption.[37] In other words, consumers were deceived into believing superfluous credit had reduced their need for precautionary savings.

Glick and Lansing (2011) find a reasonably strong correlation between the availability of household credit, which is derived from data contained in the Fed's Senior Loan Officer Survey, and household leverage, which is defined as the ratio of household debt to disposable income (Figure 2-11).[38] This is another way of saying that financial innovation played an important role in the decline in the savings rate by increasing the availability of credit. An example is the ease at which home equity withdrawals became possible—for example, by using the neighborhood ATM.

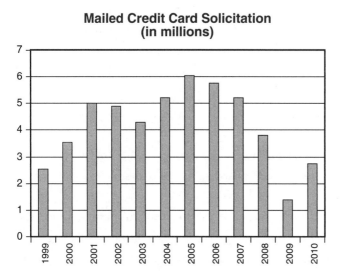

Figure 2-10 Credit growth boosts consumption.

Source: http://www.frbsf.org/publications/economics/letter/2011/el2011-01.html

Glick and Lansing construct an empirical model to compare the savings rate to two contemporaneous explanatory variables: the ratio of household net worth to disposable income (shown in Figure 2-4) and the measure of credit availability (shown in Figure 2-11). The researchers find that their model explains 90 percent of the variance in the savings rate since 1966, as shown in Figure 2-12. Underscoring the importance of credit availability as an explanatory variable, the researchers find that a model that excludes credit availability explains a relatively low 73% of changes in the savings rate and an even lower amount over the past 10 years when credit availability has moved dramatically.

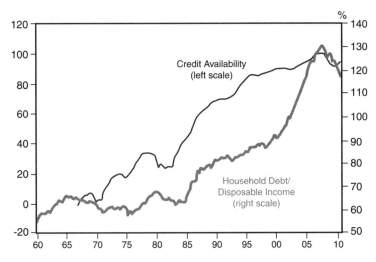

Figure 2-11 Household debt is tied to the availability of credit.

Source: Federal Reserve Bank of San Francisco (http://www.frbsf.org/publications/economics/letter/2011/el2011-01.html)

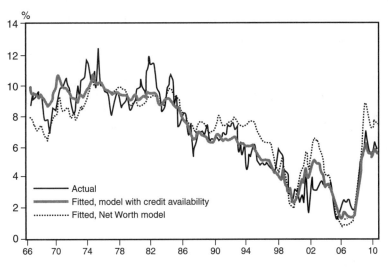

Figure 2-12 Actual and fitted savings rate, modeled to credit availability.

Source: Glick, Reuven, and Lansing, Kevin, "Consumers and the Economy, Part I: Household Credit and Personal Saving," Federal Reserve Bank of San Francisco, *Economic Letter*, 2011

These data are important to remember in the time ahead because the data suggest the low availability of credit will likely boost savings at the expense of consumption, thereby hampering economic activity.

Crippled by Capitalism

"The crippling of individuals I consider the worst evil of capitalism. Our whole educational system suffers from this evil. An exaggerated competitive attitude is inculcated into the student, who is trained to worship acquisitive success as a preparation for his future career."

—Albert Einstein

A cocktail of powerful ingredients led consumers on a spending binge over the past 30 years that resulted in the excessive use of debt and depletion of savings. Sociological, anthropological, and psychological factors combined with financial innovation, mass marketing, and mass production of goods and services to create conspicuous consumption on a colossal and unprecedented scale. The reckless behavior reflected very natural expressions of primal urges and social cravings that nary a human being can resist, especially when the opportunity for immediate gratification presents itself. There is little to nothing that policymakers can do to stymie these natural proclivities. The best they can do is work around them, shaping policies that go beyond failed constructs to reflect the basic tendencies of human beings and their yearning for attention.

3

How Politicians Carry Out Fiscal Illusions, Deceive the Public, and Balloon Our Debts

"The soulless carry out deception and betrayal with indefatigable remorselessness, dispensing of their hearts and subordinating humanity and benevolence for self-interest, carrying it out with malevolence and disdain for the greater good. Not in a quarter, a half, or a full orb's turn is man kept from deceit's dagger. The bleeding heart it leaves the eyes cannot see nor the pain felt, yet the wound left by the villain's relentless piercing of the soul is visible even in darkness. Fairness is fleeting and foulness flairs from flesh-eating fiends, they filled fully with affinity solely for themselves."
—Tony Crescenzi

Fiscal Illusion and the Hoodwinking of America

American taxpayers have been hoodwinked for decades by a fiscal illusion that has led them to believe that the cost they bear from profligate government spending is low relative to the benefits. The hoodwinkers have been many, in particular politicians in Washington, who have also led the American people to believe that the use of debt is without cost. This is the essence of fiscal illusion, whereby the victims are ill-informed and are taken advantage of by those who have control of budgetary matters and use debt to hide the true cost of their decisions. Public unions for decades have been perpetrators in this charade, strong-arming their way to support causes that shun the public good to serve their self-interests, doing so by substantially influencing fiscal and budgetary decisions, largely through collective bargaining and by engaging in political activities that support their profligate agenda. The deception has been pervasive, carried out at every level of government, in particular local government, where the ranks of public union workers has grown steadily, surpassing in 2009 that of the private sector, where union membership has been declining for decades, as shown in Figure 3-1.

The persistent growth in public union membership represents a "structural break"[1] in American labor unionism that Norcross (2011) finds has implications not for the profitability of firms, but the solvency of governments.[2] The reason is because unions play a substantial role in affecting government spending, undermining the sovereignty of government by introducing an unelected body into policy-making.[3] Public unions affect both the level of government spending and its composition, abrogating control of public finance from an unsuspecting and ignorant populous. This deception is carried out in a variety of ways, particularly by the use of debt and deferred payments to mask the true cost of their collective bargaining agreements.

> According to Oates (1988), for the deceptive nature of collective bargaining agreements to be successful, far more than imperfect information is needed to pull the wool over the public's eyes and create a fiscal illusion: Imperfect information is not, however, synonymous with fiscal illusion. It is a necessary, but not a sufficient, condition for its existence. More specifically, fiscal illusion refers to a *systematic misperception* of fiscal parameters—a recurring propensity, for example, to underestimate one's tax liability associated with certain public

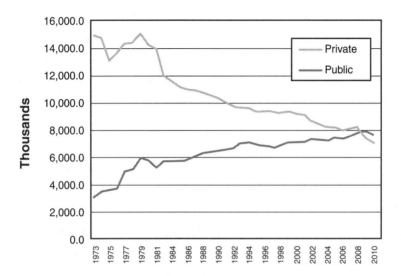

Figure 3-1 The essence of fiscal illusion

Source: Eileen Norcross, "Public Sector Unionism: A Review," George Mason University, *Working Paper*, 2011; http://mercatus.org/sites/default/files/publication/PublicSectorUnionism.Norcross_2.pdf.

programs. Imperfect information alone might well give rise to a random pattern of over- and underestimation of such tax liabilities. Fiscal illusion, in contrast, implies persistent and consistent behavior. As such, it will give rise to recurring, and presumably predictable, biases in budgetary decisions.[4]

In other words, fiscal illusion is made possible when there is both a large gap between what the public expects of fiscal initiatives and what politicians intend, as well as persistent belief by the public that the cost of fiscal initiatives is lower than it actually is.

Italian economist Amilcare Puviani first advanced the notion of fiscal illusion in 1903 in his book, *The Theory of Fiscal Illusion*, or *Teoria della illusione nelle entrate publiche*, in Italian. Puviani sought to answer a simple question: How can a politician best use his powers of the purse to promote his political projects?[5] The answer will not surprise you because you've seen this movie before. Puviani explains that what is best for the politician is not necessarily best for the public. The motivated politician conducts his office by taking credit for all that is perceived as good about public policy, whether the credit is due him or not, in pursuit of his self-interest and to self-promote. All of the politicians' actions are taken for these egocentric pursuits.

Puviani focuses in particular on fiscal matters, especially those related to taxation, which is the charlatan's main tool for deception and at the root of the definition of fiscal illusion. Puviani explains that for a politician to carry out his deceit he must make taxes seem less onerous than they actually are both in the present and the future. This is where debt use comes into play. By deferring costs; for example, by deferring income payments to union workers to a later date, or by deferring payment for current expenditures through the use of debt, politicians can focus the public on the benefits of fiscal initiatives rather than their true cost. In doing so, the politician's status is buoyed along with his chances of re-election.

James Buchanan, who in 1986 won the Nobel Memorial Prize in Economic Sciences for his work on public choice theory, advanced Puviani's groundbreaking work in 1960, following decades of only minor advancement, with work that stands as testament to the increased level of activism that took place in the 1960s, a time when fiscal initiatives, the size of government, and public union membership all increased sharply. Two very notable programs that were birthed during that time were Medicare and Medicaid, both of which were launched in 1966 and which today account for about 30 percent of all U.S. spending.

Buchanan builds on Puviani's ideas by tying fiscal illusion to the size of government, believing that politicians manipulate the gap between the public's perception about the benefits of fiscal initiatives and their costs to grow the size of government.[6] This can be done in many ways, including by the use of debt and by applying taxes that are less visible than those that are taken directly out of paychecks. Another means is by the use of regulations, which are a form of tax. Wagner (2001) cites The Competitive Enterprise Institute in a paper discussing fiscal illusion, which in 2001 estimated the cost of federal regulations at around $700 billion per year, or $2,500 per American.[7] These costs are spread over literally thousands of goods and services, absorbed by both businesses and consumers and therefore a restraining influence on economic activity. The illusory part of regulations is that their cost is almost impossible for a consumer—for a taxpayer—to quantify. There is no breakdown of the cost on any of the labels of the products they buy or the services they receive. As Wagner (2001) notes,

> Anything that can be accomplished through taxation can be accomplished through regulation, and vice versa. For instance, a school district could reduce its taxes simply by requiring parents to send their children to approved schools. The net effect, however, would be pretty much the same, whether schools are financed by taxes and provided free of direct charge, or whether parents are required to send their children to approved schools. As a first approximation, taxation and regulation are simply different means for accomplishing the same thing: government control over the use of resources in society. Our true tax burden is really a compound of taxes plus regulations. The most direct and truthful way of taxing people is to send them monthly bills, much as we pay for our utilities. Politicians never do this.

Buchanan (1967) goes beyond taxation and regulation to list numerous other ways in which politicians use illusions to gain revenue and grow the size of government.[8] According to Mourao (2010) these include obscuring individual shares in the opportunity cost of public outlays; charging explicit fees for nominal services provided upon the occurrence of impressive or pleasant events; levying taxes that capitalize on sentiments of social fear, making the burden appear less than might otherwise be the case; using "scare tactics" that have a propensity to make the alternatives to particular tax proposals emerge worse than they are; fragmenting the total tax weight on an entity into numerous small levies; and blurring the final incidence of the tax.[9] The final result of these *illusions* is having gathered higher amounts of public revenue with little resistance from the electorate.

Fiscal illusion, hence, takes on many forms, and its fungible nature is what gives the politician ample flexibility to find a means to carry out his deception. Oates (1988) summarizes the five general forms of fiscal illusion identified in literature to which the plethora of individual illusions can be applied[10]:

1. Complexity of the tax structure
2. Renter illusion with respect to property taxation
3. Income elasticity of the tax structure
4. Debt illusion
5. The flypaper effect

Let's take a look at each of these forms of fiscal slight of hand.

The Tax Structure

The U.S. tax structure is often railed for its complexity, seen by advocates of smaller government and lower taxes as a hindrance to economic growth and vitality. The complexity is the result of decades of manipulation to advance the agenda of politicians, who use the tax structure to create illusions about the true cost of the size of government. Buchanan (1967) identifies the means by which the politician accomplish this:

To the extent that the total tax load on an individual can be fragmented so that he confronts numerous small levies rather than a few significant ones, illusory effects may be created.[11]

No wonder there are thousands of pages in the U.S. tax code. To the politician, the more complicated it is the better because it makes it difficult if not impossible for citizens to determine the amount of tax actually collected for each line item of spending. In other words, who really knows the amount of money they pay annually toward Medicare, Medicaid, or for that pork project in a Congressional district in their state or even a faraway state? If people fully understood the cost of these line items, they would likely be less supportive of them. This hopefully will be expressed at the polls in due time, and if they then took action in the form of the voting out the politicians who propose and create these illusions and hidden spending, it would reduce the size of government with each broken illusion.

What is the solution to stopping this particular deception? Starve the beast. Milton Friedman (1978) and Ronald Reagan (1980) put it this way:

> Government wants to and will spend whatever is made available. If tax revenues are increased, spending will increase; if tax revenues are lowered, the beast is starved. Revenues have a positive causal relationship to expenditures. This view has led various proponents of limited government to encourage tax cuts that are not conditional on offsetting spending cuts. The ultimate goal is for eventual spending cuts as a result of starving the beast.[12]

> —Milton Friedman

> [My opponent] tells us that first we've got to reduce spending before we can reduce taxes. Well, if you've got a kid that's extravagant, you can lecture him all you want to about his extravagance. Or you can cut his allowance and achieve the same end much quicker.[13]

> —Ronald Reagan

In the aftermath of the financial crisis that began in 2007, a reduction in the complexities of the U.S. tax structure would present a means by which Washington could increase the transparency of fiscal spending, thereby enabling the public to more openly debate and refine the nation's spending priorities to produce a better outcome than existed in 2011, that is resulting in an intractable debt problem that can only be cured by revamping public policy.

Renter Illusion

People who have felt the sting of property taxes probably have a better understanding of the true cost of local public services than people who have not. Property owners, in other words, have a better sense of the cost of local public services than renters do—or at least those who have never paid property taxes. This form of fiscal illusion takes the form of local rents, where tenants fail to connect local public services to the rents they pay because it is the landlord who pays the taxes, not the tenant, but the landlord actually passes his costs onto the tenant, creating the illusion. As a result, renters are apt to support local fiscal initiatives, failing to realize they will actually end up paying for property tax increases indirectly through rent payment hikes, and they assuredly will because the primary means by which local governments fund themselves is through property taxes.

Income Elasticity of the Tax Structure

This is one where the tricksters can have a field day. Imagine a public spending initiative in which a politician seeking public support for the initiative promises to keep personal tax rates unchanged regardless of the new spending. The taxpayer's sentiment toward the project in this case is likely to be positive. Why? Did you catch the key word? In other words, did you catch the illusion? The politician said he would keep tax *rates* unchanged, giving no indication that the overall tax burden on individuals would increase as a result of the initiative, making it possible for the politician to expand public spending without sparking opposition. In reality, individuals do actually wind up paying taxes for spending initiatives begun under these conditions because their overall tax burdens might otherwise be lower if not for the spending and because a proportion of their future income gains (as determined by their tax rates) will be used to pay for the spending.

Debt Illusion

It is questionable whether government spending increases economic activity when it is financed by debt rather than taxes because taxpayers in this case are likely to fear future confiscation of their income to pay for the debts, either by means of increased taxation and/or regulation or by cuts in services, thereby reducing consumption and hampering economic activity by an amount equal to the taxpayer's expected liability for the spending. This viewpoint is the essence of Ricardian Equivalence, a theory rooted in the works of Ricardo (1888)[14] but advanced by Barro (1974), who explored whether government bonds represent net wealth, finding that "fiscal effects involving changes in the relative amounts of tax and debt finance for a given amount of public expenditure would have no effect on aggregate demand, interest rates, and capital formation."[15] More than two centuries ago, Adam Smith (1776) forwarded the idea that government bonds are not net wealth, with views that debunk the traditional Keynesian theory that debt use is beneficial and that fit well in the context of today's indebted societies.

> The public funds of the different indebted nations of Europe, particularly those of England, have by one author been represented as the accumulation of a great capital superadded to the other capital of the country, by means of which its trade is extended, its manufactures multiplied, and its lands cultivated and improved much beyond what they could have been by means of that other capital only. He does not consider that

the capital which the first creditors of the public advanced to government was, from the moment in which they advanced it, a certain portion of the annual produce turned away from serving in the function of a capital to serve in that of a revenue; from maintaining productive labourers to maintain unproductive ones, and to be spent and wasted, generally in the course of the year, without even the hope of any future reproduction. In return for the capital which they advanced they obtained, indeed, an annuity in the public funds in most cases of more than equal value. This annuity, no doubt, replaced to them their capital, and enabled them to carry on their trade and business to the same or perhaps to a greater extent than before; that is, they were enabled either to borrow of other people a new capital upon the credit of this annuity, or by selling it to get from other people a new capital of their own equal or superior to that which they had advanced to government. This new capital, however, which they in this manner either bought or borrowed of other people, must have existed in the country before, and must have been employed, as all capitals are, in maintaining productive labour. When it came into the hands of those who had advanced their money to government, though it was in some respects a new capital to them, it was not so to the country, but was only a capital withdrawn from certain employments in or to be turned towards others. Though it replaced to them what they had advanced to government, it did not replace it to the country.[16]

Smith essentially argues that the money raised from borrowing draws from a nation's productive capital and that the beneficial effects from borrowing are offset by the negative effects of the withdrawn capital. In effect, any benefit from spending that is financed by borrowing is merely a substitute for the benefits the capital would have had if left in the private sector.

Like Smith, Tobin (1971) recognizes it is an illusion to believe that increasing the government debt can increase national wealth, asking pointedly,

How is it possible that society merely by the device of incurring a debt to itself can deceive itself into believing that it is wealthier? Do not the additional taxes which are necessary to carry the interest charges reduce the value of other components of private wealth?[17]

The financial crisis has illuminated the validity of the Ricardian equivalence hypothesis advanced by Barro, putting Keynesians on the defensive. Keynesians will be challenged to explain how the increase in indebtedness in developed countries failed to make these nations wealthier and instead caused a massive destruction in wealth, output, and employment, the opposite of what the Keynesian believes will happen when government spending is increased. It is an illusion to believe that the fiscal multiplier for government spending for highly indebted nations is greater than 1.0; evidence from the root causes of the financial crisis and failed attempts to stimulate economic growth and employment in the aftermath of the crisis suggest the multiplier is below 1.0.

The Flypaper Effect

When a government body receives a grant from another government body—for example, when a state receives a grant from the federal government—there is a tendency for the recipient to increase its spending more so than if the monies were the result of revenue increases associated with income gains in the private sector. Intragovernmental aid such as this can be a potent influence in the growth of the size of government. One way it does this is by encouraging recipients of intragovernmental aid to reallocate money they otherwise would have allocated toward the expenditure toward other expenditures, some of which can "stick"—hence the name "flypaper effect." Another way in which grants spur the growth of government is through matching requirements. States and other municipalities are often given aid on the condition that they match the aid for the expenditure to which the aid is granted, increasing the amount of spending by the recipient of the aid. Importantly, sometimes the matched spending leads the recipient to permanently increase the size of government programs and expenditures associated with the grant, resulting in increases in public expenditures that exceed the size of the grant. Oates (1979) finds "Increases in income shift the demand curve outward..., while grants lower the price to the taxpayer-voter and produce a downward movement along his demand curve."[18] This is shown in Figure 3-2.

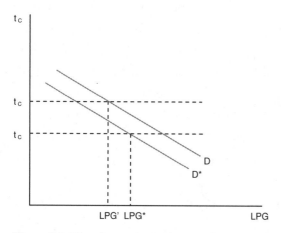

Figure 3-2 The effects of grants on the demand for recipient government services

Source: J. Patrick O'Brien and Yeung-Nan Shieh, "Utility Functions and Fiscal Illusion from Grants," *National Tax Journal* Vol. 43, no. 2 (June 1990): 201–05; http://ntj.tax.org/wwtax/ntjrec. nsf/A69A375DA53F84658525686C00686DDC/$FILE/v43n2201.pdf).

Oates also finds that "increases in personal incomes to the members of a community are not equivalent, in terms of their budgetary effects, to an equal increase in lump-sum intergovernmental revenues because, although they may generate the same true budget restraint, they do not result in the same perceived budget restraint."[19] O'Brien and Shieh (1990) find "the impact of grants on the demands for recipient government services and nonaid federal government services reflect two effects:

1. Grants change the perceived price of public goods and produce a movement along the demand curve.

2. Grants change the perceived price of recipient government services (nonaid federal government services) and shift the demand curve for nonaid federal government services (recipient government services)."[20]

The bottom-line is that that intragovernmental aid creates a fiscal illusion whereby aid recipients fail to realize the true cost of the aid, increasing demand for the services and causing the expansion of programs and expenditures associated with the aid to "stick."

In an excellent summary of the damaging elements of fiscal illusion, Buchanan and Wagner (1977) point to deep flaws in Keynesianism that inherently leads to the pursuit of political self-interest and therefore poor handling of public sector balance sheets and resulting budget deficits:

> With the completion of the Keynesian revolution, these time-tested principles of fiscal responsibility were consigned to the heap of superstitious nostrums that once stifled enlightened political-fiscal activism. Keynesianism stood the Smithian analogy on its head. The stress was placed on the differences rather than the similarities between a family and the state, and notably with respect to principles of prudent fiscal conduct. The state was no longer to be conceived in the image of the family, and the rules of prudent fiscal conduct differed dramatically as between the two institutions. The message of Keynesianism might be summarized as: What is folly in the conduct of a private family may be prudence in the conduct of the affairs of a great nation.

> What happened? Why does Camelot lie in ruin? Vietnam and Watergate cannot explain everything forever. Intellectual error of monumental proportion has been made, and not exclusively by the ordinary politicians. Error also lies squarely with the economists.

> The academic scribbler of the past who must bear substantial responsibility is Lord Keynes himself, whose ideas were uncritically accepted by American establishment economists. The mounting historical evidence of the effects of these

ideas cannot continue to be ignored. Keynesian economics has turned the politicians loose; it has destroyed the effective constraint on politicians' ordinary appetites. Armed with the Keynesian message, politicians can spend and spend without the apparent necessity to tax.[21]

As Buchanan and Wagner note, the problem with Keynesianism lies more in its political suppositions than its internal theoretical structure. The pursuit of self-interest pushes to the fore even as the politician proclaims he is acting in the interests of all. The public for its part feeds the beast by acting out of self-interest and by falling victim to fiscal illusions that the politician is inclined to create.

How Public Sector Unions Hurt the Union

The largest contributor to the 2010 election in the United States was a public union—the American Federation of State, County, and Municipal Employees (AFSCME), which contributed nearly $100 million to political campaigns, followed by the United States Chamber of Commerce.[22] The juxtaposition of these two groups captures the extraordinary ascent of public unions and their significant influence on public policy...as does the visitor log to the White House. From September 2009 through February 2011, Richard Trumka, the head of the American Federation of Labor and Congress of Industrial Organization (AFL-CIO), which represents more than 11 million workers and is the largest federation of unions in the United States, visited the White House nearly 50 times. That's a lot more visits than anyone on Main Street is likely to see in their lifetime, as well as the lifetimes of countless ordinary citizens, who will never log a single visit to the White House, let alone a visit that could be characterized as an official visit that would give the citizens of Main Street their say.

Even more striking, perhaps, is that the most frequent visitor to the White House in the first half of 2009 was Andy Stern, the head of the Services Employees International Union (SEIU), a union representing two million public and private employees. He boasts, "We spent a fortune to elect Barack Obama—$60.7 million to be exact—and we're proud of it."[23] Intriguing is what happened in the aftermath of the election. The *New York Post* reports that within two weeks of Obama assuming office, he signed a series of executive orders that were championed by union leaders.[24] In addition, in a striking illustration of the ability of public unions to infiltrate the political process and affect the fiscal plight of government, the *Los Angeles Times* reports that during negotiations for the $787 billion fiscal stimulus program that took effect in 2009, the SEIU lobbied Washington to have nearly $7 billion of the stimulus money withheld from California unless it revoked a wage cut it had already approved for unionized health care workers as part of its effort to fix its budget shortfall.[25]

The ascension of both the ranks of public union membership and their influence on public policy run counter to views expressed decades ago when public union membership was in its early stages of growth. George Meany, the former head of the AFL-CIO in 1955 said, "It is impossible to bargain collectively with the government."[26] Oh how far they've come. It didn't happen fast in the beginning, which can be traced back to the National Labor Relations Act of 1935 (NLRA), which is also known as the Wagner Act, after its sponsor, Robert F. Wagner. The NLRA increased the power of private unions, giving employees the right to form unions and bargain collectively with their employers over wages, benefits, and working conditions. It also granted workers the right to strike. Many workers were excluded from the NLRA, including federal, state, and local government workers. Amendments to the NLRA weakened the power of unions; for example, the Taft-Hartley Act of 1948 and the Landrum-Griffith Act of 1959. This weakening occurred at the same time that manufacturing activity in the United States began to shrink as a proportion of overall economic activity, giving way to the service sector, a transformation that has continued to the present day.

Amid the decline of the U.S. factory sector and as businesses shut down through the normal course of business cycles and creative destruction (business deaths), the ranks of private union membership began to fall. Adding to the decline was an increase in competitive pressures both domestically and internationally. The combination of these influences gave way to growth in public unions. Norcross (2011) cites the conversion of some private unions to public unions, notably the SEIU (formerly the Building Services Employees Union), as well as associations, which were compelled to do so by the growth of public union membership.[27] In 1959, the AFL-CIO reversed its stance on whether public sector employees could engage in collective bargaining, saying it supported it.

The 1960s then began a period of rapid growth in public union membership, which was spurred additionally by a major change in the way the U.S. courts ruled on public employees as well as new legislation. Whereas courts previously differentiated between the rights of public and private sector union workers, courts increasingly ruled to permit public sector employees the same rights as private sector employees.

One of the more important catalysts to the growth of public sector unions occurred in 1962 when President Kennedy signed Executive Order 10988, which gave federal workers the right to unionize and thus engage in collective bargaining. The Order spurred rapid growth in the ranks of union membership at the federal level and served as a model for growth at state and local levels.

Thus began the ascension of public sector unions, their meddling in public policy, and their immersion into activities meant not for the betterment of society but for self-aggrandizement. Evidencing this notion, Reid and Kurth find that between 1955 and 1978, militant job actions carried out by public unions increased by 90-fold, mostly at the local level, a tally far larger than the comparatively smaller 5-fold increase in public union membership.[28]

Militant actions by public sector unions occurred in waves at first, involving different occupations before they eventually involved politicians, who harnessed the influence of public unions, encouraging them to seek the redirection of federal money. Norcross (2011) cites a striking example of the politicization of public unions and their involvement in public policy-making, highlighting an example where "federal funds sent to the local level aimed at upgraded science education in inner-city schools prompted teacher strikes and the redirection of funds to all schools and to teachers' salaries. In other words, local politicians encouraged public sector militancy in order to redirect federal dollars."[29] Such undue influence on the distribution of national income represents an attack on the democratic process, and by directing money toward areas where public sector union workers are employed, it feeds growth in their ranks.

Public Unions Are Monopolistic

Norcross notes the major differences between the sort of monopolistic powers that private sector unions have versus those of the public sector, illuminating the viral manner in which public sector unions can grow their ranks, exert influence on public policy, and balloon public expenditures:

> In economics, a union is defined as a labor cartel. In bargaining with a private employer, the union exercises monopoly power and is able to secure a wage that is higher than the competitive or market wage. Driving up the wage rate causes the employer to purchase less labor. Thus, while private sector unions are able to increase wages for their members, these gains come with an economic tradeoff: fewer jobs for non-union employees, lower corporate profits, and higher prices to consumers.

> As in the private sector, public sector unions are able to increase their wages through employer negotiations. In addition, however, public sector unions are also able to increase demand for their labor through the political, legislative, or

regulatory process, thus increasing wages further than private sector unions are able to. Note that the effect on total employment is ambiguous: it may be more or less than employment in a competitive labor market.[30]

Norcross depicts the distinction between the effects on wages of public and private sector unions in Figures 3-3 and 3-4.

Private Sector Union Wage Effect

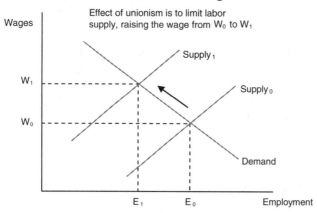

Figure 3-3 The theoretical impact of unions on private-sector wages

Source: Eileen Norcross, "Public Sector Unionism: A Review," George Mason University, *Working Paper*, 2011.

Public Sector Union Wage Effect

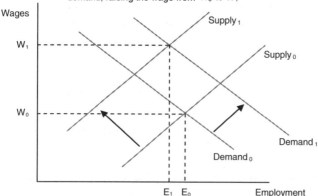

Figure 3-4 The theoretical impact of unions on public-sector wages

Source: Eileen Norcross, "Public Sector Unionism: A Review," George Mason University, *Working Paper*, 2011.

Supporting Norcross, Edwards (2010) finds that public sector union workers have much higher average wages and benefits than nonunionized public sector workers, citing data from the Bureau of Labor Statistics shown in Table 3-1.[31]

TABLE 3-1 State and Local Workers, Union Versus Nonunion, Measured by Average Compensation in Dollars per Hour Worked, June 2009

	Union	Nonunion	Ratio
Total compensation	$47.46	$33.33	1.42
Wages and salaries	29.90	22.86	1.31
Benefits	17.57	10.47	1.68
Health insurance	5.91	3.07	1.93
Defined-benefit pension	3.98	1.94	2.05
Defined-contribution pension	0.25	0.36	0.69
Other benefits	7.43	5.10	1.46

Source: Edwards, Chris, "Public-Sector Unions," Cato Institute, *Tax & Budget*, No. 61, March 2010

As the table shows, BLS data indicate that public sector union members have a 31 percent advantage in wages and a 68 percent advantage in benefits. It is important to note, however, that some of the differential reflects the fact that many of the public sector union workers reside in states that are relatively high paying, skewing the average. Nevertheless, adjusting for these influences, Edwards finds public sector union workers earn 10 percent more than nonunion public sector workers.

Above-market wage and benefit payments are just two of the many costs associated with public unions and collective bargaining. Despite such costs, the absence of market discipline in the public sector stymies the process by which it can be changed or destroyed by these and other inefficiencies in the same way that industries in the unionized private sector are when they attempt to maintain a bad status quo. Rather than adjust or die as industries in the private sector do, the public union beast is simply fed more. Nobel Laureate Paul A. Samuelson (quoted in Reynolds, 1987) puts it this way:

The whole history of unionism has been in determining how industries in decline are accelerated toward their extinction.[32]

To Samuelson's point, consider unionized public sector pension funds. Unlike the private sector, no market discipline is present to control inefficiencies in the public sector, which needn't rely on profits as the private sector must when it funds its employee obligations because the public sector derives its funding from compulsory tax payments. This is a bad state of affairs for the government sector, and it is bad news for taxpayers, who ultimately must bear the cost of funding public sector pension obligations. Holcombe and Gwartney (2010) investigated the economic impact of unions on economic freedom and growth, concluding

> In the future, the largest impact of unionization in the United States will come from public sector unionization. The burden of generous retirement benefits will crowd out other government expenditures, will be a force for higher taxes, and will impose an increasing burden on the private sector of the economy that pays those taxes.[33]

Employees in public sector unions do not have to concern themselves with cost burdens in the same way that workers in the private sector must because the burdens are not theirs. In contrast, the private sector employee must consider competitive factors that will impact his organization and ultimately his livelihood.

Fiscal Illusion as a Means of Concealing the Cost of Collective Bargaining

Norcross points to an even more disturbing proclivity among state and local public sector unions and government officials in today's capital-starved world to resort to fiscal illusion or other means to pursue their self-interests:

> As the current fiscal stress in many state and local government reveals, government negotiators share the goals of unions to increase spending and are able to conceal the full price of

bargaining agreements to voters in the form of current or deferred compensation (e.g. enhanced pension formulas and benefits). Governments may resort to debt finance, spending deferrals, or intergovernmental aid, thus enabling the government to increase employment and wages (either current or deferred) for union workers while concealing the true cost to voters. That is, the spending limit, or budgetary constraint under which governments operate may be evaded by resorting to accounting techniques or fiscal illusion.[34]

Fiscal illusion enables the public sector to avoid boundaries that exist in the private sector. Unmotivated, the public sector fails to control costs or pursue optimal efficiencies and gains in productivity, choosing instead to propagate itself, to expand through the procurement of additional taxpayer money, both out of current revenues and future revenues, through the use of debt or other forms of deferred taxpayer burdens. One might believe that this would be quite obvious to the taxpayer, but such is the essence of fiscal illusion. Norcross cites Troy (2004) in warning of the consequences of the perpetual use of fiscal illusion to mask the true cost of government spending:

> The check on excessive taxation is voter opposition at the ballot box. However, if the potential for fiscal illusion and fiscal evasion allows governments to conceal the full cost of public sector labor to taxpayers for a sustained period, then the ultimate check on the growth of public sector unionism is municipal insolvency.[35]

Norcross sums up the dynamic by which public sector unions can increase government indebtedness and harm economic activity:

> Since the employer and the employee benefit form the expansion of the public budget and increased spending, there is an incentive to grant awards that put greater demands on fiscal resources, necessitating higher levels of local taxes, greater indebtedness, or intergovernmental transfers. In this way, collective bargaining in the public sector may impede economic growth.[36]

Other Costs to Society from Public Unions

It's bad enough that taxpayers have illusory beliefs about the true financial costs of the public services that they pay for; they also bear burdens from the tendency of public unions to protect poorly performing workers. Moreover, public unions over the past 20 years have gone against the grain of the private sector by resisting efforts to restructure and reduce headcount where appropriate and possible to increase efficiencies and worker productivity. They've also been slow to adopt the many technological advances that have been adopted by the private sector ever since the mid-1990s, when technological advances accelerated and spurred above-trend productivity gains that continue to this day.[37]

Another area of harm to the public good that comes from the self-aggrandizing ways of public sector unions is strikes. New York City, for example, has experienced several strikes by sanitation workers that left the city filled with heaps of garbage on its crowded streets. One of these was in 1968 when sanitation workers complained that they were getting paid less than police officers and firefighters were and that the amount of money that they had to contribute to their pensions was too large. Although it is common in the private sector to grade one's pay against the pay others in the same occupation and in the same geographical location receive, it is uncommon for these comparisons to be made between different occupations.

Philadelphians in November 2009 felt the monopolistic powers of public union workers first hand when Local 234 of the Public Transit Union struck and left 800,000 transit riders stranded. Ironically, the strike occurred on Election Day, underscoring the view held by Holcombe and Gwartney that changes in labor laws during the twentieth century have compromised one of the freedoms democracy thrives under: economic freedom.[38] This is despite Holcombe and Gwartney's view that collective bargaining conceptually is consistent with economic freedom. The Philadelphia transit strike came just four years after the previous transit strike there, and it was the third in

11 years. (The 2005 strike lasted 7 days, and the 1998 strike last a whopping 40 days.) The president of Local 234 said that the union had disagreements over wages and workers' rights, accusing the transit authority of consistently taking money out of its underfunded pension plan.[39] The union sought protection of its pension fund, and it wanted to keep employee contributions to the cost of their health care coverage at 1 percent of pay. This is extraordinarily below the amount that private sector workers pay toward their health care insurance. To wit, a 2010 study by the Henry J. Kaiser Foundation finds that in 2010 the percentage of premiums paid toward single coverage was 19 percent, up from 17 percent in 2009, and that the percentage of premiums paid toward family coverage was 30 percent, up from 27 percent in 2009.[40] Talk about behind the times and excessive sense of entitlement!

New York City, which has the largest public transportation system in the world and is, of course, therefore heavily reliant upon it, in 2005 experienced its third transit strike. It too was untimely and therefore costly. It occurred on December 20th during the heaviest shopping week of the year and lasted seven days. The strike forced shoppers to find alternatives, and it badly hurt New York City, with estimates for the damage running at several hundred million dollars per day. This of course refers to the short-term cost of such harsh actions.

The long-term costs of strikes by public unions and the "victories" they won over the years while carrying out militant actions began to emerge during the financial crisis amid widespread strains in state and local finances, many of which were related either directly or indirectly to skyrocketing costs associated with pension and health care obligations to public sector workers that they could no longer afford. Strains in public sector finance are unlikely to result in a significant amount of defaults in the public sector. The strains are more likely to be manifested in a transformation of the municipal bond market, morphing from an interest rate market to a credit market. In other words, credit-related factors will become a greater determinant of municipal bond yields than in the past when municipal bond yields had high correlation to U.S. Treasury yields. Now there will likely be greater differentiation between the literally millions of municipal bonds outstanding, with investors paying more attention than ever before to the creditworthiness of issuers, especially now that the municipal bond insurance business has fallen apart and is no longer trusted by many.

Municipalities: Crises Loom but Not Immediately

The day of reckoning for municipalities with respect to their crippling pension and health care obligations will be delayed by a number of factors, but the delay does not negate the need for municipalities to begin tending to these problems now, lest they fester and become problems too great to bear. Standard and Poor's (2011) agrees:

> We believe that if governments consistently rely heavily on debt and other one-time solutions and continue to ignore or postpone difficult service provision, revenue enhancement, pension and other postemployment benefit funding needs in the hope that economic growth will bail out their finances, they could be setting themselves up for greater hardship in the near future.[41]

Risks to municipalities and hence the municipal bond market in the meantime will, as long as the U.S. economy continues to muddle through its secular problems, be kept down by the following factors:

1. Long average maturities for municipal debt
2. A manageable stock of municipal debt
3. Manageable interest burdens for municipal bonds
4. Pension dilemmas that escalate not for ten years time in most cases

Let's look at each of these.

Long Average Maturities for Municipal Debt

Stracke and Narens (2011) cite data from the Securities Industry and Financial Markets Association (SIFMA) indicating that at the end of 2010 the weighted average maturity of all municipal bonds outstanding was 16.2 years.[42] This is much longer than that of U.S. Treasuries, which stands at about 5 years. This is important because it means that there is no maturity spike on the horizon that would by itself cause municipalities to have a sudden need for financing. In other words, financing needs for municipalities are spread out over a long stretch of time. Certainly Lehman Brothers wishes its liabilities were stretched out over time. Many of its obligations and those of other institutions that failed at the start of the financial crisis were funded with very short-term obligations, such as overnight repurchase agreements. Reductions in short-term obligations such as these have been targeted by a variety of debtors in the aftermath of the crisis, and more balanced matching of assets and liabilities is a solution to a more stable financial system.

A Manageable Stock of Municipal Debt

Stracke and Narens cite data from the Census Bureau indicating that at the median, state debt totaled just 7.3 percent of local gross state product (GSP) in 2008, quite a bit lower than Greece at near 150 percent, Japan at 200 percent, and the United States at over 60 percent. Importantly, state-affiliated issuers that have revenue sources of their own owe some of the debt owed by states. These include universities and transportation authorities, for example. Local governments have debts totaling about 11 percent of GDP, but here, too, a meaningful portion is owed by quasi-corporate issuers such as utility companies, which also have independent revenue sources by which to pay their debt obligations.

Manageable Interest Burdens

Here the burden is not large, thanks in part to today's low interest rate levels. For perspective, when the municipal default rate reached its cyclical peak of 0.39 percent in 1991 (yes, 0.39 percent was the *peak*!), data from the Census Bureau indicate that the total amount of municipal interest costs were 6.2 percent of all state and local revenues. In recent years the figure has been closer to 4.5 percent, a tally too low by itself to put sufficient strain on municipal finances to cause a funding problem.[43]

Pension Dilemmas that Escalate Not for Ten Years' Time in Most Cases

Stracke and Narens analyzed whether public pension problems pose a threat to the near-term solvency of municipalities. They believe the problem will become untenable in the latter years of this decade if municipalities do not take significant actions to diminish the large amount of unfunded liabilities they have; kicking-the-can down the road won't work in perpetuity. Stracke and Narens find that even in cases where unfunded pension liabilities is poor (under 65 percent), in a muddle-through economic scenario, pension obligations will not be large enough to spur an immediate funding crisis for such municipalities, nor until around 2016.[44]

Defaults by municipalities are in fact quite rare, so it remains to be seen whether the burgeoning strains on municipal finance will ever reach a breaking point. Certainly demographic influences won't help, and if anything they increase the odds because in 2011 Baby Boomers (people born between 1946 and 1964) began turning 65 years old. Baby Boomers will substantially increase the number of people aged 65 and older, a cohort that will grow to 20 percent of the U.S. population in 2029 when the last Baby Boomer turns 65 (including me!), up from 13 percent in 2011. That's an increase of 32 million people, to 72 million. As the ranks of the aged grow, so will the strains on municipal finance, which will tear at the seams if municipalities fail to address their looming pension and health care obligations.

Standard & Poor's highlights the historically low incident of defaults by the public sector. Many of you will be surprised by the data, especially those of you that have fallen victim to the fear mongering by some who, well, really did not do their homework very well and seek to profit from the hype they generate:

> The actual number of defaults in the rated U.S. public finance universe has been relatively low. Of the more than 17,000 issuers we rate, there were no defaults in 2009 and only three in 2010. Taking a longer-term view, there have been only 42 defaults for non-housing issues recorded during the past 25 years, 40 of which we rated noninvestment-grade prior to default. By contrast, a total of 1,868 corporate (financial and nonfinancial) issuer defaults were recorded in the same period. In light of the difficulties faced by states, municipalities, and governmental entities, and the likelihood of greater market volatility in 2011, we have analyzed U.S. banks' exposure to this sector.[45]

The relatively placid default history of the municipal bond market does not by itself assure a similarly placid future. Any notion that past is prologue does not seem to fit at the Keynesian Endpoint, and it therefore behooves all who can influence public finances to approach the years ahead with a fair dose of constructive anxiety. This means that public sector unions need be honest about the ability of government to afford pension and health care benefits promised to them in good times. The contracts they signed have been outmoded by a substantially changed world, whereby the obligations of employers and employees alike have been redefined. For example, retirement savings are now the responsibility of employees, not employers, with the vast majority of private sector workers now in defined contribution plans, not the defined benefit plans that most public sector employees are in.

The clock cannot be unwound on the many "victories" that public sector unions have had over the years, nor can any of the debts from their victories be erased absent large-scale defaults that erase the debts. That's the doomsday scenario—don't even speak of it! We did, however, address the outlook for the municipal bond market earlier in the chapter and saw a relatively stable climate for now, with municipalities strained but having a little bit of breathing room before they are forced to make drastic changes to the way they run their finances.

There Is No Free Lunch

Dynamism has for more than two centuries brought prosperity to the United States, which has shown savoir-faire with great alacrity, always doing the right thing at the right time and creating conditions to help its capitalist-based society to thrive. The financial crisis has nonetheless exposed flaws in its system, in particular how public money is run and the far extent to which politicians have gone to deceive the public about spending initiatives. With the public sector under stress, the illusory belief that you can get something for nothing is changing. All citizens must recognize that there is no such thing as free lunch.

Buchanan summarizes well the mindset that if embraced by the politicians and the public at large would surely be beneficial to the United States. His use of the word "bondage" in the context of public debts is particularly striking. If only it would resonate and spur outrage that reverses the current course:

> In the year (1776) of the American Declaration of Independence, Adam Smith observed What is prudence in the conduct of every private family, can scarce be folly in that of a great kingdom. Until the advent of the Keynesian revolution in the middle years of this century, the fiscal conduct of the American Republic was informed by this Smithian principle of fiscal responsibility: Government should not spend without imposing taxes; and government should not place future

generations in bondage by deficit financing of public outlays designed to provide temporary and short-lived benefits.[46]

Buchanan further notes the propensity of politicians and all who play a role in the appropriation of public money to act irresponsibly toward the use of debt, particularly relative to the way in which the private debts are treated.

> Because of this difference in the specification and identifi-cation of liability in private and public debt, we should pre-dict that persons will be somewhat less prudent in issuing the latter than the former. That is to say, the pressures brought to bear on governmental decision makers to constrain irre-sponsible borrowing may not be comparable to those that the analogous private borrower would incorporate within his own behavioral calculus. The relative absence of such public or voter constraints might lead elected politicians, those who ex-plicitly make spending, taxing, and borrowing decisions for governments, to borrow even when the conditions for respon-sible debt issues are not present.[47]

Citizens, in other words, must become more acutely aware of how public money is being spent because most politicians just don't give a damn.

A Seminal Moment in Public Finance

A seminal moment in public finance was the enactment of the Sinking Fund Act of 1795, which was amended in 1802. It was the continuation of a policy begun by Alexander Hamilton in 1790 as a means of establishing credit for the United States. The fund set aside a substantial amount of revenue for the retirement of debt, and it committed the United States to paying its debt through the collection of revenues. The Act and the notion of public debts were controver-sial at that time; after all, tax collections were at the center of com-plaints by colonists against Great Britain and were a catalyst for the

American Revolution. John Watts Kearny wrote of the Sinking Fund Act, saying (as quoted by Buchanan, 1977),The fiscal resources of the country were now subjected to a clear and definite survey, and a like scrutiny was applied in ascertaining the actual nature and extent of the national obligations.[48]

Kearny describes how the Act established conditions by which a system of public debt could be sustained, as it surely has, although not quite in the way envisioned:

> The Act of the 3d of March, 1795, is an event of importance in the financial history of the country. It was the consummation of what remained unfinished in our system of public credit, in that it publicly recognized, and ingrafted on that system, three essential principles, the regular operation of which can alone prevent a progressive accumulation of debt: first of all it established distinctive revenues for the payment of the interest of the public debt as well as for the reimbursement of the principal within a determinate period; secondly, it directed imperatively their application to the debt alone; and thirdly it pledged the faith of the Government that the appointed revenues should continue to be levied and collected and appropriated to these objects until the whole debt should be redeemed.[49]

This was a system commitment to the payment of public debts that worked well until, as Buchanan noted, the advent of the Keynesian revolution when prudence toward fiscal matters was eschewed in favor of perpetual fiscal illusions that ballooned the national debt.

Leadership at the Keynesian Endpoint

In June 2011, the New Jersey State Assembly passed by a vote of 46 to 32 a hallmark bill backed by New Jersey Governor Chris Christie, a Republican, requiring 750,000 state workers and retirees to pay more toward their health care and retirement benefits, a move that Christie's administration says will save New Jersey a whopping $132 billion over the next 30 years. The move narrows the wide gap that exists between the contributions that workers in the public sector pay toward their benefits compared to that of the private sector.[50]

The approval is striking considering that Democrats control both houses of the New Jersey State Legislature and the fact that union membership in New Jersey is among the highest of any state in the United States. Decisive action is necessary in New Jersey because its pension problem is one of the worst in the country. The problems emanate from many years of politicians carrying out fiscal illusions and making promises to union workers in order to garner their support in political elections. The approval of the plan will serve as a model for other states as well as the federal government, which are grappling with similar problems.

Democrats joined Republicans in approving the bill because they recognize the most prominent feature of the Keynesian Endpoint, which is that the last balance sheet has been tapped. There is no means of funding a deficit continuum, and debt can no longer be used to mask the true cost of public spending. As New Jersey Assemblyman Patrick Diegnan, Jr., a Democrat, put it,

> These reforms are unquestionably bitter pills for us to swallow, but they are reasonable, and they are necessary. We now have towns across this state that are struggling to afford health benefits for their employees.[51]

Local unions responded with intense verve, going so far as to drape a hearse with a banner that read, "The Soul of the Democratic Party," driving it in a procession in front of the State House in New Jersey. Participants to the procession shouted, "Kill the Bill," and "We'll remember in November."[52] Do they not see that the state cannot afford to pay the benefits they were promised by politicians long gone from power and which are far above those received by workers in the private sector?

Governor Chris Christie has acted boldly, he believes, by "putting the people first and daring to touch the third rail of politics in order to bring reform to an unsustainable system."[53] He of course is referring to his stance against public unions. This boldness and attention to the greater good is why many see Christie as a potential candidate for the presidency of the United States.

The Ugly Face of Optimism

America is an optimistic nation, and its tendency to look at the sunny side of most everything has inspired it to accomplish the most amazing feats and acts of human kindness and boldness ever known to mankind. Yet its optimism has a dark side. There are many who use this optimism as a veil to hide the truth of what lies behind their endeavors, which they lace with unkindness, selfishness, and ill repute toward their fellow citizens and future generations. The optimistic nature of Americans distracts them, making them susceptible to fiscal illusions and the wanton use of public money. The hapless are hoodwinked easily by hope, however harrowing the goals of the hollow-hearted, they look through sunny lenses seeing only the outermost beauty of an ugly beast that as a vulture lurks to feast on its prey.

4

The Biggest Ponzi Scheme in History:
The Myth of Quantitative Easing

In 1920 the *Boston Post* contacted Clarence Barron, the founder of *Barron's*, to investigate a man who claimed to be racking up remarkable gains for investors in an arbitrage involving the purchase of postal reply coupons in one country and their redemption in another. Charles Ponzi, the developer of the scheme, sought to convince investors that differentials in inflation rates between countries had created an opportunity for investors to purchase the postal reply coupons on the cheap in one country—particularly Italy, and redeem them in another—chiefly the United States, an arbitrage that Ponzi said would enable investors to grow their money by several fold if they invested with him. There in fact were differences between the price of postal reply coupons postage bought in countries outside of the United States and their redemption value, but there were substantial barriers preventing any actual arbitrage, including enormous logistical challenges having to redeem the coupons, which were of low denominational value. Ponzi birthed and perpetuated the scheme nonetheless.

Barron sought to expose Ponzi's scheme, noting in articles that eventually brought the *Post* a Pulitzer Prize, that to support the claims that Ponzi's investors had on the investments he had supposedly made for them that there would have to be 160 million postal reply coupons in circulation when in fact there were only 27,000. These and other questions led an angry and suspicious crowd to gather outside of Ponzi's Securities Exchange Company, which was located in Boston on School Street, a very short street and the site of the first public school in the United States. Ponzi, who was famous for his deceptions, convinced many in the angry crowd to stay calm and leave their money with him, enticing them with little more than his charm, donuts, and coffee. It wasn't the first time that investors would be misled by the potential for future profits and simple trappings. Donuts and coffee? Really? Is it this easy to get investors to part with their money? Yes, it seems.

From Donuts to Quantitative Easing (QEI and QEII): The New Profit Illusion

Charles Ponzi offered donuts to turn back a suspicious crowd of investors before his scheme was eventually found out. The Fed would need millions of donuts to sate the appetites of the literally millions of investors worldwide that hold U.S. Treasuries in what has become the greatest Ponzi scheme of all time: the creation of a scourge of debt so large that the Fed itself has had to purchase the debt to keep the scheme going. To do so, the Fed simply pressed the "on" button to its virtual printing press, crediting the account of the U.S. Treasury with the money it needed to perpetuate the Treasury's endless borrowing. In the process, the Fed kept the demand for U.S. Treasuries deceptively high, drawing in many classes of buyers, including households, banks, pension funds, insurance companies, and, especially, foreign investors. Their combined purchases creates a profit illusion, with investors believing that they will continuously reap profits from perpetually falling bond yields and rising bond prices, just as they have had opportunity to do over the past 30 years, amid the great secular bull market for bonds.

It can't last. At the Keynesian Endpoint, the Federal Reserve's colossal bond purchases will likely, to the chagrin of millions of unsuspecting bond investors, bring about an end to the bull market in bonds. The Fed's purchases have the sweet aroma of a freshly baked jelly donut, and many a bond investor has been drawn to its savory sugary taste. The whiff of rotten eggs is what investors should instead smell, but this is easily hidden with a nose pin, which the Fed places on the noses of each investor, with the goal of creating perpetual serendipitous moments that in the eyes of investors transform the rotten stench into something far more delectable. Ultimately, the stench of the Federal Reserve's bond purchases will seep into the nostrils of investors all around the world when it becomes glaringly obvious that the Fed can't possibly continue as the Treasury's main source of demand for long. Moreover, Treasury investors will realize that the Fed's purchases themselves create financial and economic conditions that are bad news for them primarily because the purchases confiscate their inflation-adjusted returns as well as the purchasing power of their dollars. Worse are the capital losses that investors in Treasury securities may incur from having bought into the Ponzi scheme at prices inflated by the Fed's purchases, sort of like playing a game of hot potato and getting stuck with the potato when the Fed abruptly leaves the game.

The Intended Purpose of QEI and QEII

The ultimate intention of QEI and QEII differed from its initial intention, as shown in the language the Fed used to describe QEI, which was announced on November 25, 2008, and QEII, which was announced on November 3, 2010:

> "QEI," announced November 25, 2008: This action is being taken to reduce the cost and increase the availability of credit for the purchase of houses, which in turn should support housing markets and foster improved conditions in financial markets more generally.

Just how effective was the Fed in supporting the housing market? Not much! This is evident in Figure 4-1, a chart that makes it blatantly obvious why there is such a striking difference between the way the Fed described the intentions of QEI and QEII.

"QEII," announced November 3, 2010:

> To promote a stronger pace of economic recovery and to help ensure that inflation, over time, is at levels consistent with its mandate, the Committee decided today to expand its holdings of securities.

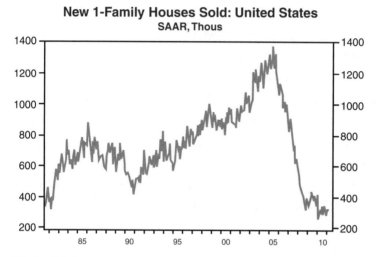

New 1-Family Houses Sold: United States
SAAR, Thous

Figure 4-1 Low mortgage rates failed to work their usual magic

Source: Census Bureau/Haver Analytics

The bottom line is that the Fed decided the best way to combat having hit the so-called "zero bound" on rates and ease financial conditions further was to endeavor to lower longer-term interest rates, which, in the Fed's vernacular are those rates that are as short as one year and beyond, although it tends to mean two years and beyond.

Pocket Pickers

With the announcements of QEI and QEII and the purchases that would follow, the Federal Reserve in essence began to pick the pockets of Treasury bond investors throughout the world. To be sure, the purchases were as sweet smelling as a dozen jelly donuts when they began because they fattened the bellies of many investors who held them through the very substantial price gains that resulted from the sharp decline in Treasury yields (Figure 4-2).

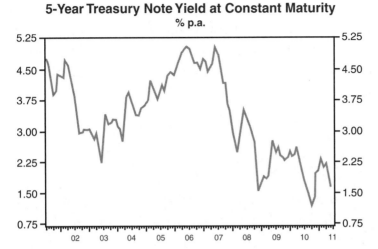

Figure 4-2 Investors reaped big gains from big declines in Treasury yields

Source: Federal Reserve Board/Haver Analytics

The problem, however, is that the Fed essentially robbed Peter to pay Paul, by pushing interest rates below the rate of inflation throughout much of the yield curve (as shown in Figure 4-3), by reducing the value of the U.S. dollar by pushing short-term interest rates below what investors could earn on investments in other currencies, and by increasing the supply of dollars in the world financial system.

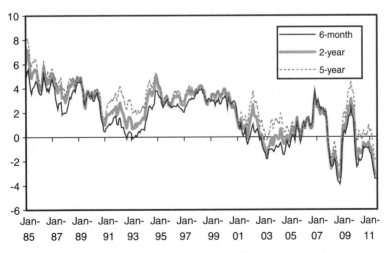

Figure 4-3 Real yields on Treasury securities have plunged

Source: Federal Reserve. Bureau of Labor Statistics

Peter was the unsuspecting investor in Treasury securities drawn into the Ponzi scheme by the allure of ever-rising Treasury prices, as well as money market investors and fixed-income investors and savers who depend on interest income to either support or enhance their livelihood; Paul was everyone else invested in everything else.

How QEI and QEII Played Out

Table 4-1 shows the various announcements associated with QEI and QEII and the schedule of long-term securities purchases the Fed engaged in.

TABLE 4-1 Announcements by the Federal Reserve of Its Long-Term Securities Asset-Purchase Programs (LSAPs), aka QEI and QEII

Date	Announcement	Period of Operations
November 25, 2008 "QEI"	$500 billion purchase of agency mortgage-backed securities and $100 billion of agency debt	December 2008 through October 2009 for agency debt; January 2009 through March 2010 for agency mortgage-backed securities.
March 18, 2009 "QEI"	$750 billion purchase of agency mortgage-backed securities; $100 billion to $200 billion of agency debt; $300 billion of Treasury securities	March 2009 through October 2009 for Treasury and agency securities.
November 3, 2010 "QEII"	$600 billion purchase of U.S. Treasury securities and the continued reinvestment of principal payments from agency debt and mortgage-backed securities	November 2010 through June 2011. Reinvestment of principal payments extended beyond June 2011 to maintain the size of the Fed's balance sheet.

Source: Federal Reserve

Numerous studies and common sense tell us that the Fed's large-scale asset purchase program (LSAP) drove interest rates lower across the fixed-income spectrum and in response lowered risk aversion substantially enough to drive investors into riskier assets and thereby loosen financial conditions. Figure 4-4 shows the cumulative changes in interest rates for various fixed-income instruments for eight "event days" associated with announcements of LSAPs studied by the Federal Reserve Bank of New York.[1] All told, the study by Gagnon, Raskin, Remache, and Sack suggest that the cumulative change for Treasury yields on days the Fed influenced expectations for the total future amount of LSAPs was a whopping 91 basis points, and the study doesn't even include the effects of QEII when rates dropped very substantially in response to its voyage! An even larger footprint was left on agency securities and agency mortgage-backed securities.

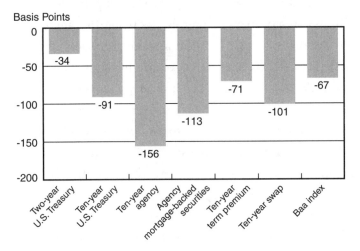

Figure 4-4 Cumulative interest changes on baseline event set days

Sources: Bloomberg L.P.; Barclay's Capital; Board of Governors of the Federal Reserve System

The decline in longer-term interest rates is the result of a decline in the so-called term premium for market interest rates, which is to say the extra yield that investors expect to receive over and above the average of expected future short-term interest rates for the many risks associated with holding a longer-term security, including the uncertain amounts of volatility, liquidity, and inflation that will occur over a longer-term horizon, in addition to numerous other uncertainties that can arise over time. The Fed's impact on longer-term rates therefore resulted more from a decline in the term premium for long-term rates than from indications the Fed would likely keep short-term rates low for an extended period, which the Fed repeatedly said it would in the policy statements it delivered following its regularly-scheduled FOMC (Federal Open Market Committee) meetings beginning in March 2009. That month coincidentally marked the bottom of the stock market following the onset of the financial crisis.

The portfolio-balance effect on term premiums for longer-term securities resulted from the perceived reduction in risks associated with holding these securities as described by Tobin (1958, 1969).[2, 3] The way it worked for the Fed is relatively simple: LSAPs removed a large amount Treasury, agency, and agency mortgage-backed securities from the secondary market, thereby reducing the amount of "duration," or interest-rate risk, that the remaining holders of these securities had to bear for changes in market interest rates. In essence, the Fed reduced the amount of assets whose direction could be subjected to influences such as those from short-term oriented investors, leaving the remaining stock of assets to those more inclined to place a premium on the assets, including pension funds, central banks, and investment managers, for example, because these entities have an intrinsic need for duration owing to their varied needs for duration. A pension fund, for example, has longer-term liabilities it must attempt to match with assets, including fixed-income assets such as U.S. Treasuries. In this way, the Federal Reserve kept the game going, encouraging traditional buyers to continue buying by using its printing press to reduce the amount of longer-term securities in circulation.

The House of Pain: How Punishingly Low Rates Bolstered Stocks, Other Assets, and the Economy

The rebalancing effect resulting from the Federal Reserve's large-scale asset purchase program stretched across the gamut of financial assets, resulting in a substantial loosening of financial conditions, as evidenced by the collective performance of corporate equities, corporate bonds, and other financial assets, which is summed up in the Bloomberg financial conditions index shown in Figure 4-5.

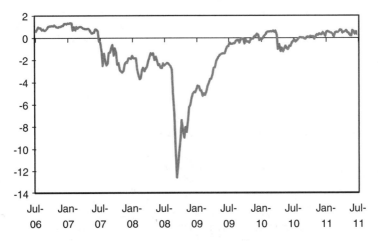

Figure 4-5 Bloomberg Financial Conditions Index. The Bloomberg Financial Conditions index combines yield spreads and indices from the money markets, equity markets, and bond markets into a normalized index. The values of this index are z-scores, which represent the number of standard deviations that current financial conditions lie above the average of the 1994–June 2008 period.

Source: Bloomberg

The movement into riskier assets that was encouraged by the Federal Reserve can be visualized by looking at a concentric circle, with the least risky assets at the center and the riskiest assets at the perimeter of the circle. Prodding investors to move out the risk spectrum to bolster the value of risk assets was a major part of the Fed's strategy, and it was highly successful, with the riskiest assets outperforming other assets amid the Fed's buying binge.

Gains in the value of financial assets helped restore a chunk of the $16 trillion in financial wealth that households lost during the financial crisis, thereby encouraging them to slow their effort to increase savings and instead do what they have cherished doing for decades: consume. These trends are shown in Figures 4-6 and 4-7.

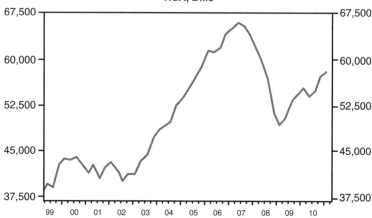

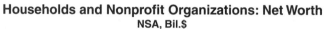

Figure 4-6 Net worth of households and nonprofits

Source: Bureau of Economic Analysis/Haver Analytics

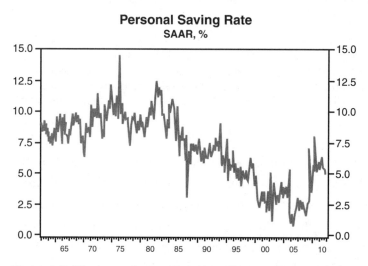

Figure 4-7 Why save when your stock and home values are climbing? Prices never fall. Surprise! Yes they do.

Source: Bureau of Economic Analysis/Haver Analytics

Now, if you are thinking that the gains in wealth are funny money, you're right because they resulted from the dual effect of the decline in term premiums for long-term assets and the migration of money out the risk spectrum, both spurred by the Fed's printing press, which has nothing to do with ingenuity or innovation or gains in national wealth. Nor were the gains the result of any increase in the three so-called factors of production that facilitate output: land, labor, and capital goods. Land refers to not only the quantity of land available for output, but the many goods that can be derived from land, such as food, energy, and metals, among others. Labor includes both the quantity of people and their productive capabilities, their skill sets, attributes these days thought of as human capital. Capital goods refer to factories, machinery, tools, technology, and buildings used in the production of goods. Each of these factors of production has proven throughout history to be vital to building the wealth of nations, but they had nothing to do with the rebound in wealth in the United States following the wealth destruction that took place from the onset of the financial crisis. It was the Fed's printing press that restored the wealth lost—wealth, mind you, that was previously built on debt. That last point is important because it suggests that the wealth that was destroyed should remain destroyed unless the decades of claims that originated as claims against future wealth are repaid and true wealth is built, either via increases in the factors of production or increases in the national savings rate, which can only occur if the U.S. eliminates it massive budget deficits and or increases its trade balance with the rest of the world by an amount larger than the size of its budget deficit.

The Biggest House of Pain of Them All: The Money Market

Much of the migration into riskier assets was encouraged by the Fed having created a "house of pain," through not only a decrease in term premia for longer-term bonds, but also its zero interest rate policy, commonly known as ZIRP. The Fed mercilessly created an investment climate in the money market so punishing that it drove investors to seek refuge in other assets. This is evident in the exodus from money market funds that in 2009 resulted in outflows of $280 billion and a whopping $392 billion in 2010. Substantial outflows continued into 2011 (Figure 4-8). These outflows helped other asset classes to flourish, just as the Fed hoped.

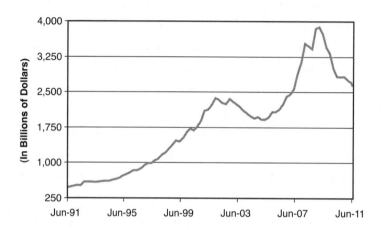

Figure 4-8 Total amount invested in money market funds

Source: Investment Company Institute (ICI)

In addition to ZIRP, further downward pressure on money market rates occurred in April 2011 when the Federal Deposit Insurance Company (FDIC) began assessing fees on not just deposits, but also other liabilities, including repurchase agreements, or repo, the market by which banks exchange their securities holdings (usually Treasuries) for cash, at a rate close to the federal funds rate, the rate targeted by the Fed at between zero and 0.25 percent since December 16, 2008. The action significantly reduced the attractiveness of the $2.5 trillion repo market (the biggest segment of the money market) as a source of bank funding because it closed the arbitrage opportunity that banks since 2008 had taken advantage of by borrowing in the repo market at rates of around 15–20 basis points and then depositing the money at the Fed to earn the 25 basis points the Fed paid on excess bank reserve, thus netting the difference. For investors in repo, which include many of the nation's top investment firms as well as money market mutual funds, the FDIC's action was like salt in their wounds because they were already taking a pounding from the relentless increase in financial liquidity resulting from QEII, which was pressuring repo lower, like a steel roll sitting atop a pancake.

Needless to say, other money market rates such as those for T-bills, commercial paper, and certificates of deposit were also sitting beneath the steel roll, as they always do when the Fed is rolling it, because these rates are very closely tied to the federal funds rate, as shown in Figure 4-9. In other words, the Federal Reserve can at any time pick investors' pockets through what to money market investors is a dastardly form of financial repression that forces them to receive rates of interest that are below the inflation rate—a negative real rate of return.

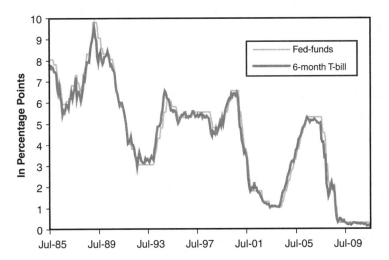

Figure 4-9 Money market rates closely follow the fed funds rate, which is controlled by the Federal Reserve.

Source: Federal Reserve

What the Fed and Yucca Mountain Have in Common and Why "Quantitative Easing" Is a Misnomer

History is laden with failed attempts at creating new money to shed debt. Greek tyrant Dionysius of Syracuse, now Sicily, at around 400 B.C. resorted to coinage debasement when his fortunes declined. Germany, of course, debased its currency before World War II, leading to hyperinflation. More recently, Zimbabwe printed massive amounts of currency, also leading to hyperinflation—I purchased trillions of Zimbabwe dollars on eBay for a few U.S. dollars! Such are the ravages of excessive use of the printing press.

Debasement of indebted nations' currencies depends importantly on the excessive creation of money. Today, the deleveraging process is preventing this from happening. This brings us to a critical point: *By themselves, increases in the quantity of bank reserves resulting from central bank activities cannot boost the money supply; only banks can create money supply.* To illustrate the point, let's look at a sample T-account (that is, a basic two-column accounting table; see Figure 4-10) for a U.S. bank and its customer.

	T-Account	
Changes in Assets		Changes in Liabilities
ABC Company		XYZ Bank
Demand Deposits	Bank Loan	Loan to ABC Co.	Demand Deposit to ABC Co.
+20,000	+20,000	+20,000	+20,000

Figure 4-10 The rule of money creation: only banks can expand the money supply

ABC Company borrows $20,000 from XYZ Bank, which, like all banks, is an intermediary between the Fed and the public. Banks, in fact, are the only entities allowed to offer checking accounts.

As the T-account shows, the immediate effect of the loan is to increase total demand deposits by $20,000, but no decrease has occurred in the amount of currency in circulation. Therefore, by making the loan, XYZ Bank has created $20,000 of new money supply.

The ability of banks to create loans and thus boost the money supply is what worries those who focus on the quantity of reserves that the Federal Reserve has injected into the financial system. Roughly $1.5 trillion of excess reserves were injected into the U.S. banking system as a result of the Fed's asset-purchase programs, which is about $1.5 trillion more than normal—banks typically would rather lend their excess reserves than leave them deposited at the Fed (Figure 4-11) where they earn next to nothing.

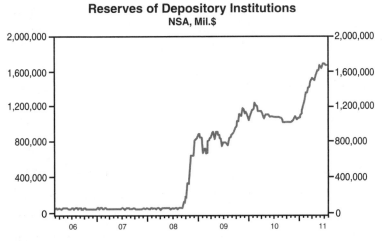

Reserves of Depository Institutions
NSA, Mil.$

Figure 4-11 Banks are depositing their reserves rather than lending them.
Federal Reserve Board/Haver Analytics

In normal times, the banking system can turn one dollar of reserves into about eight dollars of new money supply because a bank can lend 90 cents on the dollar after putting 10 cents aside at the Fed for a reserve requirement. A bank on the receiving end of the 90 cents can lend out 90 percent of that, or 81 cents, and so on and so forth until presto: One dollar becomes eight dollars. This is why the monetary base, which represents the money, or reserves, injected into the financial system by the Federal Reserve, is called "high-powered money."

Bank reserves in their enormous quantities therefore are toxic, but in the same way that nuclear waste is of no danger as long as it is tucked away either in Yucca Mountain or concrete casks, bank reserves are of no danger to fueling inflation as long as they are held at the Fed. This is why the term "quantitative easing" is actually a misnomer—no actual increase in the money supply resulted from the Fed's creation of bank reserves because banks did not lend out the reserves. Only when the concrete cracks—when banks utilize their excess reserves and lend again—can the creation of reserves be called quantitative easing. When this happens and the money thus begins to seep out of Yucca Mountain, the Fed will begin to remove the toxins, eliminating the dangerous potential for excessive coinage, or so we hope.

Draining the Toxins

How will the Fed drain the toxins? Here is the expected sequencing:

1. **Allow the run-off of agency mortgage-backed securities:** Many of the mortgage payments made by American households go toward paying off mortgages held by the Federal Reserve in the form of mortgage-backed securities. As households pay their mortgages, rather than recycle those payments with the purchase of Treasury securities, the Fed will simply hold the money, essentially removing the money from circulation. This will amount to between $15 billion to $20 billion per month.

2. **Conduct reverse repos:** The Fed will conduct open market operations whereby it will lend securities to the nation's primary dealers in exchange for cash. Primary dealers are required to participate in these operations, which will drain around $600 billion or so from the financial system.

3. **Auction term-deposits through the Fed's Term Deposit Facility (TDF):** The Fed will offer term-deposits via an auction process whereby banks bid to earn a desired yield for deposits they keep at the Fed. The rate is generally up to a few basis points at most above the interest rate the Fed pays on excess reserves and hence attractive to banks. The TDF will drain approximately $200 billion from the financial system.

4. **Raise interest rates:** In an interest-rate targeting regime, the only way to alter the interest rate is to adjust the supply of money. The Fed will therefore have to drain reserves from the banking system in order to increase the cost of money.

5. **Sell securities:** Selling securities is last in the sequencing for a number of reasons. First, the Fed has no experience selling securities of the magnitude it must sell them this time around if it is to shrink its balance sheet. This means the Fed can't be sure of the impact that its actions would have on both the financial markets and the economy. Second, the market's capacity to hold mortgage-backed securities is almost certainly lower than it was before the Fed bought $1.25 trillion of them. Third, any sale of mortgage securities could weaken an already weakened housing market by boosting the cost of mortgage finance. Fourth, the Fed likely has no appetite for selling any of its assets at a loss out of fear of political backlash.

Let's hope that when the money starts to seep out of Yucca Mountain that the Fed's Geiger counters are both working properly and in use at the Fed. If not, we will have a serious inflation problem at some point. The most likely scenario is that the Geiger counters will work, be heard loud and clear at the Fed, and prompt a swift and effective response. Again, let's hope.

Why $1.25 Trillion of Mortgage Buying Did Diddly for Housing

So far we've talked a great deal about how QEI and QEII affected economic and financial conditions. Let's now talk a bit about how little it did for housing. Recall that when the Fed announced QEI in November 2008, it said it was taking the plunge to "reduce the cost and increase the availability of credit for the purchase of houses, which in turn should support housing markets and foster improved conditions in financial markets more generally." Oh, yes, I forgot: QEI was for the housing market. Did it help? Not an iota. Let's take a closer look at what happened. It offers lessons about the challenges indebted nations face at the Keynesian Endpoint, which require a reduction in debt and in the excesses built up in the real economy by indebtedness.

There are a number of reasons why the housing market did not respond to the decline in mortgage rates shown in Figure 4-12. One of these is the very sharp tightening of lending standards that occurred in response to the onset of the financial crisis. According to the Federal Reserve, the percentage of banks that tightened were tightening their lending standards increased to about 75 percent in the second quarter of 2008. The subprime market was essentially shut down, with almost no new subprime mortgages originated in the United States in the aftermath of the crisis. This contributed to a decline in the home-ownership rate, which is shown in Figure 4-13.

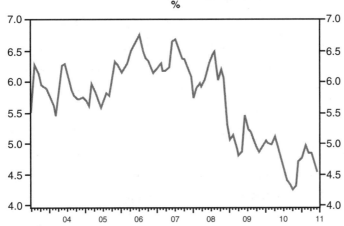

Figure 4-12 Mortgage rates fell after the crisis. Housing languished nonetheless.

Source: Federal Reserve Board/Haver Analytics

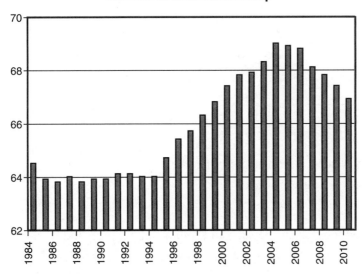

Figure 4-13 Homeownership rate in the United States

Source: U.S. Census Bureau

No amount of Fed liquidity could make banks lend to subprime borrowers after they took such heavy losses from subprime mortgages. This is one of the lessons of the post-crisis policy response, the idea that liquidity cannot solve a solvency problem. It merely forms a bridge, and often it is a bridge to nowhere.

Liquidity and the cost of money are also of no use when there is excesses in the real economy that need to be worked off. The excesses arise from debt-led consumption patterns that can't possibly be sustained without sufficient growth in real incomes and savings, including at the national level. These were lacking before the financial crisis began, and they remained barriers to the housing market's recovery in its aftermath. Figure 4-14 makes clear that the massive amount of excess supply of homes presented a formidable challenge to policymakers hoping to revive the moribund housing market.

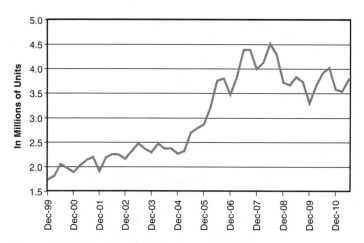

Figure 4-14 Number of existing homes for sale

Source: National Association of Realtors

Confidence was also lacking in the housing market, and it, along with income growth, is one of the two market pillars. Figure 4-15 shows the miserable level of consumer confidence that resulted from the financial crisis. No amount of liquidity can make people feel better about buying houses when they are fearful about the future both for housing and the labor market.

Figure 4-15 Housing can't bounce if consumers feel glum.

Source: The Conference Board/Haver Analytics

What Then Will Revive Housing Beyond the Keynesian Endpoint?

If the Fed and Washington can't revive the housing market, how will it recover? The answer is to look beyond foreclosures and finance to demographics and construction. In doing so keep in mind this idea: People are born short a roof over the heads, and they eventually have to recover. So as long as the population grows and the construction of new dwellings stays below the household formation rate, empty space will fill up, and prices will eventually stabilize.

A population that grows 2.7 million persons per year at a time when construction is at a standstill will be sufficient over a few years to bring the single-family vacancy rate low enough to boost rents and—much later, home prices. This is not really a prediction—it is already happening. Any downturn in prices shouldn't go far because the demographic influence will be too powerful, especially now that the U.S. economy has stabilized because household formation will increase—roommates will get tired of each other, and mama's boys will finally move out of the house (although not in Italy, where mama's boys stay at home far longer than seems normal!). Population growth of 2.7 million per year should result in about 1 million new households, a rate that far exceeds the pace of new construction, which is running under 500K per annum. (Some housing starts are actually replacement homes, which means the actual increase in the housing stock is running below the 500K annual rate for housing starts.) This will inexorably lead to a decline in the vacancy rate. So yes, the home-ownership rate will decline, but so will the vacancy rate, which will boost rents and hence the value of those empty homes.

Housing will muddle through its inventory dilemma for as long as the economic recovery continues. Economic growth is important during this time to prevent any meaningful decline in home prices. Already about 25 percent of homeowners owe more on their mortgages than their homes are worth. A drop of another 10 percentage points could put another third of homeowners below water. The second-round effects of such a decline would be extremely damaging to the economy and spark another round of deleveraging economy-wide.

Who Will Buy Treasuries if the Fed Doesn't?

QEI and QEII resulted in the purchase of about $2.5 trillion of Treasury, agency, and mortgage-backed securities, and in the first half of 2011 the Federal Reserve purchased nearly as many Treasuries as were issued by the Treasury Department. In other words, the U.S. government was heavily reliant upon the Fed to finance the U.S. government. This isn't to say the Treasury would have been unable to fund itself if not for the Fed, but what it does mean is the Treasury would have been unable to fund itself at the interest rate levels it did.

It is therefore important to ask what will happen when the Fed stops buying, particularly given the vast amount of Treasury securities the U.S. must issue in order to fund itself. It certainly is a pickle.

To answer the question, first consider who it is that owns Treasuries. Table 4-2 indicates quite clearly that the U.S. heavily relies upon foreign investors to fund itself, with foreign investors holding more than half of all U.S. Treasury securities outstanding. This cohort is therefore the most important and the one that Washington should be trying to please most. Yet, it's not doing too well in this department because it has not done anything serious to tackle the U.S. debt problem. The inability of Washington to get its financial house in order puts the United States at serious risk of losing the confidence of foreign investors. If this happens, then the cost of borrowing will skyrocket in the United States, and the United States will be forced into austerity measures that will lower the standard of living for all Americans.

TABLE 4-2   The Major Holders of the $9.62 Trillion of U.S. Treasuries Outstanding as of March 31, 2011

Holder	Amount Held, in Billions of Dollars	% of Treasuries Outstanding
Foreign investors	4,445	46.0
Federal Reserve	1,340	13.9
Household sector	959	9.9
State and local governments	506	5.3
Private pension funds	505	5.2
Money market mutual funds	338	3.5
State and local retirement funds	188	1.9
Federal retirement funds	133	1.4

Source: Federal Reserve

Threats to the U.S. Dollar's Reserve Status

Probably the biggest savior for the U.S. in terms of its ability to finance itself is the fact that despite all of the problems the U.S. faces, the U.S. dollar remains the world's reserve currency, which means that more of the world's transactions are conducted in dollars than any other currency. This provides an enormous amount of support to the U.S. dollar because it creates a large set of natural buyers, in particular, foreign central banks. Moreover, the United States is a superpower, and hence it is the world's greatest power militarily, politically, and economically. The combination of these influences gives foreign investors confidence when investing in the United States.

Still, as ever present as these conditions have always seemed, the lines between the United States and other nations is blurring largely because of the ascension of other nations—China in particular. The root of this transformation is economic, but it is also political, with the rest of the world seen as having lost some of its confidence in the United States' ability to lead following troubles in the Middle East.

On the economic front, the idea that investments in the United States are completely safe has lost some of its luster and is under threat. While the rest of the world is in the midst of a secular upswing, the United States is arguably in the midst of a secular downturn, brought on by an unwinding of the excess use of financial leverage, a lack of national savings, and large fiscal deficits.

In the past, investors did not question actions taken by the fiscal authority to assist the private sector. Times have changed. Today, investors have made sovereign credit risk their risk factor du jour. No longer are investors sitting ready with blank checks to underwrite fiscal profligacy. Like a banker, investors are asking themselves, "Would

I rather lend money to nations such as the United States whose debt burden is worsening, or to nations where it is improving and in many cases already very low?" To many investors, including those in the United States, the answer is patently obvious.

For the United States, its hegemony in vital areas looks likely to be retained for quite some time, so any erosion of the U.S. dollar's reserve status is likely to take many years, perhaps a generation or more. Where, for example, if not in U.S. dollars can the world house its roughly $10 trillion of international reserves? In the euro? Not likely given that Europe is also working through a sovereign debt dilemma. Investors can't turn to China, either, despite its strong fiscal situation because China's currency is not yet a free-market currency, and China has no bond market to house the world's reserves.

Central Banks Are Diversifying Away from U.S. Dollars

Although the U.S. dollar looks likely to retain its reserve status for quite some time, it has been losing its status slowly but surely for nearly a decade now, with more of the world's reserves flowing to other currencies and into the real economy. For example, as shown in Figure 4-16, the U.S. dollar in early 2011 represented 61 percent of the world's reserve assets, down from 71 percent ten years earlier. The euro during this time ascended from 20 percent of the world's reserves assets to 26 percent. No speeding up of this trend is likely given Europe's problems, but what is important to infer from these data is that they indicate the world has grown less confident in the United States, particularly now that it has reached the Keynesian Endpoint, because the United States can't solve its problems by endlessly borrowing from the rest of the world.

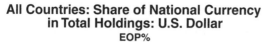

**All Countries: Share of National Currency
in Total Holdings: U.S. Dollar**

EOP%

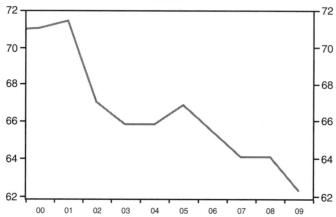

Figure 4-16 The U.S. dollar is slowly losing its standing abroad.

Source: International Monetary Fund/Haver Analytics

Excessive U.S. Debts Will Drive Cash Flow Decisions Globally

The gradual loss of the U.S. dollar's reserve status is driven by a conscious decision by the world's central banks to diversify their reserve assets to not only minimize the risks associated with holding the currency of a heavily indebted nation—the United States—but to more closely align their reserves with trends in international trade, where the U.S. shares the stage with formidable players and is slowly seeing its influence erode. For example, China and Brazil in 2009 agreed to settle their trade invoices in their respective currencies bypassing the U.S. dollar as a means of settling trade between the two countries.

Facing losses from both a decline in the value of the U.S. dollar and low investment returns in dollar-denominated assets such as U.S. Treasuries, the world is actively seeking alternative investments. For example, China is investing in mining companies and commodities, and it is carving out shipping lanes, seeing these as better places to put their money. China knows that it will need commodities to produce goods it will sell to the world, so it seems it is making a surefire bet on its own future. It certainly seems a better bet than U.S. Treasuries.

Other nations are sure to follow China's lead, recognizing that at the Keynesian Endpoint investments in indebted nations such as the United States, Japan, and those in Europe are unlikely to return as much as they used to. In this way, sovereign debt is likely to be a powerful influence that will the movement of global cash flows for many years to come.

It's Time to Make the Donuts

QEI and QEII were necessary evils at a time when the U.S. financial system was on the brink, but they are unsustainable means of funding the U.S. government. Ultimately, the United States must own up to its past sins and let the deleveraging process play itself out. It can't pretend that previous levels of demand can be restored simply by turning on the printing press at the Federal Reserve. The United States instead must recognize that only by increasing investment in its people, its land, and its infrastructure can it promote economic growth rates fast enough to justify consumption levels previously supported by a wing and a prayer—by debt.

For the Federal Reserve and the U.S. Treasury, it is time to make the donuts because there is a crowd standing outside, and although there is no wrongdoing to make them as angry as the crowd that stood outside of Charles Ponzi's office before he was busted, they are just as anxious, and it is going to take a lot of convincing to get them to show up at the next Treasury auction and the one after that, and the one after that, and....

5

How the Keynesian Endpoint Is Changing the Global Political Landscape

The scene: A walkway in a tree-lined park on lovely summer afternoon

The players: A dark-suited man, ostensibly politician Republican Congressman Paul Ryan (who wishes to reform Medicare) and grandma, 80 years old

In a finely appointed dark suit, a man is walking an elderly and frail white-haired woman in her wheelchair through a park on a glorious afternoon, where the sun's rays can be seen bursting through the park's leaf-covered skies. The woman is closed-lipped but smiling, turning her head ever so gingerly toward the seemingly kind man, whose smug face seems out of tune with the melody playing both in the background from an unknown source and in the heart of the woman, whose smirk casts an outward glow of the joyful feeling she has inside, no doubt from the memory of a life filled with thousands of similarly blissful days.

In haste, the smug man quickens his steps, but he says nothing to the old woman; she sustaining her smile, although now only with her lips—her eyes opening wider, her knees touching, and her shoulders hunching like a cat at the ready. The melody is still playing, but now only in her ears, her heart sullen with fear.

Faster still go the steps of the man, whose dark hair holds still even as the woman's flowered apron wrinkles, matching the lines on her face. The stroll darkens as the walkway brightens, where through the trees an opening is ahead. There's a cliff there. The pair moves toward it. It is the woman's final glimpse at the sun and the open skies as she is ushered to the cliff where her wheelchair is tipped forward like an applecart, and she tumbles out over the cliff.

What you ask is this horrifying scene? (Don't worry, the elderly actress is just doing fine; a mannequin was tossed over the cliff). It is a commercial made by a group of "concerned citizens," better known to some as "liberal attack dogs." The message in the commercial is obvious, but the attack dogs leave nothing to chance, flashing onto the screen the message, "America can't be beautiful," pausing for a moment and then adding, "Without Medicare." The ad was uploaded to the Internet and could be found on Youtube.com in the spring of 2011. It was meant to alarm senior citizens about proposed cuts to Medicare, in particular to changes in the program proposed by Representative Paul Ryan, the chairman of the U.S. House Budget Committee, who ostensibly is the protagonist in the shocking commercial.

This particular attack ad is an attempt by politicians to summon the powerful dynamics of gerontocracy to gain the support of senior citizens and get re-elected. A less sinister view would be that politicians are attempting to support policies they believe are best for the United States. The latter thesis in a different era would be more believable than the former, but it has become difficult to put blind faith in politicians in recent years, they acting so irresponsibly with public money.

The ad is a sign of the times and indicative of the immensely powerful impact that government indebtedness is having on the political landscape throughout the world and the many dramas that going to continue to play out on the world stage. Protests against cuts to salaries, pensions, and healthcare benefits have already become commonplace in countries worldwide, including in Greece, Spain, Portugal, London, Sri Lanka, Romania, France, as well in the United States, where there have been protests in Wisconsin, New York, Washington, Michigan, and New Jersey, among many other states, cities, and smaller towns.

Public furor over fiscal austerity will make it difficult to implement the austerity needed to rehabilitate the public sector's poorly situated balance sheet. The scene described here is one example. In the United States, politicians are under pressure to maintain existing entitlement programs and the promises they made over many years with public sector unions. Consider what happened in New York in May 2011 when the state held a special election for an open congressional seat in the 26th Congressional District in the western part of New York. Astoundingly, a Democrat won in a district widely known to be conservative. Kathy Hochul, the Democratic candidate and a country clerk, beat Republican opponent Jane Corwin, an assemblywoman, by a margin of 47 percent to 43 percent, with the balance of the vote going to independent candidates. Hochul ran openly against Paul Ryan's plan to slow the growth rate of Medicare. Her victory is widely seen as evidence of the political pressure that politicians face in attempts to control entitlement spending and by extension the U.S. debt problem.

In her victory speech, Hochul shed light on her campaign strategy, which was to focus beyond the cohort of people aged 65 and older, by focusing on those who are not far from senior citizenry. Hochul said sarcastically of her victory that night,

> Yes, we are all future seniors, that's for sure. It's the future seniors they were going after, and we didn't like that did we?[1]

Hochul added a specific reference to Medicare, as many others did that night and in its aftermath:

> The voters of this district have sent me to Washington because I said I'm willing to fight for them on Medicare, make sure the lobbyists pay for their fair share and get our budget under control. The question is: Did I have the confidence and faith of Republicans, Democrats and independents who listened to our message loud and clear? We're going to protect seniors, we're going to protect the middle class and small businesses.[2]

Nancy Pelosi, the former Speaker of the House in the U.S. House of Representatives and widely cast as a liberal, said,

Kathy Hochul's victory tonight is a tribute to Democrats' commitment to preserve and strengthen Medicare, create jobs, and grow our economy, and it sends a clear message that will echo nationwide: Republicans will be held accountable for their vote to end Medicare.[3]

Oh, the pressure today's politicians must bear for having to be the ones who have to shrink the scope of entitlement programs after their predecessors for 50 years did nothing but expand them! Never mind that entitlement spending accounts for close to 60 percent of all U.S. spending—the U.S. can solve its debt problem by cutting everything else! Not! The fact is, it will be exceedingly difficult if not impossible to trim the budget deficit without cutting spending on entitlements because there is no meat on the bone to cut from these other areas. For example, the one area presidents often say they are going to cut or "freeze" is nondefense discretionary spending. This is one of the few areas they can exert any control over. The problem is nondefense discretionary spending represents a very small slice of the overall spending pie, totaling just $689 billion in 2010 compared to overall spending of about $3.5 trillion.[4] The meat is on the entitlement spending bone, so any politician that says he or she can reduce the U.S. budget deficit as much as is necessary to stabilize the U.S. fiscal situation is either lying or a magician.

No Grand Bargain on the U.S. Deficit Problem Until After the 2012 Election

Saddled with worry over how the public will respond to any proposals that would reduce the growth rate of entitlement spending (as opposed to reducing the actual amount of entitlement spending, which is extremely unlikely owing to factors related to demographics and inflation), politicians are likely to sit on their hands and do very little ahead of the 2012 election. In other words, there will be no grand bargain between Republicans and Democrats that strikes a balance between the Ryan plan or any other Republican plan and any plan the Democrats might put forth. Instead, both parties are likely to continue to kick the can down the road, content that by having raised the debt ceiling for about the eightieth time in U.S. history, that they will have again staved off a problem—for themselves at least.

Failure to do more than agree to an outline for future deficit reduction constitutes another in a series of abuses of the U.S. reserve status privilege. It is another step in the eventual loss of the U.S. reserve status of the U.S. dollar—it will be a process, not an event. The process has actually been underway for quite some time, with the U.S. dollar falling from 71 percent of the world's reserve assets at the start of the millennium to 61 percent in early 2011.[5]

The world, in other words, is already diversifying out of U.S. dollars, a process that is likely to continue for two reasons. First, the U.S. is likely to experience a slower rate of economic growth than many other parts of the world, in particular the emerging markets, owing to its massive debts, poor demographics, large current account deficit, and poorly comprised public spending. (Compared to nations with healthier balance sheets, the U.S. spends very little on infrastructure, R&D, and education, allocating a large share of national income toward healthcare.) As the U.S. economy shrinks as a share of global trade, so will use of the dollar, which is currently the world's medium of exchange. Second, the inattentiveness of U.S. policymakers to address the structural factors that are worsening the fiscal position of the United States will compel foreign investors to behave as any good banker would by derisking their reserve portfolios, increasingly allocating money away from the United States toward countries whose balance sheets are improving rather than deteriorating. This will further reduce the proportion of the world's reserve assets that are held in U.S. dollars.

The diversification process will be sped up by continued recklessness toward budgetary matters, such as what was seen in 2011 when policymakers took a battle over the debt ceiling to the brink, with

Democrats and Republicans playing a dangerous game of chicken over whether deficit reduction should be comprised of spending cuts, tax increases, or some combination of the two. This oft-repeated game of Russian roulette occurring at a time when the world has tapped the last balance sheet is the height of recklessness. Foreign central banks will not be party to this sort of fiscal irresponsibility and will use it as a wakeup call to the tail risks they face in holding vast amounts of sovereign money in U.S. dollars.

Certain events have a way of waking people up to risk, and it changes their behavior for years afterward. September 11th of course woke up the United States and other nations to glaring security lapses that previously went undetected. And it resulted in widespread changes in security measures on a variety fronts, including efforts to protect borders, airports, and buildings, as well as intelligence collection. In a far different vein, but one that speaks to how certain events act as markers for changes in the way things are done, the devastating earthquake that occurred off the coast of Sendai, Japan, on March 11, 2011, illuminated the heavy dependence that much of the world has on Japan for supplies in major industries such as the automotive industry and the technology sector. In fact, economic data throughout the world showed a very significant impact on industrial output from cutbacks in the production of automobiles and high-tech equipment in the aftermath of the earthquake. It is felt that in the aftermath of "3/11" (in the same way that many refer to the tragic events of September 11, 2001 as "9/11," many in Japan refer to the tragic events of March 11, 2011 as "3/11," or "three-one-one") many global companies that depend on Japan for supplies will diversify and add new suppliers to reduce the risk of future disruptions to their production schedules.

Although the battle over the U.S. debt ceiling can hardly be called a seminal moment in the evolution of the U.S. dollar as the world's reserve currency, it will reinforce and perhaps hasten slightly the diversification of the world's reserve assets away from U.S. dollars toward alternative currencies by alerting investors to the folly of U.S. policy toward its fiscal situation. Although no individual currency stands ready to take the mantle (Europe is a mess, Japan has too much debt, and China doesn't have fully convertible currency nor a bond market to house the world's reserve assets), continued abuse in Washington of the reserve-status privilege of the U.S. dollar will speed the diversification process, which at some point could result in the dollar falling to under 50 percent of the world's reserve assets, with a plurality of other currencies thereby becoming more dominant.

If a plurality of currencies become the dominant global reserve asset, real interest rates will likely rise in the United States, crimping economic growth and lowering investment returns on riskier assets such as corporate equities. Increases in funding costs will require further austerity, harming economic activity still further. An increase of just a percentage point on the roughly $10 trillion of public debt outstanding in July 2011 amounts to an additional $100 billion of annual interest expense, holding the debt load constant and pushing aside the cost of interest on interest, which of course we can't because both the debt load and the amount of interest paid on interest will increase as long as the United States has a budget deficit—as it surely will for many, many years to come.

The political pressures Washington will feel ahead of the 2012 election will result in mini bargains containing outlines at best for future deficit reduction. For example, there will be no provision that states Part D of the Medicare program (the prescription drug program begun in 2003) will be reduced because that would scare seniors, and anything that scares seniors politicians will not touch. No meaningful specificity is likely until after the 2012 election. In other words, the U.S. is likely to continue to kick the can down the road on its fiscal dilemma and further abuse its reserve currency privilege, opening the door to further depreciation of the U.S. dollar, higher real interest rates, lowered investment returns, and weaker economic activity. To the politician, these costs do not seem to have resonated much, as is evident by the fiery and consequential battle that took place over the debt ceiling in the summer of 2011, which is why many believe Washington won't wake up unless or until there is a crisis.

Beyond the Keynesian Endpoint Leaders Must Lead

The political battles playing out on the world stage are therefore a major problem for indebted countries. Politicians are inclined to give in to pressures applied from their constituency on major issues—it is the essence of democracy to do so and to let the will of the people decide, after all, but this a rare time when letting the people decide what is best for a nation may not be what is best for a nation, or a state, or a city, for that matter. Instead, this is a time when policymakers have to make honest assessments of the actions they believe are necessary to right the ship. It is a time for leaders to lead, in other words.

Take Greece, for example. When George Papandreou became Prime Minister of Greece in November 2009, he discovered that his nation's budget deficit was much greater than he previously believed. Papandreou proclaimed to the world in December 2009 that his predecessor had disguised the size of the deficit, which in 2010 reached 10.5 percent of the nation's gross domestic product. Combined with an already-high stock of debt, the deficit created an intractable problem for Greece. Recognizing the dilemma, investors saw Greece as a bad credit, forcing Greece to pay high interest rates to investors in order to be compensated for the risk of owning Greek bonds. This worsened the problem because interest rate levels exceeded the growth rate in Greece's economy. In such a situation where the interest rate on a nation's debt is higher than the growth rate for its gross domestic product (in nominal terms), its debt-to-GDP ratio will rise in perpetuity.

In 2010 Greece faced a deep crisis that required it to borrow $140 billion from the European Union and the International Monetary Fund in exchange for austerity measures that would stabilize Greece's finances. It still wasn't enough, despite the loan package amounting to almost half the size of Greece's economy about $14,000 per person for each of Greece's 10.7 million citizens.[6]

In 2011, Greece needed another bailout, but lenders would not agree to one unless Greece took more drastic actions than it did the previous year. Facing political pressures of their own, Germany and France and the rest of the European Union demanded Greece implement additional austerity measures before they were given additional aid because the European Union risked losing support from their constituencies for not just the support package but also for the euro.

Papandreou crafted a $113 billion austerity plan for Greece that would inflict a great amount of pain onto its people, who rose up in objection to the harshness of the plan, defined as much by the change it would impose on its people's way of life, especially for public sector employees, which accounts for about 25 percent of employment in Greece.

On June 29, 2011, Greek citizens took to the streets by the thousands to protest an impending vote on the austerity plan. Many protestors were dressed ominously in all-black clothing, covered fully except for their hands and above the noses of their face, their menacing eyes peering through their covering. The protestors hailed rocks and bottles, lit fires to cars, and charged at uniformed police with wooden sticks and metal pipes, shouting at them with great passion and verve. All the while the protestors fended off a constant dispersion of tear gas and the risk of serious physical harm, which is a constant risk amid the madness of crowds. The crowd amassed outside of the Hellenic Parliament in Athens, where 300 parliament members were holed up inside to vote on the $113 billion austerity plan that lenders wanted to see Greece approve before divvying out any additional loans. In a fine display of bravery and sense of duty to their nation, the members of parliament were completely undeterred by vociferousness of the crowd and the tear gas that could be seen outside of the parliament building, where the stench of the gas was seeping inside. They voted in favor of the plan by a count of 155 to 138, with a few abstentions.

As part of the $113 billion austerity plan, public sector workers would be asked to pay more into their pension plans, have their pension and health care benefits cut, and retire later in life. Tax rates were increased, the income threshold for paying taxes was lowered to $11,600 from $17,400, and the number of people employed by the public sector was cut. Greece would also privatize about $70 billion of public assets.

Figure 5.1 Protesters fill the rotunda of Wisconsin's capital, February 2011.

Source: *Antenna*, University of Wisconsin

Figure 5.2 Protesters at the Hellenic Parliament in Athens, Greece, June 2011

Ironically, Papandreou sought to reverse course on policies begun by his father, Andreas Papandreou, who, following two decades of harsh rule in the 1960s and 1970s, including a dictatorship from 1967 to 1974, was elected prime minister of Greece in a landslide victory in 1981. He was Greece's first socialist prime minister, and his mandate was to restore the income inequality that had built up in Greece while it dealt with right-wing leadership. Andreas Papandreou immediately began efforts to redistribute income, increasing pensions and wages, and establishing a welfare system that provided substantial increases in coverage for welfare, health care, and retirement. This was a sharp turn from previous policies, and in fact Greece until the 1970s had one of the smallest public sectors of any European country.[7] The expansion of government services and social programs occurring in the absence of efforts to offset the costs put Greece on a path to indebtedness that Andreas Papandreou's son is now having to alter.

Beyond the Keynesian Endpoint, entitlement-oriented societies such as Greece can no longer fund their large entitlement programs nor sustain levels of public spending that exceed revenue sources. For George Papandreou, this means he must be a stalwart and do the opposite of his father and reduce the size of government. Leaders such as Papandreou have a calling unlike those of any leaders of recent decades, to formulate and then implement policies that are apt to be extremely unpopular with the very people that voted them into office and which can result in their removal from office. In short, politicians must change their stripes and put the longer-term interests of their respective political jurisdictions before their own, and they must fend off virulent opposition wherever it may lurk, as it surely will.

Power Is Shifting at the IMF and Away from the G-7

In addition to the changes that will be seen in political leadership throughout the world and in every level of government, there will also be major change in the structure of the International Monetary Fund (IMF) and vastly more influence for the G-20—the Group of Twenty nations, which accounts for 90 percent of global gross national product.[8] The G-20 has now supplanted the outdated G-7 as the world's most powerful cooperative group of finance ministers and central bank chiefs. G-20 nations that were not part of the G-7, including China, Brazil, Indonesia, Mexico, Russia, Turkey, and South Korea, now have strong voices in shaping policies more consistent with the makeup of the global economy than possible with the G-7.

At the IMF, voting rights have been altered to better reflect this makeup, but the allocation of these rights remain outdated, as evidenced by the voting rights that individual countries have relative to the size of their economies. For example, China's voting share ranks sixth even though China's economy is the second largest in the world. Meanwhile, ancient post-WWII voting rights given to relatively small European nations remains stubbornly high. For example, Belgium's voting share in July 2011 was 1.86 percent of all votes compared to 1.72 percent for Brazil, despite Brazil's economy being five times larger than Belgium's.

The declining economic prowess of developed countries and their shrinking share of world economic activity are part of a handoff of power and influence to the developing world that is likely to continue for many years to come owing to the debt burdens the developed world must work through before it can return to faster economic growth rates. Institutions such as the IMF must continue to evolve to reflect the true composition of the global economy if they are to represent their members and therefore the global economy more fairly and in a way that best promotes sustainable economic growth and stable financial conditions.

6

Age Warfare: Gerontocracy

Dramatis personae:

Alonso, the elder, 65 years old, retired

Angelo, son to Alonso

Lucy, daughter to Angelo, 10 years old

Act I

Scene 1. The kitchen table at Alonso's home, on Main Street, USA

Alonso. Son, my longevity requires prosperity, but my wages have fallen as I have ripened; surely you will help me.

Angelo. Father, your longevity is assured by your active life; you require no recompense from me.

Alonso. Enumerate your words and your estimate, son, for I wish to live the same as I have in all of my years, and my exit is far beyond a stone's throw away.

Angelo. I wish you years beyond your wishes, father, but my purse is also for our treasured Lucy.

Alonso. Lucy is wealthy in her stock of years; I am poor. Her recompense in time you will earn, and she will live as you wish.

Lucy. (*Aside to Angelo*: Father, why does grandfather wish to borrow the coins we keep for my schooling?)

Alonso. (*Aside to Lucy*: Grandfather and his generation have known only one sort of life and the debts of their years have not wrought the troubles the debts would bring to your years. While we shall bear no malice to his fog, we shall seek his better judgment to secure your good days henceforth.)

At the Keynesian Endpoint, indebted nations face a monumental challenge in finding ways to reduce their debts and in appropriating their spending, particularly because the populations of developed countries such as the United States, Japan, and those in Europe are demographically aging. Poor Lucy in our mock play is at a considerable disadvantage in being able to maintain the same rate of increase in living standards as the generations before her, as well as in being able to compete with the rest of the world. She is burdened by the debts piled up by previous generations as well as a powerful reality that previous generations did not face: gerontocracy, rule by the elderly. Of course, what is meant here is not actual rule out of some sixteenth century English novel, but a sizeable shift in voting power so substantial that the priorities of the young and of future generations are at risk of being subordinated to senior citizens. When they are, tax dollars are allocated toward healthcare and other priorities near and dear to seniors rather than toward education and infrastructure, two major factors that heavily influence a nation's economic growth potential. How fast can a nation grow if such a large part of its public expenditures is put toward healthcare rather than toward investing in its future? The question is excruciating to many who hear it because to them spending money on healthcare is investing in the future—of their loved ones, that is.

Never before has public policy been subject to age warfare as it is today and will be in the years ahead. In the United States it is simple arithmetic: In 2011, the numbers of people turning age 65 began to grow exponentially, reflecting the aging of the Baby Boomers, who were born between the years 1946 and 1964. Like every other generation, voters in this group will choose candidates who are aligned with their personal interests, such as preserving Social Security and Medicare at a time when these programs need to be cut, especially Medicare. This elevates the importance of the 2012 election in the United States, and it will play a substantial role in determining the outcome of the nation's fiscal plight. If seniors in their plentiful numbers back spineless politicians who without a mandate from their constituency will vote to maintain the current trajectory on mandatory spending programs such as Medicare, the United States will sink deeper into debt, its economic growth potential will shrink, and its standard of living will decline.

In addition to the threat to growth that the misallocation of a nation's income presents, a demographically aging nation has more difficulty paying down its debts because the older people get, the less they save, and the less people save, the more difficult it is for a nation to find buyers of its debt. This boosts the cost of borrowing and thereby makes it more difficult for a nation to liquidate its debts because the interest rate on the debt must be below the rate of economic growth in order for the amount of debt outstanding to grow at a slower pace than the amount of GDP to thus bring down a nation's debt-to-GDP ratio.

This is a battle of the aged for the ages.

The Inexorable Numbers on Aging and How They Worsen the Debt Crisis

From Figure 6-1 it is abundantly evident that the rate of increase in the number of Americans 65 and older turned sharply higher in 2011, reflecting the beginning of a tidal wave of Baby Boomers who will turn 65 during the years 2011 through 2029, when the youngest of the Baby Boomers reach the illustrious age.

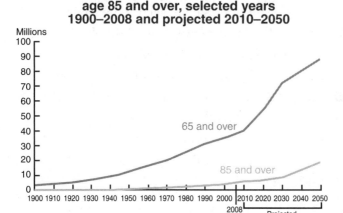

Figure 6-1 2011 was the year the Baby Boomers began turning 65; America is aging.

Source: http://www.agingstats.gov/agingstatsdotnet/Main_Site/Data/2010_Documents/Docs/OA_2010.pdf

Table 6-1 gets a bit more granular with the actual statistics, and when you stop and think of the numbers, their implications are staggering. As Table 6-1 shows, data from the Census Bureau indicate that the number of Americans who were aged 65 and older in 2010 was 40.23 million. By 2020 the tally is expected to reach 54.8 million, a whopping increase of 14.6 million seniors. Mind you, in the previous ten years, from 2000 to 2010, the increase was a far smaller—5.3 million. From 2020 to 2030 the increase will be far larger, with the number of Americans aged 65 and older leaping by 15.3 million to 72.1 million, an increase of about 80 percent from today's level.

TABLE 6-1 Throngs of Seniors, Many of Whom Will Need Healthcare and Receive Social Security Checks

Year	Number of Persons 65 and Older	Total Population
1900	3,080,498	75,994,575
1910	3,949,524	91,972,266
1920	4,933,215	105,710,620
1930	6,633,805	122,775,046
1940	9,019,314	131,669,275
1950	12,269,537	150,697,361

Year	Number of Persons 65 and Older	Total Population
1960	16,559,580	179,323,175
1970	20,065,502	203,211,926
1980	25,549,427	226,545,805
1990	31,241,831	248,709,873
2000	34,991,753	281,421,906
2010	40,228,712	310,232,863
2020	54,804,470	341,386,665
2030	72,091,915	373,503,674
2040	81,238,391	405,655,295
2050	88,546,973	439,010,253

Sources: This table was compiled by the U.S. Administration on Aging using the Census data noted.

Figures for projections from 2010 through 2050 are from: Table 12. Projections of the Population by Age and Sex for the United States: 2010 to 2050 (NP2008-T12), Population Division, U.S. Census Bureau; Release Date: August 14, 2008

The data for 1900 through 2000 is from Appendix Table 5, Census 2000 Special Reports, Series CENSR-4, Demographic Trends in the 20th Century, 2002.

Note: Due to Census rounding differences, the totals in this table may be slightly different from the totals in the other sheets in this workbook.

It is important to compare the projected increase in the number of older Americans to the projected rate of increase in other age cohorts and note the sizeable difference, recognizing that it represents a dramatic shift in the influence that each cohort will have over the political process and hence America's fiscal situation.

Let's look at these data in percentages in order to gain a better perspective on how the increase in the number of Americans aged 65 and older is dramatically changing the landscape of America's fiscal future.

Figure 6-2 shows the increase in the percentage of Americans aged 65 and older. The chart makes clear that not only is the absolute number of older Americans increasing, their numbers are increasing relative to other age cohorts. This is extremely important because it suggests that senior citizens' political might will strengthen, as is discussed shortly.

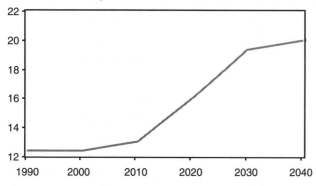

Figure 6-2 The growing ranks of the aged

Source: Projections of the Population by Age and Sex for the United States: 2010 to 2050 (NP2008-T12), Population Division, U.S. Census Bureau; Release Date: August 14, 2008. Data from the U.S. Administration on Aging using Census data; http://www.aoa.gov/AoARoot/Aging_Statistics/Census_Population/Index.aspx.

Data that underlie the chart indicate that in 2010 the percentage of Americans who were aged 65 and older was 13 percent and that the percentage is projected to increase sharply over the next 20 years, to 16.1 percent in 2020 and 19.3 percent in 2030 before leveling off to about 20 percent in subsequent decades.

These data suggest that the voting power of Americans aged 65 and older is rising at a time when spending on senior citizens must decrease in order to fix the U.S. fiscal situation. If this theory is to hold any water, it is important to decipher whether the increase in the number of seniors will translate into an increase in the number of likely voters in the seniors demographic relative to other cohorts. The way to do so is to examine the voting history of the various age demographics. In other words, we need do as *psephologists* do and study public elections.

Table 6-2 shows the voting record for the 2008 election. What stands out is the strong proclivity of senior citizens to vote. This is extremely important given their growing numbers, as it suggests a high proportion of this growing cohort will vote, further suggesting that the influence of senior citizens in American politics will climb. As the table shows, the percentage of registered voters aged 65 and up that voted in the 2008 election was quite high, at around 78 percent for those aged 65 to 74 years and around 77 percent for those aged 75 and older. These are the highest percentages of all of the age cohorts, and the voting rate is as much as 20 percentage points higher than the voting rate for the youngest cohort.

TABLE 6-2 Older People Vote More Than Younger People Do

Sex and Age	Total Population	U.S. Citizen						
		Total Citizen Population	Reported Registered Number	Percent	Not Registered Number	Percent	Reported Voted Number	Percent
Both Sexes								
Total 18 years and over	225,499	206,072	146,311	71.0	59,761	29.0	131,144	63.6
..18 to 24 years	28,263	25,791	15,082	58.5	10,708	41.5	12,515	48.5
..25 to 34 years	40,240	34,218	22,736	66.4	11,482	33.6	19,501	57.0
..35 to 44 years	41,460	36,397	25,449	69.9	10,949	30.1	22,865	62.8
..45 to 54 years	44,181	41,085	30,210	73.5	10,875	26.5	27,673	67.4
..55 to 64 years	33,896	32,288	24,734	76.6	7,553	23.4	23,071	71.5
..65 to 74 years	20,227	19,571	15,290	78.1	4,280	21.9	14,176	72.4
..75 years and over	17,231	16,724	12,810	76.6	3,914	23.4	11,344	67.8

Source: U.S. Census Bureau, *Voting and Registration in the Election of November 2008*; http://www.census.gov/hhes/www/socdemo/voting/publications/p20/2008/Table%2001.xls.

The election of John McCain as the Republican Party's nominee for president in 2008 is an example of the influential role that senior citizens are playing in deciding the outcome of elections. McCain won his party's nomination with the help of strong backing from seniors, and he even received a larger share of their vote in the presidential election than Obama did, besting him by receiving 53 percent of the vote from those aged 65 and older compared to 45 percent for Obama.

It is certainly not a given to believe that senior citizens will vote to maintain Medicare and to a lesser extent, Social Security, in their current form, no matter how unsustainable the projected spending path is for each program in light of the size of the U.S. budget deficit. Seniors, having built up significant wealth in the 1980s and 1990s, and many still working, may worry more about the possibility that the large U.S. budget deficit will result in both a confiscation of their future income and a reduction in services and their standard of living more generally. In other words, many seniors and those approaching age 65 may well subordinate their concerns about cuts in entitlement spending to concerns about taxation and the ability of government to provide essential services deemed important to their quality of life—for example, transportation systems, parks, national security, and local security. Patriotic seniors may also wish to see the nation right itself in the autumn of their years.

More likely, many senior citizens will vote to maintain the status quo, even though it will likely be many years before any changes to entitlement programs are implemented. This is more likely now than before the financial crisis because households in every age group lost a considerable amount of wealth during the financial crisis due to declines in the value of their homes, equity holdings, and other assets. Figure 6-3 shows the decline in household net worth in the aftermath of the financial crisis as well as the subsequent rebound, which has been relatively small compared to what was lost. This puts retirees behind the eight ball and is why they will vote for the status quo and keep a stranglehold over America's fiscal plight.

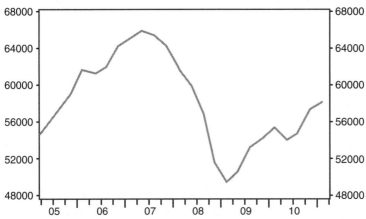

Figure 6-3 Seniors have seen their nest eggs disappear.

Source: Federal Reserve Board/Haver Analytics

There is another dimension to the financial crisis that will compel senior citizens to vote for candidates who are leery about overhauling entitlement programs. Many seniors are unhappy about the way their tax dollars were dealt with during the financial crisis, witnessing many large and prominent companies getting either bailed out or assisted with public money during the crisis. This will provoke a "what about me" and "it's my turn" attitude, with self-sacrifice and patriotism taking a back seat. In turn, entitlement spending will drown the nation in debt and reduce its economic vitality.

The Tribe of the Elders

Social anthropologists study a wide range of subject matter, taking a holistic view of the wide range of diversity that exists between groups of people because of differences in age, culture, income, skills, and other group-related classifications. The work of social anthropology can be applied to the debt dilemma that the United States and other demographically aging societies are confronting—in particular the very significant political realities that will dictate how indebted nations resolve their respective debt problems.

Social anthropologists take a 35,000-foot view of society and can analyze, for example, the extent to which a society is either fragmented or cohesive. Japan, for example, is a cohesive society that has shown a willingness to engage in shared sacrifice. The United States is viewed as less cohesive than Japan, which, many believe, explains the income inequality that exists in the U.S. This lack of cohesion has built up over the years. For example, consider the way the nation pulled together during the1940s during World War II. Fast-forward to today, and we see a more divisive nation, which is manifested in a lack of political consensus in Washington. That said, America in the 1940s was tested in an extraordinary way, and it is not fair to compare today to those times, which contained a stress and threat that most of us can't begin to fathom. We can't know the extent to which the nation would bond in a common cause if it were faced with a deeper crisis.

Nevertheless, at a time when cohesion is needed most, many powerful groups of people within society will stand in the way. The rich will seek to protect their interests by opposing higher taxes; the poor will oppose cuts in government spending; and senior citizens will seek to protect their interests by opposing cuts in entitlement spending. A social anthropologist would say that senior citizens represent a modern form of "tribe," and their large and growing numbers make them a very powerful one. Each tribe is in fact powerful in the sense that each has the ability to disrupt efforts to devise much needed solutions to the U.S. debt problem.

The challenge for the United States and other indebted nations is to show cohesion at a time when fragmentation is the more powerful force. This requires leadership, where leaders act boldly in the interests of the nation rather than by doing what is popular or by doing things that will help them to win re-election. This means standing up to a very large tribe—the tribe of elders—and telling them that it must make changes to entitlement programs in order for America to stay solvent. It needn't be a hard sell because the existing tribe of elders, those aged 65 and up, are not likely to see their benefits cut much. The largest cuts will affect younger tribes, which are likely to put up less resistance than the tribe of elders. Politicians nonetheless will have to be bold and stand up to both if the United States fails to bond and address its fiscal dilemma in a timely manner.

Entitlement Programs Can No Longer Be Sacred Cows

If the United States is to solve its fiscal dilemma, it must have no sacred cows and therefore stop protecting its overgrown entitlement programs. The Congressional Budget Office (CBO), a nonpartisan agency created in 1974 to provide Congress with estimates on the budgetary implications of proposed and enacted legislation, estimates that Social Security, Medicare, Medicaid, and other health programs will account for 70 percent of mandatory spending in 2011 and that by 2021 these programs will account for more than 80 percent of mandatory spending, owing to rapid increases in the cost of health care. As a percentage of GDP, by 2021 these programs will account for 12.7 percent of the economy, up from 10.6 percent in 2011. Historical context and the projected growth in mandatory spending programs relative to other forms of spending are shown in Figure 6-4.

Outlays, by Category

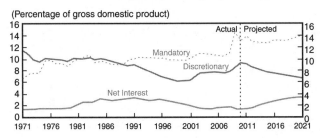

Figure 6-4 Entitlement programs are soaking up U.S. spending power.

Source: http://www.cbo.gov/ftpdocs/120xx/doc12039/01-26_FY2011Outlook.pdf.

Drilling down a bit further, Table 6-3 shows the staggering numbers and their projected growth. As the table shows, the U.S. federal government had total outlays of $3.456 trillion in 2010, an amount equal to 23.8 percent of the U.S. gross domestic product. Of the $3.456 trillion in total outlays, $1.9 trillion was spent on mandatory programs, of which Social Security payments was the largest individual program, with outlays of $701 billion, although medical care represented a larger share of the pie, as shown in the combined outlays for Medicare and Medicaid.

CBO's Baseline Projections of Outlays

	Actual, 2010	2011	2012	2013	2014	2015	2016	2017	2018	2019	2020	2021	Total 2012-2016	Total 2012-2021
Mandatory						In Billions of Dollars								
Social Security	701	727	761	799	842	889	940	997	1,059	1,126	1,196	1,267	4,231	9,876
Medicare	520	572	566	610	645	679	738	771	806	885	949	1,021	3,238	7,670
Medicaid	273	274	264	278	329	371	416	447	474	508	544	587	1,659	4,219
Other spending	600	726	657	641	616	647	692	698	701	748	767	796	3,253	6,963
Offsetting receipts	-184	-191	-211	-222	-230	-240	-249	-267	-285	-302	-317	-338	-1,151	-2,659
Subtotal	1,910	2,108	2,038	2,106	2,203	2,346	2,538	2,647	2,757	2,964	3,138	3,333	11,230	26,070
Discretionary														
Defense	689	712	710	725	738	752	773	787	801	827	848	869	3,698	7,830
Nondefense	660	663	643	638	640	645	653	666	680	697	714	731	3,219	6,707
Subtotal	1,349	1,375	1,352	1,364	1,378	1,397	1,426	1,453	1,482	1,524	1,562	1,600	6,917	14,538
Net Interest	197	225	264	325	394	459	527	592	646	697	751	792	1,969	5,447
Total	3,456	3,708	3,655	3,794	3,975	4,202	4,491	4,691	4,885	5,185	5,451	5,726	20,117	46,055
On-budget	2,901	3,210	3,073	3,150	3,294	3,481	3,730	3,884	4,029	4,276	4,485	4,702	16,727	38,103
Off-budget	555	498	581	644	682	721	761	807	856	909	966	1,024	3,390	7,952
Mandatory						As a Percentage of Gross Domestic Product								
Social Security	4.8	4.8	4.9	4.9	4.9	4.9	4.9	5.0	5.1	5.1	5.2	5.3	4.9	5.0
Medicare	3.6	3.8	3.6	3.7	3.7	3.7	3.9	3.8	3.9	4.0	4.2	4.3	3.7	3.9
Medicaid	1.9	1.8	1.7	1.7	1.9	2.0	2.2	2.2	2.3	2.3	2.4	2.5	1.9	2.2
Other spending	4.1	4.8	4.2	3.9	3.6	3.6	3.6	3.5	3.3	3.3	3.4	3.3	3.8	3.5
Offsetting receipts	-1.3	-1.3	-1.3	-1.4	-1.3	-1.3	-1.3	-1.3	-1.4	-1.4	-1.4	-1.4	-1.3	-1.4
Subtotal	13.2	14.0	13.0	12.8	12.8	12.9	13.3	13.2	13.2	13.6	13.8	14.0	13.0	13.3
Discretionary														
Defense	4.7	4.7	4.5	4.4	4.3	4.1	4.0	3.9	3.8	3.8	3.7	3.6	4.3	4.0
Nondefense	4.5	4.4	4.1	3.9	3.7	3.5	3.4	3.3	3.3	3.2	3.1	3.1	3.7	3.4
Subtotal	9.3	9.1	8.6	8.3	8.0	7.7	7.4	7.3	7.1	7.0	6.8	6.7	8.0	7.4
Net Interest	1.4	1.5	1.7	2.0	2.3	2.5	2.8	3.0	3.1	3.2	3.3	3.3	2.3	2.8
Total	23.8	24.7	23.3	23.1	23.0	23.1	23.5	23.4	23.3	23.7	23.9	24.0	23.2	23.5
On-budget	20.0	21.4	19.6	19.2	19.1	19.1	19.5	19.4	19.2	19.6	19.7	19.7	19.3	19.4
Off-budget	3.8	3.3	3.7	3.9	4.0	4.0	4.0	4.0	4.1	4.2	4.2	4.3	3.9	4.1
Memorandum:														
Gross Domestic Product (Billions of dollars)	14,513	15,034	15,693	16,400	17,258	18,195	19,141	20,033	20,935	21,856	22,817	23,810	86,686	196,138

Table 6-3 U.S. Spending: Where It Goes

Source: CBO; http://www.cbo.gov/ftpdocs/120xx/doc12039/01-26_FY2011Outlook.pdf.

The growth rate in outlays for Medicare and Medicaid is expected to exceed the growth rate in outlays for Social Security. As a result, a decade from now Medicare and Medicaid are expected to represent 6.8 percent of the U.S. gross domestic product, compared to today's

5.5 percent. Highlighting the main trouble spot on the spending front, outlays for Social Security are expected to move up by a smaller amount, to 5.3 percent of GDP from today's 4.8 percent.

Another way to view the albatross that the Medicare and Medicaid programs represent is to express their total annual cost in terms of cost per household and to then compare the cost to household income. To say the least, viewed this way the figures are more unsettling. At a cost of about $850 billion in 2011, the cost per household for Medicare and Medicaid was about $8,000. The cost for all mandatory spending programs, which includes Social Security, among others, the CBO estimates the total cost in 2011 at $2.1 trillion, or about $18,000 per household. This is a staggering percentage of household income, which runs on average at about $50,000 per year.[1]

The hefty price tag for mandatory spending programs supports a very large and growing number of people, almost certainly far more than was intended when the programs were established, in particular Medicare and Medicaid, which were created in 1965. A startling statistic in this respect is that today roughly 1 in 6 Americans receives Medicaid, up from 1 in 50 in 1965. Translation: A substantial number of people have a vested interest in seeing to it that America keeps its Sacred Cows, including older Americans, who are the sole beneficiaries of Medicare spending.

Let's take this a step further and preview the discussion we will have later in the chapter on the composition of U.S. spending and compare what the U.S. spends on healthcare to what it spends on education. The sobering fact is that the U.S. spends about four times as much on its mandatory programs than it does on elementary and secondary education, and the trend will only worsen in the years ahead owing to the demographic story. How can investing in health care rather than education be good for America's place in the world? Yes, we must also invest in our health; our humanity and indeed our economy behoove us to do so. The vexing issue is over how to contain the growth of these programs so that there remains ample money for other priorities.

The massive and growing size of these Sacred Cows is thus set to deal a crushing blow to the United States unless their growth rates are arrested. The demographics present a significant threat to removing this threat, and Washington hasn't shown any courage to tackle the dilemma without first having the support of the general public. Washington could well agree to targets for future cuts, but the most we can expect from Washington is for it to do as it always has on this issue and kick the can down the road, this time to the 2012 election. It will lack the backbone to agree to the specifics of a deal until then, with politicians fixating on the powerful voting bloc of senior citizens they would have to answer to if any cuts in entitlement spending were to be announced before the election.

Markets Will Devour the Spineless

The daunting challenge America faces is to stop the growth rate of its entitlement programs at a time when throngs of people benefit from them and vast numbers more are standing in the wings to get their share. Congress has obviously never impeded their growth; this is how they came to be so large. So as long as Congress is a willing supplier of funds for these programs, there will be plenty of demand to keep up their growth rates. It will be an intractable problem until someone leads. Will Washington lead? It must, or the financial markets will force the issue.

Is this fear mongering? Not a chance. The financial markets have already shot their first arrow across the bow of the United States and other indebted nations. Indeed, the financial crisis was a tacit recognition by market participants of the problems facing the developed world—the decline in the value of financial assets reflects a markdown in expectations on future cash flows, itself a damning verdict on the outlook for economies and markets for developed countries. The financial markets have rebounded you say? Indeed they have, but not enough to recoup even half of the $16 trillion that American households lost (out of a total of $65 trillion) in the crisis.

What might happen next? Did someone say oink, or "PIG," the tender but serious acronym for Portugal, Ireland, and Greece? Investors were unwilling to take a leap of faith toward these countries in part because they are serial defaulters. For developed countries, investors have been more willing to take the leap, hoping for a different outcome and one that reflects the storied histories of these nations, as well as the more dynamic political and economic systems they have demonstrated over many decades. For investors to keep their faith, they will expect politicians to stop playing games of chicken with their constituency and do so before each reaches their doom at the end of the cliff. If they attempt to continue their games of chicken, investors will sniff it out faster than an army of ants can sniff out a melting ice cream cone on a burning sidewalk in the middle of a hot summer day. The response would not be pretty, and the pressure put on governments to act would be immense, via sharp increases in market interest rates, declines in share prices, and weaker foreign exchange rates. The tightening of financial conditions and increased inflation would weaken real incomes and set in motion a vicious cycle of self-reinforcing decreases in production, income, and spending—the opposite of what drives economic expansions and increases a nation's standard of living.

There's No Meat on the Discretionary-Spending Bone

If the United States is to reduce its massive annual budget deficits, it has no choice but to reduce the growth rate of its spending on mandatory spending programs because there is little else to cut. Table 6-3 makes helps make this clear. It indicates that spending on discretionary items, which is controlled by annual appropriations from Congress, is much lower than spending on mandatory items.

More important, about half of discretionary spending is on national defense, a category that is unlikely to be cut substantially given the superpower status of the United States and its desire to maintain its hegemony. This leaves nondefense nondiscretionary spending, a category where there is very little meat on the bone to cut and pretty much the only category that politicians ever take on. In fact, "cuts" to this category are a running joke, with headlines proclaiming all too often of spending "freezes" that hardly amount to a hill of beans. For example, many a politician (including presidents) has walked up to the microphone to announce either a freeze or cut in federal spending of as much as 5 percent or so, but the public doesn't fully understand that this sort of announcement only applies to discretionary spending. Moreover, it applies only to the nondefense portion of discretionary spending, which means that there is even less meat to cut off the bone than people realize.

Making the picture even bleaker is the fact that much of what is in the discretionary spending category is unlikely to be subjected to meaningful cuts, including the following:

- Law enforcement
- Highway and motor carrier safety
- National parks
- Disaster relief
- Foreign aid
- Public transit

Relying on cuts in discretionary spending to cut an annual deficit of $1.4 trillion is tantamount to squeezing water from a stone. It is impossible. Americans deserve better and more responsible thinking as well as more mature behavior than it gets from Washington. The U.S. Treasury is running on empty, and there is little room between here and the cliff.

The leadership void in Washington on fiscal matters requires a groundswell of support for action that will give politicians a mandate for change. This mandate should have been sought long ago when the demographics were more favorable than they are today and before the entitlement programs grew to be so encumbering. Now that the Baby Boomers are turning 65 and will be for the next 20 years,

America faces an uphill climb cutting its spending at a time when the aging of the population is causing it to accelerate and Boomers will be inclined to see to it that Washington does not break its social contract with them. Boomers have shaped their lives around these social contracts, as evidenced by the decline in the savings rate in recent decades. The savings rate presumably has fallen as entitlement spending has increased because entitlement programs have created a social safety net that has reduced the proclivity to save.

People have come to expect that government will support them in their retirement, for both income and healthcare. This is the opposite of what is happening today in China and other nations that lack a social safety net (see Figure 6-5). In these countries, the savings rate is very high, reflecting the belief by citizens that when they age they will have to fend for themselves because the amount of support they have been promised is either little or nothing. Having lost a substantial amount of wealth as a result of the financial crisis, seniors more than ever will expect Washington to honor its social contracts with them. This will increase their proclivity to vote for candidates who will protect the entitlement programs.

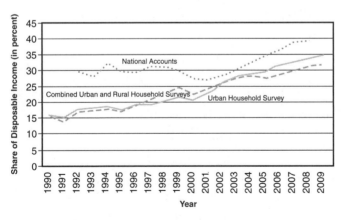

Figure 6-5 The lack of a social safety net boosts China's household savings rate.

Source: International Monetary Fund (IMF) from the National Bureau of Statistics, Flow of Funds data and Urban and Rural Household Survey. Saving rate from national accounts is significantly higher than that from the household surveys. This discrepancy is common (it is present in most countries), and can be due to differences in definitions of income and consumption, methodology and sample coverage; http://www.imf.org/external/pubs/ft/wp/2010/wp10289.pdf.

The Phoniest Savings Accounts of All Time

It is difficult to know how much money is inside of a piggybank without cracking it open and counting all that was put in it, but we can at least shake it or peek inside of the small opening atop the pig's back to see what's inside and wager a guess. If it's empty, one shake or peek will do. Not so with the piggybank that holds the U.S. government's trust funds because the rattling you hear deceives; it's not real money. You see, dear reader, the United States has been "investing" money it does not actually have in so-called trust funds that represent nothing more than promises, or I.O.U.s to future generations. There is no money in the piggybank; it was spent a long time ago. The U.S. government says there is indeed money invested in the trust funds. Let's take a closer look.

There are two trust funds, the Social Security Trust Fund, which is known as the Old-Age and Survivors Insurance (OASI) trust fund, and the Disability Insurance (DI) trust fund. According to the Social Security Administration (SSA), the purpose of these trust funds is as follows:

1. To provide an accounting mechanism for tracking all income to and disbursements from the funds.
2. To hold the accumulated assets.

The SSA adds that "these accumulated assets provide automatic spending authority to pay benefits." Accumulated assets? Where? Well, our trusted government assures us that

> By law, income to the trust funds must be invested, on a daily basis, in securities guaranteed as to both principal and interest by the Federal government. All securities held by the trust funds are "special issues" of the United States Treasury. Such securities are available only to the trust funds.[2]

Table 6-4 shows the so-called investment holdings held by the SSA in the two trust funds:

Table 6-4 Funny Money: The Investment "Holdings" of the Old-Age and Survivors Insurance (OASI) and Disability Insurance (DI) Trust Funds

Investments held at the end of June 2011 by type of investment, interest rate, and trust fund (Amounts in thousands)					
Investment Type	Interest Rate (%)	Maturity Years	Total	OASI	DI
Special issues (available only to the trust funds)	Bonds 2.500	2012	$13,094,944	$5,971,788	$7,123,156
	2.500	2013 - 2026	244,180,617	244,180,617	—
	2.875	2012 - 2025	255,013,207	255,013,207	—
	3.250	2012 - 2013	21,256,541	21,256,541	—
	3.250	2014 - 2020	80,540,810	74,397,892	6,142,918
	3.250	2021 - 2024	185,195,973	185,195,973	—
	3.500	2012 - 2013	19,027,502	19,027,502	—
	3.500	2014 - 2018	140,794,894	124,956,000	15,838,894
	4.000	2012 - 2013	24,150,385	24,150,385	—
	4.000	2014 - 2023	271,638,320	251,359,621	20,278,699
	4.125	2012 - 2013	21,033,892	21,033,892	—
	4.125	2014 - 2020	186,662,971	169,687,376	16,975,595
	4.625	2012 - 2013	18,335,328	18,335,328	—
	4.625	2014 - 2019	158,418,342	141,906,974	16,511,368
	5.000	2012	12,454,232	12,454,232	—
	5.000	2013 - 2022	260,615,797	242,695,789	17,920,008
	5.125	2012	11,567,866	11,567,866	—
	5.125	2013 - 2021	229,593,728	210,696,300	18,897,428
	5.250	2012	9,235,912	9,235,912	—
	5.250	2013 - 2017	130,047,777	114,330,889	15,716,888
	5.625	2012	9,621,437	9,621,437	—
	5.625	2013 - 2016	110,490,392	97,015,642	13,474,750
	5.875	2012	6,169,273	6,169,273	—
	5.875	2013	48,620,674	43,258,869	5,361,805
	6.000	2012	6,693,628	6,693,628	—
	6.000	2013 - 2014	63,399,864	56,646,125	6,753,739
	6.500	2012	8,577,396	8,577,396	—
	6.500	2013 - 2015	85,693,783	75,684,685	10,009,098
	6.875	2012	37,089,596	37,089,596	—
Total amount invested			2,669,215,081	2,498,210,735	171,004,346
Average interest rate [a]			4.250%	4.220%	4.693%

[a] The average is weighted by the amount invested at each rate.

Source: U.S. Social Security Administration; http://socialsecurity.gov/cgi-bin/investheld.cgi.

Not too shabby for a government with $10 trillion in publicly held debt that spends $1.4 trillion more than it takes in! Please, Uncle Sam, tell how you stuffed so much money into your piggybank!

Even Funny Money Runs Out

The SSA says that the Disability Insurance fund will be depleted by 2017, which would make it the first of the trust funds to run dry. The Old-Age and Survivors Insurance fund will deplete in 2040, the SSA says, and when it does, the OASI will nonetheless be able to fund about 75 percent of OASI expenditures through the year 2084 from the money it takes in from the taxes collected out of people's paychecks dedicated to OASI.

The reality looks far different for both the Disability Insurance fund and the Old-Age and Survivors when viewed through the prism of actual money because who but debtors have ever heard of paying for bills with money they do not actually have? This sort of perspective is what makes this little nugget from the SSA quite relevant to my point:

> Social Security expenditures are expected to exceed tax receipts this year (2010) for the first time since 1983.[3]

In other words, the piggybank emptied in 2010, and the rattling you hear inside are not fake coins; they're slugs.

The Medicare program has run at a deficit for far longer than the Social Security program, having been underfunded by a whopping $1.9 trillion since the program's inception in 1966 through 2009.[4] The deficit is the result of 35 years of Medicare expenses exceeding Medicare-related tax receipts. There are actually several parts to the Medicare program, each with its own accounting nuance. Medicare Part A, for example, receives dedicated revenues from payroll taxes, amounting to 2.9 percent of payrolls. It went into deficit in 2008. Medicare Parts B and D are funded through yearly federal expenditures, which is to say that they are completely unfunded.

Medicaid tops them all. It has been operating at a "loss" ever since its inception in 1966—there are no dedicated taxes or any form of revenue associated with the program. As a result, the program has been underfunded to the tune of (close your eyes) $3.7 trillion over the past 45 years.[5] Earlier I mentioned that 1 in 6 Americans receives Medicaid, an astounding figure that in 2010 amounted to $273 billion in expenditures, reflecting continuous mission creep, a common problem following the creation of government programs, especially those in which the benefits are "free" and where politicians are more than willing to provide the funding for them.

So the next time your hear a politician say that a government program is fully funded through some point in the distant future, check the facts. Better yet, crack open the piggybank to see what is really inside.

America Is at a Crossroads, and the Elderly Are at the Wheel

Throughout our lives, we reach many crossroads and must make difficult choices, often with great consequence. For America this is one of those times. It is at a crossroads that will determine the outcome of its debt plight, its economic vitality, and its standard of living. America must decide whether it will go down a path that for the next 20 years directs an ever-increasing share of its resources toward healthcare, or a path where it reinvents itself by reversing the decades-long trend of increased spending on healthcare and directs a larger share of public money toward the skills of its people, its land, and its capital. If the U.S. takes the latter path, it will be better positioned to compete in a world that is becoming decidedly less U.S.-centric. Otherwise the U.S. will slowly lose its hegemony politically, economically, and militarily, as well as risk losing the reserve status of the dollar.

Just how America will decide is of course up to its citizens, who for more than two centuries have made countless decisions that have led to peace and prosperity for America and indeed the world. Americans once again are being asked to lead. Which path will they choose? Will they be informed enough to know that the financial costs of the aging of the Baby Boomers will in the context of the current framework for Medicare, Medicaid, and Social Security be perilous to not only America's fiscal health but its status in the world? Will Americans care? Or will they turn inward, taking a narrow view of it all and think only of the benefits they individually have been promised?

At the Keynesian Endpoint, to Run Faster the Car Needs a Better Mix of Fuel

In addition to the obvious need for the United States to reduce its spending, it must also change the composition of its spending. It must invest more in its future by investing in the many endeavors that have demonstrated long lasting economic benefits. A few examples include highways, railways, airports, and other transportation-related projects, as well as education, worker training, and research & development. This will require a reduction in the growth rate of healthcare spending, the politics of which for the reasons cited throughout the chapter are a hard sell and because the benefits of spending in these other areas aren't immediately obvious to most people. This mindset has kept the United States on the wrong path for decades, with healthcare being made the top spending priority. The financial crisis has exposed this mistake and illuminated the path the nation must take if it is to reduce its debt burden and realize its economic growth potential as well as compete in the global economy.

Mind you, this is hardly an endorsement of Keynesian government stimulus, certainly not of the variety that the United Sates for decades has used whenever it wished to stimulate economic activity. Rather, this is a recommendation for the United States to *shift* its spending priorities and avoid increasing its spending because at the Keynesian Endpoint it can't increase its spending. Spending initiatives that are either financed by deficits or taken from other priorities having similar efficacy in terms of stimulating economic activity could be torpedoed. This is another way of saying that the fiscal multiplier of new spending initiatives at the Keynesian Endpoint is likely to be less than 1.0 or negative if the funding for the initiatives is derived from deficit spending. Keynes himself saw limitations to the efficacy of government spending, saying it is important to consider the many factors that could reduce the fiscal multiplier, including the impact that the sourcing of the funds could have on interest rates and inflation and the potential impact that government spending could have on liquidity preferences.[6]

A study by the International Monetary Fund (IMF) examining the impact of government expenditure shocks supports the idea that while the fiscal multiplier of government spending initiatives is larger in industrial countries than in developing countries, in highly indebted countries (those with debt-to-GDP ratios above 60 percent) the fiscal multiplier is not significantly far from zero in the very short run and apt to be below 1.0 in the long run. In fact, the IMF finds that 60 percent "is indeed a critical value above which fiscal stimulus may have a negative, rather than a positive impact on output in the long run."[7] Figure 6-6 makes this abundantly clear.

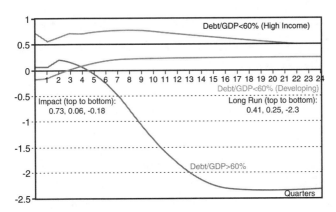

Figure 6-6 Keynesian economics fails high-debt countries: the cumulative multipliers of high- and low-debt countries.

Source: International Monetary Fund (IMF). Ilzetzki, Ethan, and Mendoza, Enrique G., and Végh, Carlos A., "How Big (Small) are Fiscal Multipliers?", IMF Working Paper, March 2011.

The negative fiscal multiplier that tends to exist for high-debt nations provides damning evidence against those who would say the United States and other high-debt nations should continue to attempt to stimulate their economies through deficit spending. This is especially true at the Keynesian Endpoint because the deleveraging imperative reduces the inclination to spend and invest and therefore reduces the effectiveness of government spending aimed at stimulating economic activity. The concluding remarks from the IMF's study (2011) supports this idea:

> Our results suggest that seeking the Holy Grail of fiscal stimulus could be counterproductive, with little benefit in terms of output and potential long-run costs due to larger stocks of public debt. Moreover, fiscal stimuli are likely to become even weaker, and potentially yield even negative multipliers in the near future, because of the high debt ratios observed in countries, particularly in the industrialized world.[8]

In addition to considering how a country's indebtedness can affect the efficacy of its efforts at stimulating economic activity, policymakers should also consider whether their spending initiatives merely shift spending from one level of government to another and thereby nullify the potential benefits.

A study by the Congressional Budget Office finds that federal spending sometimes is just a substitute for state and local spending, erasing the benefits of the federal spending:

> The available information suggests three conclusions: some investments in public infrastructure can be justified by their benefits to the economy, but their supply is limited; some (perhaps substantial) portion of federal spending on infrastructure displaces state and local spending; and on balance, available studies do not support the claim that increases in federal infrastructure spending would increase economic growth.[9]

These and other considerations behoove policymakers to revamp and reformulate public spending by designing budgets that seek to get the most bang for the taxpayer's buck. Budgets should be designed with the goal of increasing appropriations toward outlays that have relatively high fiscal multipliers. The most effective way to do this is not by increasing aggregate spending, but by changing the composition of existing spending.

Spending on Infrastructure Can Drive Economic Growth

Shifting money toward infrastructure is one way for a nation to boost the efficacy of its spending because infrastructure spending boosts a nation's productivity and therefore its standard of living more so than spending on other priorities, including healthcare. This is the sort of thing we sometimes take for granted because the innovations occurred many generations before us. The advent of trains, planes, and automobiles each has contributed substantially to increasing the standard of living in the United States and the rest of the world.

Adam Smith (1776) saw government investment in infrastructure so important that in his *Wealth of Nations* he said

> The third and last duty of government was that of erecting and maintaining those public institutions and those public works which, although they may be in the highest degree advantageous to a great society, are, however, of such a nature, that the profit could not repay the expense to any individual or small number of individuals, and which it therefore cannot be expected that any individual or small number of individuals should erect or maintain.[10]

In other words, Smith argued that it was necessary for government to fund public works because individuals would not, owing to the loss they would incur if they did. Society as a whole therefore should foot the bill, given that public works benefit the masses.

Infrastructure spending is relatively easy to ramp up, and it has proven to be effective in boosting economic activity in both the short and long run. It nonetheless is important to keep in mind this analysis, which shows that attempts by high-debt nations to stimulate economic activity through deficit spending are apt to fail. This means that government spending initiatives should be selected based not only on their need and their utility to society, but by their ability to kindle economic activity that in the long run will equal or exceed the amount spent on the initiative, which is to say when their fiscal multiplier is at or above 1.0.

A study by the Federal Reserve estimating the "job multiplier" of fiscal spending that resulted from the 2009 American Recovery and Reinvestment Act (ARRA) finds that "spending on infrastructure as well as other general purposes had a large positive impact, while aid to state governments to support Medicaid may have actually reduced state and local government employment."[11] Any analysis of the impact of fiscal spending enters the realm of what economists call the counterfactual, where reality is judged against what the reality would otherwise have been without the variable or policy analyzed. Congressman Barney Frank put it well:

> Not for the first time, as an elected official, I envy economists. Economists have available to them, in an analytical approach, the counterfactual.... They can contrast what happened to what would have happened. No one has ever gotten re-elected where the bumper sticker said, "It would have been worse without me." You probably can get tenure with that. But you can't win office.[12]

Nevertheless, a large amount of these counterfactuals exist in economics, and the consistency of the conclusions provides substantial support for the idea that spending on infrastructure is superior to other forms of spending in terms of stimulating economic growth in both the short and long run. Much of this is intuitive, and it is just plain common sense to believe that when a nation improves or expands its existing infrastructure that it will improve its ability to move its people and goods faster and more efficiently than before.

A study by Texas A&M University estimates that the average cost per automobile commuter in the 439 urban areas they examined cost $808 in 2009, the result of the wasting of 3.9 billion gallons of fuel, time, and other factors, as shown in Table 6-5.[13] As logic dictates, the study finds that changes in roadway supply affects the amount of highway congestion, with additional roadways reducing travel time. Figure 6-7 contrasts the increase in congestion that occurred in the studied areas by comparing the increases in demand for roadways (based on travel growth) relative to supply (based on roadway expansion).

TABLE 6-5 Traffic Wastes Time and Money! The Congestion Effects on the Average Commuter in 2009.

Congestion Statistics per Auto Commuter			
Population Group	Average Cost ($)	Average Delay (hours)	Average Fuel (gallons)
Very Large Areas	1166	50	39
Large Areas	726	31	26
Medium Areas	508	22	18
Small Areas	436	18	16
Other Urban Areas	445	18	16
439 Area Average	808	34	28
439 Area Total	**$114.8 billion**	**4.8 billion**	**3.9 billion**

Source: Texas A&M University; http://mobility.tamu.edu/ums/report/congestion_cost.pdf.

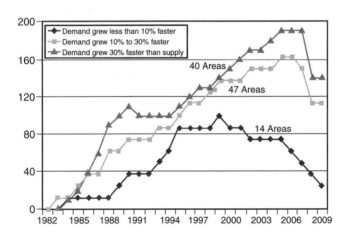

Figure 6-7 It's simple economics: When demand for roadways outstripped supply in the studied areas, congestion increased.

Source: Texas A&M Urban Mobility Report, December 2010. See http://tti.tamu.edu/documents/mobility_report_2010.pdf.

Another form of congestion all too familiar to travelers is airline congestion, which causes flight delays, cancellations, and the like, rooted in a clogged system badly in need of new capacity. In fact, data from the U.S. Department of Transportation and the Bureau of Transportation Statistics indicate that about 25 percent of airport delays can be attributed to volume-related factors.

In addition to reducing congestion, infrastructure spending is important to the production of goods and services. It facilitates the delivery of raw materials, parts, and manufactured goods, via road-ways, railways, airports, and maritime ships. China's investment in its roads and high-speed rail makes sense in this context, and it is cost effective. To wit, the American Society of Civil Engineers (ASCE) estimates that a freight train is three times as fuel efficient as a truck,[14] which means the increased use of rail can help the United States to reduce its dependency on foreign sources of energy.

The ASCE estimated in 2009 in its Report Card on America's Infrastructure that the United States needed to spend $2.2 trillion over five years in order to restore the nation's infrastructure to good condition (Table 6-6). Suffice it to say this money will be difficult to come by, especially with an ever-increasing share of taxpayer money going toward entitlement programs such as Medicare and Social Security. This means that, seniors, who drive far less than younger people do, are clearly in the drivers seat on this one, as we discussed earlier.

Table 6-6 America's Infrastructure is Badly in Need of Attention.

Category	5-Year Need (Billions)	Estimated Actual Spending-	American Recovery and Reinvestment Act (P.L. III-005)	Five-Year Investment ShortFall
Aviation	87	45	1.3	(40.7)
Dams	12.5	5	0.05	(7.45)
Drinking Water and Wastewater	255	140	6.4	(108.6)
Energy	75	34.5	11	(29.5)
Hazardous Waste and Solid Waste	77	32.5	1.1	(43.4)
Inland Waterways	50	25	4.475	(20.5)
Levees	50	1.13	0	(1.13)
Public Parks and Recreation	85	36	0.835	(48.17)
Rail	63	42	9.3	(11.7)
Roads and Bridges	930	351.5	27.5	(549.5)
Discretionary grants for surface transportation			1.5	
Schools	160	125	0*	(35)
Transit	265	66.5	8.4	(190.1)
	2.122 trillion***	903 billion	71.76 billion	(1.176 trillion)
Total Need****	**$2.2 trillion**			

* 5 year spending estimate based on the most recent available
  spending at all levels of government and not indexed for inflation
** The American Recovery and Reinvestment Act included $53.6 billion
   for a State Fiscal Stabilization Fund for education, as of press time,
   it was not known how much would be spent on school infrastructure.
*** Not adjusted for inflation
**** Assumes 3% annual inflation

Source: American Society of Civil Engineers (ASCE), *2009 Report Card for America's Infrastructure*; http://www.infrastructurereportcard.org/sites/default/files/RC2009_full_report.pdf.

R&D: Sowing the Seeds of Future Growth

Very similar to the economics of investing in infrastructure, the economics of investing in research and development (R&D) are often unfavorable, making it necessary for government to fill the void left by the private sector. This is especially important today given the increased competition posed by countries that are on the rise and those that have money to burn and are seeking to make a bigger footprint on the global scene. Supporting this idea are data from the

Organization for Economic Cooperation and Development (OECD) indicating that developing nations are grabbing an increasing share of global spending on R&D,[15] a trend that at the Keynesian Endpoint is likely to continue, given the inability of debtors to increase their spending. This is why the only solution for indebted nations is to change the composition of their spending.

Government spending for R&D is particularly important at the early stages of the R&D process when the economics of investing in R&D are very unappealing. It is easy to think of a few examples, including biotechnology, waste management, nanotechnology, medical technology, pharmaceuticals, and energy. Each of these categories has an area of R&D that requires a very large amount of investment to achieve enough advances in their respective fields to entice the private sector to enter the market with R&D of its own. Ben Bernanke (2011) agrees, finding that

> The economic arguments for government support of innovation generally imply that governments should focus particularly on fostering basic, or foundational, research. The most applied and commercially relevant research is likely to be done in any case by the private sector, as private firms have strong incentives to determine what the market demands and to meet those needs.[16]

The vast amount of wealth destroyed during the financial crisis increases the need for innovations that will drive economic growth and restore lost wealth. This is especially important now because many industries are structurally impaired and will be unable to drive economic growth for a very long time. Structurally impaired industries include residential and commercial construction, automotive, finance, and retail, all of which have seen their levels of economic activity fall well below peak levels. The inability to expand existing industries means that new ones must take the mantle and drive economic activity in the years ahead. This regeneration process is popularly called "creative destruction," a phrase coined by Austrian-American economist

Joseph Schumpeter to describe how the creation of products, business models, inventory controls, marketing strategies, shipping methods, and other innovations foster economic activity to replace the loss of activity resulting from outmoded or impaired products or industries.[17] Schumpeter believed that the essence of capitalism was innovation, underscoring the importance of investing in basis research.

Innovation is at the root of gains in productivity, which advances a nation's standard of living. It is obviously better, therefore, to have more productivity than less, which supports public policies such as investment in R&D that are designed to enhance a nation's productivity. A nation that grows its productivity by 2.5 percent per year doubles its standard of living in 28 years. By comparison, if its productivity advances at a slower rate of 1.5 percent its takes 47 years to double the standard of living.

Throughout America's storied years, innovation has led America to prosperity. In today's competitive global marketplace, America more than ever must continue to innovate if it is to remain prosperous. Thomas Edison said that "Genius is one percent inspiration, and ninety-nine percent perspiration." At the Keynesian Endpoint, scarceness of money means that in the absence of a shift in spending priorities, perspiration will be needed more than ever!

Teaching Old Dogs New Tricks

There are many other ways the United States and other indebted nations can shift their spending priorities in order to minimize the negative economic effects that result from fiscal austerity. Education is an obvious one, and it is the realm of what economists call human capital, which has been studied in depth for decades ever since the concept was introduced in 1964 by Nobel Laureate Theodore W. Schultz.[18] Human capital refers to the skills and knowledge of individuals that when attained increase the value of an individual in the labor markets.

There are two ways in particular that education promotes economic growth. First, it increases the amount of human capital that exists in a society, doing so by increasing the number of highly skilled individuals in society—scientists, teachers, technicians, researchers, doctors, and inventors, for example. These individuals contribute to the development of innovations that promote increases in productivity and therefore national income. This is often called *Schumpeterian growth,* which is growth attributable to increases in human capital.[19]

The second way that education promotes economic growth is by facilitating, diffusing, and transmitting knowledge. An excellent example of this is the computer industry. Imagine if the abundance of innovation developed in the computer industry over the past 20 years went unused, underutilized, and unexploited because individuals did not know how to use any of the new hardware or software that were developed as a result of the innovation. In such a world, the benefits to economic growth would have been far less than was realized. Just think of the plethora of ways computing power has affected society because individuals invented ways to exploit the innovation. Heck, even Hollywood has been changed forever because someone figured out how to use computers to create special effects and animation that look like the real thing. Televisions have been changed forever, too, as nary an electronics store sells televisions any more than a few inches thick—a far cry from the 2-foot deep televisions sold not long ago.

Edward Denison conducted a comprehensive study of the effects of education on economic growth in the United States from 1929 to 1982. Denison attributes 16 percent of the growth in nonresidential business to education per worker.[20] Many other studies arrive at similar findings. If we therefore assume that the effects of education account for 16 percent of economic growth, the $2.2 trillion increase in real GDP seen during the period 1959 to 1987 would have been cut by $1.26 trillion, leaving real GDP at $6.01 trillion instead of $7.27 trillion in 1987.

When we think about education, one of the first things that comes to mind is the young because it is in our youth that we attain the bulk of our education. Our school years leave an indelible mark that stays with us throughout our lives, and it is difficult to imagine how life would be if we had not gone to school.

The preciousness of children and the brevity of youth is a feature of life that captivates the hearts of every generation, and it is especially adored and cherished by the aged, who in the twilight of their years become sentimental toward life and the memories of their own youth. Far be it from them, therefore, to deny the juvenescent the privilege of inheriting an education system as good or better as the one they had. It is unfathomable to believe that they would. The problem, however, is that they unwittingly could cause harm to our precious young, by their very substantial demand for government-sponsored medical care and the money that it takes to pay for the care. Little do seniors know that their demand for and support of entitlement spending creates a black hole that pulls money away from the young and that the black hole is growing massively and will continue to do so for the next 20 years.

Nicolo Machiavelli said of change:

> It must be remembered that there is nothing more difficult to plan, more doubtful of success, nor more dangerous to management than the creation of a new system. For the initiator has the enmity of all who would profit by the preservation of the old institution and merely the lukewarm defense in those who gain by the new ones.[21]

If the United States is to change and chart a more prosperous course, it will need its elders to show their wisdom and recognize that by subterfuge—by the power of the aged in elections as well as by their demand for health care and other entitlements—the future of the United States is being dictated by gerontocracy.

7

The Hypnotic Power of Debt

Jenny Wants a Doll

The setting: An attic playroom in a middle-class household in Anywhere, USA.

The players: Four 7-year-old girls; all are from typical middle-class households except one—she is from a household that earns a bit less than the national average.

The scene: The girls are playing with their dolls, having a tea party.

Prologue (aside from author): As a father of three girls and brother to three sisters, I know of few moments in life that capture the fleeting nature of youth and the brevity of life than when a little girl is playing with her dolls. I have always taken a step back in my mind when I've watched my girls play, knowing it is but a moment in time. Sometimes I imagine myself 10 or 20 years hence wishing I could have that time again. Then I bring myself back to reality to savor the moment. I know it will never come again.

Narrator: Seated on foot-high chairs at a round wooden table covered by a white tablecloth are four young girls. It's teatime. Three of the girls are each holding an American Girl doll, a very popular but relatively expensive doll that their parents bought for them not long ago. The fourth girl, Jenny, doesn't own an American Girl doll, so she is holding a different sort of doll. It is cute and in many ways it looks similar to the American Girl doll, topped with long wispy blonde hair and covered with powdery, plump skin and displaying a bright white smile. Jenny's doll nevertheless looks different than the other dolls.

It is a bit smaller, and its features don't look as real as those on the American Girl dolls. The other girls know that Jenny's doll is not an American Girl doll, but they make nothing of it. Jenny nonetheless feels a bit sad and wishes for the day when she, too, will have an American Girl doll.

Jenny couldn't possibly have known that that her desire to have what others had would sow the seeds for her consumption habits in the years to come. She would do what millions of Americans have done for decades: try to keep up with the Joneses. Americans for many years have peered outside of their windows to look at the driveway next door and across the street to see what their neighbors were driving and if their neighbors were showcasing a new car, chances were they would want one, too. Heaven have mercy on us who chose to stay within our means and drive our cars into the ground! Have pity on us! Forgive us for purchasing three-year-old cars and for taking a pass on the haircut we would have taken off of the sticker price of a new car the minute we bought it and took it off the dealer's lot!

Money and Credit Hasn't Bought Happiness

For many Americans, keeping up with the Joneses for many years meant turning to credit because their income levels did not support their consumption habits. These poor souls—and oh so many of them!—put their relative levels of consumption above all else, subordinating income when in fact income should be the driving force. Economists would say that the *absolute income hypothesis* developed by John Maynard Keynes lost to both the *permanent income hypothesis* developed by Milton Friedman[1] and the *relative income hypothesis* developed by James Duesenberry.[2]

Keynes believes that the *absolute*, or current level of income drove consumption and that future spending relative to income would depend on the consumer's marginal propensity to consume. Sir Keynes, perhaps this is the way consumption patterns in a perfect world *should* evolve, at least if consumers are to spend prudently, but it is not how they actually evolved because poor Americans just had to keep up with the Joneses; they just had to!

Milton Friedman, who believes that consumption was driven by far more than just current income, solves a major weakness of Keynes's absolute income hypothesis. Friedman believes that consumption is driven primarily by a household's expectation for future income, including its permanent income, which is determined by the accumulation of assets of many sorts, stretching beyond just current income to include assets such as stocks, bonds, bank deposits, and real estate, as well as human capital, which is derived from intangibles such as education, training, and experience. Wealth, in other words, matters, and the consumption of those that have it tend under Friedman's theory to be affected most by it. Friedman's permanent income hypothesis helps us to understand the mega consumption binge that took place from the 1980s until the financial crisis. Rising asset values and an expectation that they would continue rising hypnotized Americans into believing they could stop saving and max out their credit cards until the cows came home—and eventually they did. Game over!

Friedman's permanent income hypothesis combines well with Duesenberry's relative income hypothesis, which theorizes that a household's consumption pattern is driven by how it views its consumption relative to others in its income cohort. Duesenberry explains:

> ...for any given relative income distribution, the percentage of income saved by a family will tend to be a unique, invariant, and increasing function of its percentile position in the income distribution. The percentage saved will be independent of the absolute level of income. It follows that the aggregate saving ratio will be independent of the absolute level of income.

In the meshed version of the permanent and relative income hypotheses, a household can justify keeping up with the Joneses if it believes it is on a permanent glide path with respect to its income. Alvarez-Cuadrado and Van Long (2009) support the idea of meshing the hypotheses, finding that

> an individual's consumption is driven by the comparison of his lifetime income and the lifetime income of his reference group; a permanent income version of the Duesenberry's (1949) relative income hypothesis.[3]

In their work, Alvarez-Cuadrado and Van Long cite an intriguing study by Neumark and Postlewaite (1998) that attempts to explain the "striking rise" in the employment of married women in the United States over the past century. One can almost visualize this one, and many readers I am sure will relate to it. To explain the rise, Neumark and Postlewaite introduce a version of the relative income hypothesis that uses—get this—a sample of married sisters. The researchers find that married women are 16 to 25 percent more likely to work outside the home if their sisters' husbands earn more than their own husbands. In other words, the jealousy that young sisters often display toward each other over their toys, their bedtime, their clothes, their shoes, and oh so much more reflects a deeply entrenched emotion that many researchers believe begins in a child immediately after the birth of a sibling,[4] when the older sibling attempts to differentiate herself and to gain her share of her parents' attention. The younger sibling eventually attempts to do the same. The problem is compounded by societal pressures, not the least of which is the immense pressure in the United States to compete for top honors in, well, just about everything.

The pressures to compete, to stand out, to be noticed, and indeed to be loved foster envy, resentment, and jealousy, emotions that manifest in a wide variety of ways, including the way people dress, how they eat, who they date or marry, where they work, and the type of cars they drive. It is a major factor underlying the desire to consume, and it promotes the use of credit because people view credit as providing a means of satisfying and reconciling emotional discontent and mental unease.

Incomes Are up, but Why Aren't We Happier?

The question therefore begs: Can consumption resolve deeply rooted emotional problems? In other words, can money buy happiness? This age-old question is usually put in the context of religion, and it is a recurring theme in both the New and Old Testaments of the Bible. A passage in the New Testament describes an encounter between a rich man and Jesus, who tells the man that if he wishes to follow him, he must sell all of his possessions and give the proceeds to the poor. The rich man refuses, walking away sorrowful. Jesus then turns to his followers and says,

> It is easier for a camel to go through a needle's eye than it is for a rich man to enter the kingdom of God.[5]

Perhaps if there were a tax deduction to reduce the rich man's taxable income and thereby enable his further consumption, the rich man might have agreed! Maybe leaving his credit cards open would have sealed the deal!

USC Professor Richard Easterlin in 1974 attempted to measure the correlation between income and happiness, developing a theory that has come to be known as the *Easterlin Paradox*.[6] It is a fascinating theory that suggests that although people with higher incomes tend to be happier than those of lesser income, happiness does not increase within nations when they grow wealthier. This concept is depicted in the striking illustration of Easterlin's findings in Figure 7-1.

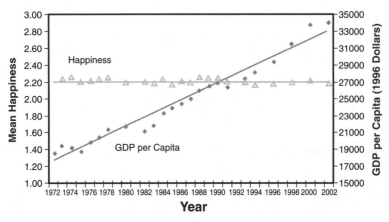

Figure 7-1 Money doesn't buy happiness; the Easterlin Paradox.

Sources: Davis and Smith (2002); U.S. Bureau of the Census; via Easterlin (2004)

Davis, James Allan and Tom W. Smith: 2002. General Social Surveys, 1972–2002 [machine-readable data file]. Chicago: National Opinion Research Center.

Easterlin, Richard, "Feeding the Illusion of Growth and Happiness: A Reply to Hagerty and Veenhoven," University of Southern California, University of Southern California Law and Economics Working Paper Series, No. 8, 2004.

As the chart shows, real income in the United States has steadily climbed for decades, owing to increases in standard of living associated with steadily rising productivity levels. What is striking is that happiness held flat during the period, suggesting income growth by itself does not result in increased happiness. Easterlin draws from Duesenberry to explain why people within wealthier nations are not happier than those in poorer nations, reinforcing Duesenberry's relative income hypothesis:

> In the simplest cast, in which the expenditures of every other person are given equal weight, the utility gained by a given individual depends on the ratio of his expenditure to the national per-capita average. The farther he is above the average, the happier he is; the farther below, the sadder. Moreover, if the frame of reference is always the current national situation, then an increase in the national level of income in which all share proportionately would not alter the national level of happiness. A classical example of the fallacy of composition would apply: An increase in the income of any one individual would increase his happiness, but increasing the income of everyone would leave happiness unchanged.[7]

It is striking and extraordinarily illuminating to view how people respond in different countries when asked about their aspirations for future income, consumption, savings, and leisure, as Cantril did in 1965 when he posed the question to people in the United States and India and then drew comparisons.[8] Although Cantril's survey is almost 50 years old, the findings almost certainly would be similar today for surveys of people in countries having vastly different per capita income levels. The responses to Cantril's survey reinforce the relative income hypothesis and in doing so show the predisposition that people have within indebted countries toward consuming as much as they feel is necessary to bring them up to par with their neighbors.

The eye-opening results of Cantril's survey (1965) are summarized as follows:

India: I want a son and a piece of land since I am now working on land owned by other people. I would like to construct a house of my own and have a cow for milk and ghee. I would also like to buy some better clothing for my wife. If I could do this then I would be happy (35-year-old man, illiterate, agricultural laborer, income about $10 per month).

United States: If I could earn more money I would then be able to buy our own house and have more luxury around us, like better furniture, a new car, and more vacations (27-year-old skilled worker).

India: I wish for an increase in my wages because with my meager salary, I cannot afford to buy decent food for my family. If the food and clothing problems were solved, then I would feel at home and be satisfied. Also if my wife were able to work, the two of us could then feed the family, and I am sure would have a happy life, and our worries would be over (33-year-old sweeper, monthly income around $13).

United States: I would like a new car. I wish all my bills were paid and I had more money to myself. I would like to play more golf and to hunt more than I do. I would like to have more time to do the things I want to and to entertain my friends (24-year-old bus driver).

India: I would like to have a water tap and a water supply in my house. It would also be nice to have electricity. My husband's wages must be increased if our children are to get an education and our daughter is to be married (45-year-old housewife, family income about $80 per month).

United States: Materially speaking, I would like to provide my family with an income to allow them to live well—to have the proper recreation, to go camping, to have music and dancing lessons for the children, and to have family trips. I wish we could belong to a country club and do more entertaining. We just bought a new home and expect to be perfectly satisfied with it for a number of years (28-year-old lawyer).

India: I hope in the future I will not get any disease. Now I am coughing. I also hope I can purchase a bicycle. I hope my children will study well and that I can provide them with an education. I also would sometime like to own a fan and maybe a radio (40-year-old skilled worker earning $30 per month).

Cantril (1965) sums up these fascinating and enlightening results as follows:

> People in highly developed nations have obviously acquired a wide range of aspirations, sophisticated and expensive from the point of view of people in less-developed areas, who have not yet learned all that is potentially available to people in more advanced societies and whose aspirations concerning the social and material aspects of life are modest indeed by comparison.

Easterlin and Cantril's work help us to have a better understanding of what drove Americans households in recent decades to consume the way they did. Debt was the instrument by which households made their attempt at buying happiness, but it was doomed to failure not only because the debt well eventually ran dry, but also because consumers in America and indeed throughout the world are on an everlasting treadmill trying to keep pace with the rest of society. Moreover, even as people move up the rung of the income ladder, their consumption standards increase accordingly, making it less likely they will ever feel as happy as they believe ex-ante they will feel. Most of you probably can relate to this. I sure can.

When I was 10 years old, I delivered newspapers in New York City, one of which was the *New York Daily News*. The most vivid day I can recall from those days was the day after the Viking spacecraft had landed on Mars. I awoke that morning to a bundle of papers that showed the first ever photograph from the surface of Mars, filled as it was with rocks all around the spacecraft as far as the Viking could see. I was enormously excited to see the black and white photo of the red planet on the front page of the newspaper. I for years wanted to be an astronaut, having watched on television the Apollo astronauts land on the moon.

Anyway, my excitement was doubly so because I was receiving my first paychecks, maybe about $20 per week, a massive amount given that my biggest expenditure was at the Time Out video arcade and the Sunset bowling alley. A number of years later when I was 16, I began working at a supermarket as a so-called checker, working the registers (before supermarkets had scanners, by the way!). I earned the minimum wage at the time, which was $3.35 per hour, and I was working about 20 hours per week. My total earnings therefore had leapt higher compared to my days as a paperboy. True to form, my expenditures increased as well, as did my desire to earn and consumer even more. It's the American way, after all, isn't it?

Soon enough I had bought my first car—on credit no less, because as a Tony from Staten Island New York, and 100 percent Italian no less, I just had to have what every other Tony, Vinny, and Joey on Staten Island had, a Chevy Camaro! Okay, yes, some of us owned a Trans Am (the black and gold one with the giant bird decal on the hood—what else!), a Firebird, or a Corvette. No matter, the point is that I did whatever it took to get my Camaro, which, by the way, was seven years old and cost $2,000 because that, it seemed, was what red-blooded Italians did.

So while I was earning more than ever, it didn't *feel* like more—I wasn't getting any further satisfaction compared to my paperboy days because my consumption standards increased along with my earnings. This continued as the years went on. Along the way it has been amazing for me to discover that even though my paychecks have gotten larger, they have felt the same as they did when I awoke that glorious morning to see on the front page of the Daily News something that no human being had ever seen before. The joy I felt had nothing whatsoever to do with what I would earn that day delivering the papers—I was a happy astronaut, and I felt privileged and proud to be a paperboy and to have the opportunity to deliver to many a story they, too, would never forget. There's obviously a lesson to be learned here.

The increase in consumption standards that tends to occur as people move up the income ladder holds a lesson for the developing world, as well, which is in the midst of a secular period of accelerating income growth. Developing nations must be careful about assuming that income growth by itself will translate into increased levels of national happiness and overall satisfaction with the national standard of living. Developing nations must recognize that as incomes accelerate, people will shift their consumption standards upward, offsetting the positive effects on the acceleration in income growth, potentially leaving the general sense of well-being little changed. In other words, even as per capita income increases, people will continue to judge their position in society not by their absolute level of income but by their relative income level, by comparing themselves to others.

The Hypnotized Consumer:
How We Are Hardwired to Spend

Both the temptation to spend and the desire to keep up with the Joneses represent a form of hypnosis because each has the ability to distract, which is an essential element in hypnosis. Temptation and a desire to keep up with the Joneses puts individuals into a state of hypnosis and distracts them from properly assessing how their spending decisions might affect their financial situations. The hypnosis lulls individuals into spending decisions that they would otherwise avoid if not for the distraction.

The words *hypnosis* and *hypnotism* were coined by James Braid, a surgeon, in the early 1840s. The words are derived from the term *neuro-hypnotism*, a condition known as nervous sleep. Braid defined hypnotism as

> ...a peculiar condition of the nervous system, induced by a fixed and abstracted attention of the mental and visual eye, on one object, not of an exciting nature.[9]

Braid (1843) describes his method of inducing people into a hypnotic state—a means of putting people into a trance, you could say— as follows:

> I take any bright object (I generally use my lancet case) between the thumb and fore and middle fingers of the left hand; hold it from about eight to fifteen inches from the eyes, at such position above the forehead as may be necessary to produce the greatest possible strain upon the eyes and eyelids, and enable the patient to maintain a steady fixed stare at the object. The patient must be made to understand that he is to keep the eyes steadily fixed on the object, and the mind riveted on the idea of that one object.

Hyppolyte Bernheim defines hypnotism as follows:

> I define hypnotism as the induction of a peculiar psychical [i.e., mental] condition which increases the susceptibility to suggestion. Often, it is true, the [hypnotic] sleep that may be induced facilitates suggestion, but it is not the necessary preliminary. It is suggestion that rules hypnotism.[10]

The hypnotic state that Braid and Bernheim describe seems a lot like the one that consumers enter when they enter a dealer's showroom to buy a new car. The moment a consumer walks inside a showroom, wham! Out walks an overenthusiastic salesman who puts the consumer into a mental state that increases his susceptibility to suggestion. The consumer becomes so fixated on the many temptations presented by the salesman that soon enough the consumer is adding on all sorts of bells and whistles to the car (especially the "comfort package," the sun roof, the heated mirrors, the plush mats, the rear-seat video system, and the fancy rims!). The price tag zooms, and the consumer walks out of the showroom having purchased a car he really can't afford.

When we think about how consumers tend to behave when they make purchase decisions such as they do in, for example, considering the purchase of a car, Bernheim's belief that "suggestion rules hypnotism" is better understood. In America, and indeed much of the developed world, suggestion does indeed rule, and the purveyors of goods and services exploit it, recognizing that consumers have weak knees, which is to say that they are susceptible to temptation as well as exploitations of their own inner struggles and outward attempts to satisfy their desires to keep up with the rest of society.

Both Braid and Bernheim believed suggestions were to be applied to a subject's conscious mind. In contrast, Sigmund Freud believed that suggestion applied to the subconscious mind. Freud in fact is known for his focus on the subconscious mind in his studies and in his practice. Subliminal suggestions and messaging by the Freudian way of thinking therefore present another means by which marketers can and do exploit distracted consumers. Never mind that the Federal Trade Commission considers subliminal advertising a deceptive business practice and that it is illegal also in England and Australia, advertisers as well as businesses can easily exploit the subconscious mind without subliminal references in their sales and advertising practices because the subconscious mind is predisposed to tipping the consumer toward a purchase decision regardless.

Karremans, Stroebe, and Claus (2006) believe a predisposition toward reaching a goal increases the effectiveness of subliminal messaging, suggesting that when consumers are fixated on a goal, they can be influenced into taking actions (such as consuming) to fulfill that goal.[11] The researchers conducted two experiments to assess whether subliminal priming of a brand name—for example, a quick flashing of a brand name across a movie screen—could affect people's choices for the primed brand and whether the effect is moderated by an individual's degree of thirst. The researchers conclude the studies demonstrated that "subliminal priming of a brand name of drink positively affected participants' choice for, and their intention to, drink the primed brand, but only for participants who were thirsty." This is another way of saying that the many subconscious predispositions that individuals have toward satisfying particular goals creates a tendency to consume as a means of doing so.

Figure 7-2 depicts the results of the experiment conducted by Karremans, Stroebe, and Claus (2006), which relied on the use of Lipton Ice, a brand of iced tea, as the conduit for the researchers to test whether they could induce a goal-directed action (choosing a drink) on the subjects to fulfill a goal (quenching one's thirst). Lipton Ice was chosen in part to test a claim made famous by a private market researcher named James Vicary, who in 1957 said that he was able to substantially increase sales of Coca Cola and popcorn in a movie theater by using subliminal advertising.[12] Vicary said that he flashed the messages "Drink Coca Cola" and "Eat Popcorn" across the movie screen for each showing of a movie titled, *Picnic*, which starred William Holden and Kim Novak. Vicary said he flashed the message for 1/3000 of a second every five seconds and that it resulted in a big increase in sales of both Coke and popcorn, to the tune of 18 percent and 58 percent, respectively. Vicary's claims created quite a stir that led to the ban of subliminal advertising by the National Association of Broadcasters in June 1958. It also created a great deal of fear among the general public, which came to believe that if Vicary could be successful in his brainwashing, so could the government—and the communists, which of course were feared back in the day. Vicary's claim was never substantiated, and attempts to recreate his experiment went flat. Vicary eventually admitted his experiment was a hoax, telling *Advertising Age* as much in 1962. Nevertheless, Karremans, Stroebe, and Claus believe Vicary's claim "has some basis in reality"; hence their study.

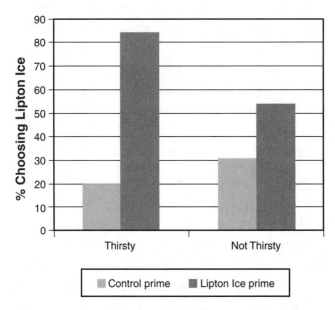

Figure 7-2 Percentage of participants who chose Lipton Ice as a function of thirst or priming for the choice

Source: Karremans, Karremans, J.; Stroebe, W.; Claus, J., "Beyond Vicary's Fantasies: The Impact of Subliminal Priming and Brand Choice, *Journal of Experimental Social Psychology*," Vol. 42 (6) (2006): 792–798.

The study helps illustrate how easily influenced people are by conduits that they believe can help satisfy their inner cravings and emotional voids. For example, having a "goal" of "keeping up with the Joneses" creates a predisposition toward consumption that people facilitate by using credit. Karremans, Stroebe, and Claus (2006) put it this way:

> People often have multiple means available to reach a particular goal, and we hypothesize that they will be more likely to select the means that is highly accessible at the moment of attempting to attain that goal.

Look no further than to that handy dandy credit card in your pocket for a highly accessible means of attempting to keep up with the Joneses. Consumers see credit cards as a quick means of reaching their goals, casting aside any negative consequences associated with the use of credit.

Mirror Neurons: You Yawn, I Yawn—You Buy, I Buy

A remarkable and very recent discovery was made in Italy in 1992 at the University of Parma that further helps us to unlock the copycat behavior of consumers. Giacomo Rizzolatti and four others conducted an experiment on macaque monkeys, trying to learn more about how the brain processes motor functions. The researchers placed electrodes on the monkeys so that they could measure the reaction in a single motor neuron. (A neuron is a cell that transmits information throughout the body, both electronically and chemically; for example, from the brain to the muscles.)[13] Neurons "fire," or transmit information through electrochemical signals when a muscle is moved or contracted.

In the fascinating and groundbreaking study, Rizzolatti and his colleagues wanted to observe how motor neurons trigger hand movements in macaque monkeys, so they watched the monkeys perform tasks, such as popping peanuts into their mouths. When the monkeys would perform the tasks, electronic monitoring devices would sound off as a result of the electrochemical signaling set off in the monkeys' motor neurons.

As is often the case with great discoveries, the researchers stumbled upon theirs. It happened while a researcher went to grab an item. Remarkably, the equipment that was monitoring the monkeys sounded off at the very same time, with the monitoring device making exactly the same sound as when a macaque had moved its own hand. Up until that point, researchers believed that when a neuron was fired, it did so to perform a unique task. In other words, only specific neurons were thought to fire for their respective tasks. That the neuron fired in a macaque when it was observing the same action in a primate other than itself (the researcher) was new to scientists. The result indicated that individual neurons could be ignited for both an action and an observation of that same action. These neurons are now known as *mirror neurons*.

A very wide range of hypotheses developed about human behavior following the discovery of mirror neurons. Scientists begin referencing mirror neurons to explain why babies stick their tongues out when they see someone else do it, why people yawn when others do, why we have difficulty watching someone else experience pain, why we feel exhilaration when watching sports. Mirror neurons are why people say that smiling and laughter is contagious.

I'll never forget an experience I had in sixth grade with my great friend Neil. We were brought together into the dean's office in I.S. 24 on Staten Island for one of our devilish but harmless pranks. When we arrived in the dean's very small office, we were seated in front of him across from his desk against the wall immediately at the doorway. The dean started giving us the third degree as we sat silently. Until one of us started to laugh. Soon enough Neil and I broke out laughing as the dean was talking. Neither of us could control ourselves. It was so hard to be serious! We were laughing so much we fell off our chairs. Neil and I never stopped laughing and left the room laughing. Did we get in trouble? Thank goodness no, but it would have been worth it for the lifetime of laughs we have had over the experience.

Many of you I am sure can think of experiences in your own lives where you have found your behavior influenced by the behavior or experiences of others around you. For example, does your skin crawl as mine does when you see a bug crawl across someone else? Do you cringe or wince when you see someone experience pain? These connections, researchers believe connect human beings to each other and promotes learning vital to life, including on a social basis.

Let's connect the dots and think about how mirror neurons influence consumer behavior. The easiest example of copycat behavior that can probably be attributed to mirror neurons relates to fads. Over the years there have been all sort of fads, including all sorts of weird hairdos and clothing styles, cars, Hula Hoops, Cabbage Patch dolls, Beanie Babies, Tickle-Me-Elmo, among many more. People for years have been buying what others buy, and many are willing to pay a hefty price to get the items. Never mind that in the vast majority of cases people soon after they buy the times wonder why they bought them in the first place and why they paid so much.

The same sort of imitation takes place when consumers shop. Consider what happens when you walk by an Apple store. Every one that I have ever walked past is buzzing with people, and the stores are brimming with excitement and are extremely inviting. The stuff inside, the cool looking people, all of it enormously alluring, and soon enough you are drawn in.

Inside of every shopping mall are a wide variety of stores offering unique experiences. The main goal for each store is to attract a target audience by creating an image that consumers want to mimic. Even the mannequins inside the store are meant to appeal to your inner mirror neurons. As soon as you see one, you want to look just like it (save for the wig and the stoic face), so moments later you are buying what he or she is wearing. Plenty of bad clothing and ugly hairdo fads have resulted from this sort of copycat behavior, but we can't help ourselves. We were born this way.

The movie-going experience is also affected by our mirror neurons, and we needn't know much about the movies we choose as long as others are choosing them for us! It seems the mirror neurons do not apply to movie critics, however, because who no one ever goes to see the movies they tell us to see!

The same impulse that makes people want to buy an item can also work in the opposite way and discourage people from buying one—if other people are signaling to steer clear. This is why bad word of mouth can be so viral and hurt a product or company. As the saying goes, the most powerful means of communication is word of mouth.

All of this is part of the amazing way in which we stay connected to each other, even if we do not know why. Mirror neurons help explain it, so the next time you find yourself feeling what others are feeling, or if you find yourself wearing the same clothes as the people you pass along the street, you'll know why.

I Want It Now! Our Insatiable Need for Immediate Gratification

> *I want the works*
> *I want the whole works*
> *Presents and prizes and sweets and surprises*
> *Of all shapes and sizes*
> *And now*
> *Don't care how*
> *I want it now*
> *Don't care how*
> *I want it now*

—Veruca Salt, *Willy Wonka and the Chocolate Factory*

In the 1971 movie, *Willy Wonka and the Chocolate Factory*, Veruca Salt is a spoiled young rich girl who is one of five lucky young kids to find a Golden Ticket inside of a Wonka bar. The Golden Tickets give the recipients the privilege of a tour inside of Willy Wonka's chocolate factory, which for years has been cloaked in mystery and shut to the public. No one has seen Wonka in many years. To find the Golden Ticket, Veruca's rich father purchases 760,000 Wonka Bars and makes his workers work day and night to open them. Never mind the cost—whoever thinks of the cost when they want instant gratification? Just listen to Veruca and keep in mind that she, like most people, can't help herself.

Veruca Salt: I wanted to be the first to find a Golden Ticket, Daddy!

Mr. Salt: I know, angel. We're doing the best we can. I've got every girl in the place to start hunting for you.

Veruca Salt: All right, where is it? Why haven't they found it?

Mr. Salt: Veruca, sweetheart, I'm not a magician! Give me time!

Veruca Salt: I want it now! What's the matter with those twerps down there?

Mr. Salt: For five days now, the entire flipping factory's been on the job. They haven't shelled a peanut in there since Monday. They've been shelling flaming chocolate bars from dawn till dusk!

Veruca Salt: Make them work nights! They're not even trying! They don't want to find it! They're jealous of me!

Mr. Salt: Sweetheart, I can push them no harder; 19,000 bars an hour they're shelling; 760,000 they've done so far.

Veruca Salt: You promised, Daddy! You promised I'd have it the very first day!

Mrs. Salt: You're going to be very unpopular around here, Henry, if you don't deliver soon.

Mr. Salt: It breaks my heart, Henrietta. I hate to see her unhappy.

Veruca Salt: I won't talk to you ever again! You're a mean father, you'll never give me anything I want! And I won't go to school till I have it!

Mr. and Mrs. Salt suffer from the same problem that we all have: We can't control our brains, and our desire for instant gratification is far stronger than our will to delay it. McClure, Laibson, Lowenstein, and Cohen (2004) link this desire to activity in the brain, in particular in the limbic system (Figure 7-3), which is sometimes known as the brain's pleasure center—what else would they call the part of the brain that loves to go shopping! Using a Magnetic Resonance Imaging (MRI) machine, the researchers measured the brain activity of participants as they made a series of intertemporal choices between early monetary rewards and later monetary rewards. Their intriguing study finds that the prefrontal cortex lights up on the MRI when participants are presented with the two choices. When participants choose the early reward, the brain's pleasure center lights up.[14]

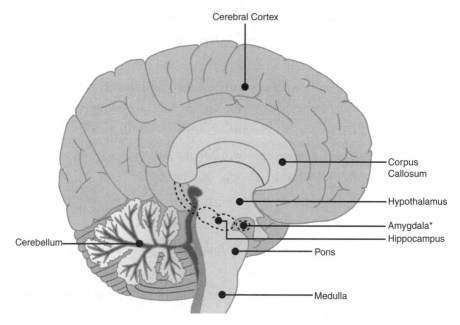

Figure 7-3 The Limbic System

Source: National Institute of Health

Here for you science buffs is the scientific explanation followed by one in English for us, uh, non-scientists:

> Parts of the limbic system associated with the midbrain dopamine system, including paralimbic cortex, are preferentially activated by decisions involving immediately available rewards. In contrast, regions of the lateral prefrontal cortex and posterior parietal cortex are engaged uniformly by intertemporal choices irrespective of delay. Furthermore, the relative engagement of the two systems is directly associated with subjects' choices, with greater relative fronto-parietal activity when subjects choose longer term options.[15]

In other words, we are anatomically built to choose immediate pleasure rather than delay it. For example, the researchers note that someone offered the choice between $10 today and $11 tomorrow might be tempted to choose the immediate option. However, if asked today to choose between $10 in a year and $11 in a year and a day, the same person is likely to prefer the slightly delayed but larger amount.

The dangers of this sort of behavior were manifested during the financial crisis, with households paying a heavy price for having chosen immediate gratification all too often. Perhaps now households will have learned the lesson they were taught in elementary school in one of *Aesop's Fables* in the story of "The Ant and the Grasshopper":

> *In a field one summer's day a Grasshopper was hopping about, chirping and singing to its heart's content. An Ant passed by, bearing along with great toil an ear of corn he was taking to the nest.*
>
> *Why not come and chat with me, said the Grasshopper, instead of toiling and moiling in that way?*
>
> *I am helping to lay up food for the winter, said the Ant, and recommend you to do the same.*
>
> *Why bother about winter? said the Grasshopper; we have got plenty of food at present. But the Ant went on its way and continued its toil.*
>
> *When the winter came the Grasshopper had no food and found itself dying of hunger, while it saw the ants distributing every day corn and grain from the stores they had collected in the summer.*
>
> *Then the Grasshopper knew:*
>
> *It is best to prepare for the days of necessity.*

McClure, Laibson, Lowenstein, and Cohen believe that their study combined with evidence of our ability to reason and show patience

> suggest that human behavior is often governed by a competition between lower level, automatic processes that may reflect

evolutionary adaptations to particular environments, and the more recently evolved, uniquely human capacity for abstract, domain-general reasoning and future planning. Within the domain of intertemporal choice, the idiosyncrasies of human preferences seem to reflect a competition between the impetuous limbic grasshopper and the provident prefrontal ant within each of us.

The researchers' work helps us to understand a number of behaviors, not the least of which is why people use credit—they just can't help themselves; they were born this way.

Temptation: As Old as Adam and Eve

If you were asked to memorize a seven-digit number as part of a memory study and then were told you had a choice between a fruit salad and a delectable piece of chocolate cake, which would you choose? Chances are you would choose the chocolate cake, even if you, like most people, are health conscious. Such are the results of a study conducted by Baba Shiv (1999), who finds temptation drives decision making when the cognitive part of a person's brain is busy or distracted.[16] Think of it as another form of hypnotism. In the experiment, Shiv asked a separate group of people to remember a two-digit number, and they were then given the same food choices. The majority of this group chose the fruit salad. In all, twice as many people who had the more challenging task of memorizing the seven-digit number chose chocolate over fruit. The results indicate that when the brain is busy—when, as Shiv says it has a high "cognitive load," it becomes more difficult for a person to fight temptation. "In other words," Shiv says, "willpower is so weak, and the prefrontal cortex is so overtaxed, that all it takes is five extra bits of information before the brain starts to give in to temptation." In Shiv's technical explanation, he assumes there is a negative element to eating chocolate cake, although some of us would disagree!

Findings from the two experiments suggest that if processing resources are limited, spontaneously evoked affective reactions rather than cognitions tend to have a greater impact on choice. As a result, the consumer is more likely to choose the alternative that is superior on the affective dimension but inferior on the cognitive dimension (e.g., chocolate cake). In contrast, when the availability of processing resources is high, cognitions related to the consequences of choosing the alternatives tend to have a bigger impact on choice compared to when the availability of these resources is low. As a result, the consumer is more likely to choose the alternative that is inferior on the affective dimension but superior on the cognitive dimension (e.g., fruit salad).

As one would expect, those who had a tendency toward giving in to temptation ("impulsives") had a greater likelihood of choosing the chocolate cake when they had to memorize the seven-digit number than did those who tended to be more prudent. Marketers focus on people who are impulsive. Supermarkets certainly are. Have you ever noticed that after the bombardment of temptations you gave in on throughout the supermarket, the additional bombardment you get while you wait impatiently on the checkout line? Somewhere along the line you almost certainly did, giving in to the temptation to purchase a magazine, a cold drink, candy, chewing gum, batteries, eyeglass repair kits, potato chips, and a wide assortment of things you could have done without but probably were so distracted (and bored) by the waiting and all of the stimuli all around you that you were more susceptible to temptation.

The excesses in consumer spending that occurred in the time leading up to the financial crisis were the result of consumers giving in to many temptations, but not all of these can be explained by the distractions created by cognitive overload. For example, the decision to obtain a credit card has little to do with cognitive overload and far more to do with other influences. Consumers are of course inundated with mail tempting them to apply for credit cards, but the decision to apply for credit has little to do with cognitive overload. In fact, the number of mailed credit card solicitations was over 5 billion in 2005, about five times as much as a decade earlier.[17] Only after consumers apply for and then receive the credit cards do they find themselves in predicaments where cognitive overload becomes a factor in their consumption decisions. In these cases, the decision to give in to temptation and consume is linked to the bombardment of distractions consumers are hit with from marketers, advertisers, salesmen, and the like, as well as the consumers' personal struggles to fit in, to feel accepted, to be a somebody by keeping up with the Joneses, and whatever it takes to feel secure.

Just as Adam and Eve believed they could survive if they gave in to temptation and ate fruit from the Forbidden Tree, Washington for years has believed it could do the same, feasting on the tree's succulent fruit and its delightful juices that to politicians work miracles, keeping them alive and in power like the overflowing waters of a fountain of youth. Never mind that one too many bites on the luscious fruit put the tongue onto the fruit's rotten and deeply poisonous core; this from the first bite the politician has found his antidote to survive, by taking to the garden and hiding from his constituency. The financial crisis has exposed the nakedness of the politician, and he no longer leaves the cherry blossom gardens of Washington unclothed and is thus draped with an apron of fig leaves, sewn by the sticky substance dripping from the bitten apples.

Why Put Off Buying Today What You Should Be Buying Tomorrow?

Before there was ever a shopping mall or a credit card, John Rae, a Canadian schoolmaster by day and economist by night, in 1834, understood well the allure of spending and the choices people had to make between receiving a benefit today or in the future. In stylish writing, Rae eloquently states,

Such pleasures as may now be enjoyed generally awaken a passion strongly prompting to the partaking of them. The actual presence of the immediate object of desire in the mind by exciting the attention, seems to rouse all the faculties, as it were to fix their view on it, and leads them to a very lively conception of the enjoyments that it offers to their instant perception. The prospects of future good, which future years may hold out to use, seem at such a moment dull and dubious, and are apt to be slighted, for objects on which the daylight is falling strongly, and showing us in all their freshness within our grasp.... Everywhere to see, that to spend is easy, to spare, hard.[18]

The inclination to overweight the short-term benefits and underweight the long-term costs of a particular decision perpetuates onto itself. In other words, people are more likely to choose immediate gratification even when delay might be the better option simply because they lack confidence they will have the control to delay the gratification. Battaglini, Benabou, and Tirole (2001) document the impulse toward short-run gratification in a study of self-control in peer groups, finding people tending to have much less self-control when making decisions on their own versus doing so in a group setting. The researchers provide a vivid illustration of the lack of self-control that people show when they face a choice between immediate or delayed gratification:

> The canonical example is that of an alcoholic who must decide every morning whether he will try to abstain that day, or just start drinking right away. If he was sure of his ability to resist his cravings throughout the day and evening, when temptation and stress will reach their peak, he might be willing to make the effort. If he expects to cave in and get drunk before the day's end anyway, on the other hand, the small benefits of a few hours' sobriety will not suffice to overcome his initial proclivity towards instant gratification, and he will just indulge himself from the start.[19]

In this context, it can be said that consumers choose instant gratification, recognizing their inability to delay it. They know they won't
be able to hold off on that new car, the nifty electronic, the new jewelry, and so forth, so they give in, even if their wallet or purse has been
emptied of cash, leaving plastic as the only option.

Laibson, Repetto, and Tobacman (2001) shed additional light on
what causes people to turn to plastic. In their study, which is appro-
priately called, A *Debt Puzzle*, the researchers attempt to reconcile
the high rate of credit card borrowing relative with lifecycle wealth
accumulation, finding five conditions that spur the use of credit card
borrowing:

> First, the calibrated labor income path slopes upward early in
> life. Second, income has transitory shocks. Third, consumers
> invest actively in an illiquid asset, which is sufficiently illiquid
> that it cannot be used to smooth transitory income shocks.
> Fourth, consumers may declare bankruptcy, reducing the ef-
> fective cost of credit card borrowing. Fifth, households have
> relatively more dependents early in the life-cycle.[20]

Using these five conditions, the researchers then constructed a
quantitative model that would predict the percentage of the population that would use credit cards at any time in their lives. Their
model predicts that 20 percent of the population will borrow on their
credit cards at any point in time, much less than the actual rate of
over 60 percent, as shown in Figure 7-4 by age cohort and by level of
education.

The "puzzle" in the Laisbon, Repetto, and Tobacman study
(2001) lies in the discount rate that consumers apply to their retirement savings and to their credit card borrowing. On the one hand,
consumers are rational, applying a discount rate of just 5 percent to
project how much they need save today in order to have the assets they
desire when they retire. On the other, a discount rate of 18 percent is
implied for those who use their credit cards frequently. The researchers also measure the value people place on immediate gratification,

finding that "consumers have a short-run discount rate of 30 percent and a long-run discount rate of 5 percent. In other words, delaying a reward by a year reduces its value by 30 percent, but delaying the same reward an additional year only generates an additional 5 percent devaluation." The researchers conclude from these observations that "It does not appear to be possible to calibrate realistic lifecycle models to match both observed levels of voluntary retirement savings and the observed frequency of credit card borrowing. We call this apparent paradox, The Debt Puzzle."

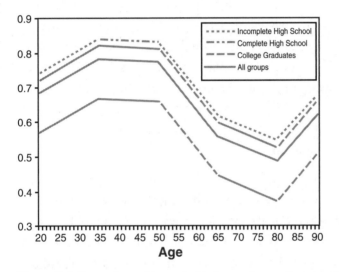

Figure 7-4 Percentage of households borrowing on their credit cards by age and education level

Source: Laibson, David; Repetto, Andrea; and Tobacman, Jeremy, "A Debt Puzzle," NBER Working Paper Series, 2001.

A telling finding in the study is that it shows the tendency for people to leave themselves with very little liquidity, even as they save for their retirement. These consumers "live hand to mouth in their checking accounts, but hold large stocks of illiquid assets like home equity and defined contributions pension plans." The point is that consumers invest in illiquid assets, where the benefits are spread out over many years, without regard for the high cost they will bear for being illiquid, not the least of which is the high cost of credit card borrowing. In other words, consumers are willing to pay a high price for immediate gratification.

How Employers Can Channel the Desire for Instant Gratification to Help Their Employees Save

Recognizing that people have insatiable and primal needs for instant gratification, employers can utilize these tendencies to help their employees save. Thaler and Benartzi (2004) devised a plan called Save More Tomorrow, which allows employees to contribute a portion of their *future* pay increases toward their retirement savings. Employees are also asked if they would like to enter the program three months from now and that they commit to doing so if they go that route.[21] This feature enables employers to take advantage of the tendency of people to procrastinate, which is a good thing. And after people have joined the plan, they will tend to stay in then, not wanting to take the time to get out.

The idea behind delaying increases in contributions until future pay increases is to keep people from feeling the sense of "loss" that would come if the additional contribution were taken out of their current paychecks. Done this way, people's tendency to avoid losses is taken into account, with the increased contributions not seen as either a loss or a reduction in their pay, even though it is relative to their *new* pay.

Consumption Versus Debt

We have seen in this chapter the powerful role that primal motives play in decisions to consume and thus to use debt. We have seen also that it is extraordinarily difficult to satisfy these human cravings, which go beyond the basic needs of living creatures to more complex elements related to our existence in a social framework. It will therefore be challenging to fend off the urges to give in to temptation, to consume excessively, and to use debt. The basic human elements that have for centuries caused bubbles to repeatedly surface in the world of finance and trade will be the same ones that undoubtedly will cause consumers to forget the lessons of the recent financial crisis and eat again from the Forbidden Tree and know again the curse of debt.

8

When Is Being in Debt a Good Thing?

Which of the two scenes presented as follows best exemplifies the gold standard by which American families should run their finances and fulfill their pursuit of happiness while also best promoting their good standing as responsible members of society? In both scenes, the families are of slightly above average income, are educated, have good credit histories, and have favorable income prospects.

Scene One:

It is a sunny Friday morning in April 1981 on Main Street in Anywhere, USA. Birds are chirping, and they are whizzing about as a newly married couple, aged 28, spring from their compact cars and like magnets are quickly joined at the hip and shoulder, their hands clasping together with a firmness and sense of togetherness that itself will make the day even more memorable—they are closing on the purchase of a new home. They are chuckling as they merrily walk toward a red brick building ahead, occasionally glancing at one another, their eyes smiling. Joy and optimism fill their hearts and minds. They know that today begins a journey that will last many years.

The couple walks into the brick building up two flights of stairs, feeling weightless even as they make the climb up to room 331, where they enter knowing that when they exit they will begin a lifetime of building memories in their new home, a finely appointed place where some day they will build their nest and share life's greatest joy and look into the twinkling eyes of their children.

There is the tussling of paperwork to be had, but it's just a formality—the excitement of the day passes the time. The room is well-lit

217

from sunshine bursting through the blinds, even as dark-suited men blanket the room. There is one last page for the couple to sign, and they do so with a flare, quickly lifting their pens off the page. The suited men stand, cap their pens, and shuffle their papers together like decks of cards. They for the thousandth time still gain pleasure in seeing yet another couple realize their dream. The suits watch as the couple embraces and their eyes brim with happy tears, their hands again clasped together, this time holding the source of day's joy: the keys to their new home.

A short drive away the couple turns onto their new street, which is lined with cherry blossoms and homes bustling with well-tended shrubbery. The sprinklers are on, and the mist captures the brilliance of the day's sunshine. Pulling up to their driveway in their sprite, little car the couple stops and darts out, laughing robustly, cross over their deep green grass and leap toward the door. Their hearts racing, they fumble the keys, which fall onto the red wooden porch, garnering more laughs. A moment later and with a turn of the key, they open the door and stand in the doorway, staring at the empty space. Both know the empty rooms will be filled soon enough, not just with their possessions, but with memories that last a lifetime. And so it was.

Scene Two:

It is a cloudy autumn day in November 2041 (yes, 30 years from now) on Main Street in Anywhere, USA, where a mature couple, both about 57 years old, are on their way to a bank to withdraw money they saved over their nearly three decades of marriage. They want to use the money to purchase a home. When they arrive at the bank, they pull into its busy parking lot, where cars are crisscrossing to and fro near the drive-through ATM located on the side of the bank. After they've parked, the husband reaches into the glove compartment for the couple's savings passbook, and then he and his wife begin to exit their car. Each swivels sideways, reaching upward to the top of their respective car doors to gain their footing. The husband reaches back into the car—he forgot his reading glasses. Heavy winds have the couple scurrying inside, their hands holding their jackets closed, their heads tucked downward. Once inside, they walk toward the teller's line and wait their turn.

When at the teller's window, the couple slips their passbook under the window's thick glass. The husband makes a request to the teller, handing her a note and saying, "We would like to withdraw all but $20,000 (about $250,000) of our money for this account and have it made payable to the party shown on this slip," Uncharacteristically the teller probes and comments and says, "That's quite a sum!" The wife leans toward the window, replying, "Yes, we are purchasing a new home, our first. Now we will have more rooms to have room for our grandchildren to play in." It is a lovely thought, but the woman feels a ping in her chest again having to ponder whether she and her husband's decision to wait such a long time to purchase a home was the right one, especially now that they are empty nesters. They never did get the home they wanted with the white picket fence adorned by deep green grass in the backyard, where the pattering of little feet and laughter of children tickles the soul. No matter, the woman lifts up her chin and is confident in her belief that in the autumn of her and her husband's years, they will find plenty of joy.

The Utility of Debt Use Is Different for the Private Sector Versus the Public Sector

The decision to purchase a home is both a financial one and a personal one. Far be it from any of us to judge whether the decision by one household to borrow money to purchase a home versus the decision by the other to save for it is the right one. That said, when juxtaposed against the quantity of years the average person lives as well as the life cycle theory of consumption proposed by Modigliani and Brumberg (1954), the utility of purchasing a home early in life has merit, as long as "utility" is defined as the enjoyment typically associated with homeownership in the United States.[1] Granted, the recent experience of many people has been decidedly worse than the longer-term experience, but it is drowned out by the throngs of people who have had positive experiences—homeownership was called the American Dream for generations for a reason. Moreover, those who had poor experiences in recent years are widely believed to have been victims to a poisonous mix of financial conditions and bubbling hysteria that for housing is not likely to repeat for at least a generation.

Defining utility is itself difficult because it depends on individual preferences and levels of satisfaction that aren't easily measured. Nevertheless, we can judge utility at least on part based on the way people perceive their income and consumption relative to others in their neighborhoods. As was discussed at length in Chapter 7, "The Hypnotic Power of Debt," this "keeping up with the Joneses" tendency forwarded by Dusenberry (1949) posits that people make consumption decisions based on what others in their locale purchase.[2] So if a neighbor were to purchase a new car, an individual would by this theory be more inclined to purchase a car than if the neighbor hadn't. These sorts of social cues are what drive consumption trends in many areas of spending and other categories including the length of women's hemlines, the waistline and style of blue jeans, hairstyles, automobile purchases, housing, furniture, music, and much more. It follows, then, that relative levels of consumption can be used to measure the utility of a purchase to an individual or household. In the United States, given that approximately 65 percent of households own a home, it is reasonable to conclude that the utility gained from owning a home is likely to be viewed as favorable versus not owing a home. This means that in our example the young couple likely made the better choice to borrow rather than save for their dream home. Keep in mind that we put all other elements of utility aside, so the analysis must go much deeper if we are to make a full judgment.

> From a macroeconomic perspective, the importance of aggregate decisions to consume rather than save has been debated ever since Keynes (1936) proposed the notion that lapses in aggregate demand play a critical role in determining

the aggregate level of output and employment.[3] In fact, excess saving amid a decline in household wealth and increase in liquidity preferences played a major role in the Great Depression. Modigliani (1986), who was awarded the Nobel Prize in economic sciences in 1985 for his work on his life cycle concept, notes that fear of excessive saving continued well beyond the Great Depression and into the 1950s: Not only was oversaving seen as having played a major role in the Great Depression, but, in addition, there was widespread fear that the problem might come back to haunt the post-war era. These fears were fostered by a widely held conviction that, in the future, there would not be too much need for additional accumulation of capital while saving would rise even faster than income. This combination could be expected to result, sooner or later, in saving outstripping the "need" for capital. These concerns were at the base of the "stagnationist" school which was prominent in the 40s and early 50s.[4]

Figure 8-1 illustrates Modigliani's life cycle theory of consumption and savings.

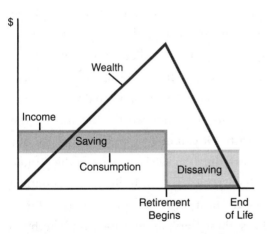

Figure 8-1 The Life-Cycle Hypothesis of Savings and Consumption

Source: Modigliani's Nobel Prize Lecture; http://nobelprize.org/nobel_prizes/economics/laureates/1985/modigliani-lecture.pdf

Modigliani makes an important point with respect to how a nation's debt will affect personal consumption. He believes that personal consumption (and by extension, the personal savings rate) will be independent of a nation's fiscal situation because it is instead dictated by an individual's life cycle. This is in contrast to the Ricardian Equivalence theory advanced by Barro (1974), which contends that budget deficits compel individuals to save a greater proportion of their income, fearing future confiscation of their income, as well as increases in government regulations, and or cuts in services.[5] Modigliani believes that to the extent deficits are used to finance productive investments, future generations will also benefit from the expenditure, creating intergenerational equity for the expenditure. In other words, debt spending that burdens future generations can be rationalized on the basis that they would also be receiving a benefit from the spending.

These days, it is exceedingly difficult to argue that the sort of deficit spending that the United States, Europe, and Japan are currently engaging in is viewed by their citizens as beneficial to future generations because no major initiatives have been made toward increasing the proportion of national income to investments that could by any shape of the imagination be considered productive. For example, as part of the $787 billion American Recovery and Reinvestment Act of 2009, $89.3 billion was spent on a program called Making Pay Work, which doled out $400 tax credits to qualified working individuals and $800 to qualified working married couples,[6] monies that went to anything but productive investments. In other words, the money was wasted; that is, consider it wasted if you believe in the existence of a Ricardian Equivalence or in Friedman's (1957) concept of the permanent income hypothesis, which posits that an individual 's spending behavior is driven by both current income and projections of his or her future income.[7] It follows, then, that the question over whether a nation should engage in deficit spending requires a thorough examination over the extent to which it will affect consumption in the private sector, both in the personal sector and the business sector.

All of this is another way of saying that government should curtail its activism and get out of the way of the private sector. Greenspan

(2011) argues that excessive government activism negatively affects investments in illiquid assets, which in the aftermath of the financial crisis reached its lowest point since the Great Depression.[8]

James M. Buchanan (1986), an advocate for a balanced budget amendment to the United States Constitution, and who in 1986 won the Nobel Prize in economic sciences for his theories on public policy, argues that deficit spending by the federal government is excessively skewed toward consumption rather than investment, which reduces its effectiveness and is actually harmful to society because no future benefit is provided to offset future liabilities:

> The public debt incurred by the U.S. government during the regime of ever-increasing, and apparently permanent, budgetary deficits has financed public or government consumption rather than public or government investment. The classical rules for fiscal prudence have been doubly violated. Not only has government failed to "pay as it goes"; government has also failed to utilize productively the funds that have been borrowed. There has been no offsetting item on the asset side to match the increase in net liability that the debt represents. The capital value of the income stream of the national economy has been reduced, dollar for dollar, with each increase in present value of liabilities represented by the debt instrument issued.[9]

Buchanan believes that in the absence of moral or constitutional constraints, "democracies will finance some share of current public consumption from debt issue rather than from taxation and that, in consequence, spending rates will be higher than would accrue under budget balance."[10] Buchanan traces this loss of discipline to Keynes and the perpetual abuse of Keynesianism by politicians, who propagated fiscal illusion to hide the true cost of deficit spending:

> In order to sell the Keynesian policy prescriptions, the moral onus on government debt and deficits had to be exorcised from public consciousness. For this purpose, the intergenerational effects of public debt financing had to be denied.[11]

One could say that Keynesianism and its reckless use of debt to achieve its lofty goals numbed the public's senses to the cost of debt, and that with each post-Depression era generation the traditional sensitivities to the use of debt faded. Buchanan notes this transformation, saying,

> The pre-Keynesian norm of budget balance served to constrain spending proclivities so as to keep governmental outlays roughly within the revenue limits generated by taxes. The Keynesian destruction of this norm, without an adequate replacement, effectively removed the constraint. Predictably, politicians responded by increasing spending more than tax revenues, by creating budget deficits as a normal course of events[12]

Buchanan, who provides some of the most stinging quotes on the ravages of Keynesian economics, points his finger at Keynes himself for legitimizing the use of debt:

> The legacy or heritage of Lord Keynes is the putative intellectual legitimacy provided to the natural and predictable political biases toward deficit spending, inflation, and the growth of government.[13]

Where's the Good in Debt Use?

Just as we showed in our example of the two couples who purchased a home at much different times in their lives, Tempelman (2007) argues that not all debt is bad, placing emphasis on the utility the debt provides in consuming today versus in the future, the common trade-off that must be considered whenever debt is used to finance current consumption:

> That borrowing has a cost does not mean that it is undesirable. Borrowing allows economic actors to align their actual consumption pattern more closely to their intertemporal consumption preferences. So long as no one is forced to borrow,

borrowing merely allows the borrower to reach a higher utility curve, as depicted by the standard microeconomic diagram. A potential borrower weighs the greater utility of shifting some amount of consumption from the future to the present against the long-term reduction in living standard. He may decide to borrow money to finance an investment or an expensive durable consumer good, but not to finance a vacation. For example, an individual may choose to purchase a residence in the present by incurring mortgage debt rather than by saving for many years to accumulate enough cash to purchase the residence without debt.[14]

There are other uses of debt that have utility for those who use it prudently. For example, debt can be utilized as a means of transferring wealth. A borrower might give the proceeds of a loan to a third party, in essence transferring his or her future income to the third party. Second, those who borrow money might in the face of their pending liabilities be more aggressive about improving their income prospects. The more responsibilities a prudent person has, the more likely it is he or she will hone up to them by taking actions that make it possible to do so; for example, by pursuing a college degree, working extra hard for a promotion, and so on.

It is intriguing to consider debt from the bondholder's perspective. Buchanan (1958) emphasizes that those who purchase bonds do so voluntarily and that they therefore make no sacrifices with respect to the use of their resources. This runs somewhat counter to the view that public debts "crowd out" the private sector, but Buchanan in this instance is referring to the utility function of the bondholder in isolation, not the impact of debt on the economy at large. The true burden from debt is its affect on current uncertainties and taxpayers, who eventually must repay the debt:

> If an individual freely chooses to purchase a government bond, he is, presumably, moving to a preferred position on his utility surface by so doing. He has improved, not worsened, his lot by the transaction.... The economy, considered as the sum of the individual economic units within it, undergoes

no sacrifice or burden when debt is created.... The fact that economic resources are given up when the public expenditure is made does not, in any way, demonstrate the existence of a sacrifice or burden on individual members of the social group.... It is not the bond purchaser who sacrifices any real economic resources anywhere in the process. He makes a presumably favorable exchange by shifting the time shape of his income stream."[15]

Summary Thoughts on the Use of Public-Debt Finance

Tempelman (2007) sums up Buchanan's findings on public-debt finance with the following seven propositions, which clearly lean toward the view that the decision to use public debt should be given far greater consideration than it has ever since the advent of Keynesian economics:[16]

1. The burden of public debt falls on future generations.

2. Public debt constitutes negative capital formation.

3. Ricardian equivalence does not hold because of fiscal illusion.

4. Keynesian macroeconomics is the principal cause of the disappearance of the unwritten balanced-budget norm that existed prior to the 1930s.

5. Barring constitutional constraints, public deficits will be a permanent phenomenon.

6. Public debt is immoral because future generations bear a financial burden as a result of spending and borrowing decisions in which they did not participate.

7. A constitutional balanced-budget amendment is required to remedy the tendency in elective democracy for government to borrow and spend rather than to tax and spend, and to spend much rather than little.

Perhaps this quote from Buchanan best sums up the long-term cost of public indebtedness:

> By financing current public outlay by debt, we are, in effect, chopping up the apple trees for firewood, thereby reducing the yield of the orchard forever.[17]

The debate over whether public debt should be used to counter deficiencies in aggregate demand continues to rage, despite the apparent costs, which at the Keynesian Endpoint have become more obvious. Whether policymakers have gained an understanding of this cost has not been established yet. The wrangling seen over the U.S. debt ceiling throughout 2011 is evidence of this. Politicians continue to abuse the reserve status of the U.S. dollar by behaving as if investors will in perpetuity fund fiscal profligacy in the United States. A better idea is to return to the pre-Keynes mindset established at the dawn of America when it enacted the Sinking Fund Act in 1795, which established the precept that debts should be repaid and not accumulate. Today's generation is unfamiliar with this mindset and far more comfortable believing debt can be used to solve every ill. It behooves the public to exorcise this sinister belief from their minds and beware of efforts by politicians to deceive them with fiscal illusions that make the use of debt appear to nourish the land when in fact it leaves it barren.

9

The Investment Implications of the Keynesian Endpoint

When you are driving your car and one of its tires bursts, you immediately know that your day has changed. Suddenly you are thrust into actions you didn't at the onset expect to take. The same can be said when you are traveling steadily on a long trip and suddenly realize that the road you are on will leave you at a wayward destination. You therefore change course.

When you are investing do you do the same? Do you know when a tire has burst, and do you take the actions necessary to get your portfolio back into working condition so that you can take it where you want it to go? When financial and economic conditions significantly change and they put your portfolio off course relative to your long-term investment objectives, do you take the fork in the road and change your path?

At the Keynesian Endpoint, nary a car is without a flat tire, and investors are driving with old maps. Many investors nonetheless are stubbornly unwilling to learn how to fix their flats, and they mistakenly believe their maps will take them to their destinations. These are in normal times common mistakes that differentiate good investors from bad. Today they are mistakes that can be catastrophic from an investment and quality-of-life perspective. The solution is to identify the likely drivers of investment returns going forward—for example, the new direction that global cash flows are likely to take in response to sovereign debt burdens—and to construct portfolios that reflect a recognition of the very important idea that asset diversification does not equal risk diversification. We talk more about both of these ideas later in the chapter.

The Six Big Investment Implications of the Keynesian Endpoint

Throughout our lives we face many situations we must adapt to in order to either sustain life as we know it, to better our lives, or in the most trying of circumstance, to survive. It is human nature to adapt, and we do in so many situations, often to our surprise and to our relief. Investors must also adapt if they are to survive and thrive, but the natural instinct to adapt doesn't lend itself to investing in the same way that it does to everything else. Adapting in this case requires a conscious effort that explores the new landscape so that a new road-map for can be drawn.

There are six overriding investment implications of the Keynesian Endpoint that provide clarity for investors to construct portfolios that will help them to achieve their objectives of maximizing their returns while minimizing risks. I list them and then explain each in the sections that follow.

1. Sovereign debt will be the main driver of global cash flows into stocks, bonds, commodities, real estate, and foreign direct investments.

2. The deleveraging of sovereign debts will spur numerous forms of financial repression, resulting in a wide range of effects on financial markets and economies, including low policy rates and steep yield curves, for example.

3. Investment returns will be lower for most investors except those who throw away their old maps and take roads they are skeptical about taking.

4. Central banks will continue to diversify their international reserves, affecting foreign exchange values, the value of financial assets, and the performance of economies.

5. Benchmark centricity is endangering portfolios more than ever, requiring investors adopt a style of investing that is less constrained than is the case for many widely followed benchmarks.

6. The world has been turned upside-down financially and economically—yesterday's losers are today's winners and vice versa—investors must drop their home bias if they are to achieve desirable risk-adjusted portfolio returns.

These are the big macro themes that are likely to persist over the secular horizon, which is defined as at least the next three to five years, but usually much longer than that, which is likely to be the case for each of these investment themes. These themes can be applied to a wide variety of investments, and we focus on specifics later in the chapter when we look at individual asset classes such as bonds, stocks, and commodities, among others.

Let's now examine each of the six investment themes.

Sovereign Debt as a Driver of Global Cash Flows

Throughout history money has flowed to where investors believed they could profit most, even if their reasoning has been more than a bit flawed at times. A classic example of this was the great tulip mania that occurred in Holland in the period 1634 to 1637 when tulip bulbs were bought as both a status symbol and for financial gain. Local market exchanges developed from the craze, and bulbs were widely traded. Single bulbs were sold for items that in normal times had substantially greater value: two tons of butter, four oxen, twelve sheep, 1,000 pounds of cheese, eight pigs, and four tons of wheat. It is amazing to see what people will do to get what everyone else wants—even if they are unsure of why they want it themselves! Tulip mania is one in a litany of episodes where the vagaries of human nature were on display. Back in the day it was the central driver of cash flows.

To be sure, not all major drivers of cash flows are rooted in speculative fervor, but it is fair to say that since human behavior is not going to change any time soon, we should expect it to continue to play a major role periodically. People by their nature will adopt a herd mentality when they see a herd running, and when they do, money will fly until the herd stops. People can't help themselves—from tulips to the beginnings of the airline, radio, and automobile industries, to dot-com stocks in 1999 and 2000, there is always fodder to see the foibles of human desire.

Can you remember what the major driver of global cash flows was? You certainly do. It was the housing market, in particular the cash that flowed from home equity withdrawals, which were garnered and ultimately transmitted throughout the global financial system and world economy. Many homeowners took out home equity loans that were as convenient as the neighborhood ATM, with homeowners able to go to just about any ATM to draw on their home equity lines of credit (HELOC). You can't make this stuff up! Others extracted money from their homes when they sold them, usually at a price that was well above the amount owed on the mortgage.

In a study, Greenspan and Kennedy (2007)[1] identify three channels by which homeowners extract equity from their homes: home sales, home equity loans, and cash-out refinancing. The study also captures the remarkable ascension that the U.S. housing market took as a driver of global cash flows in the early 2000s, noting that from 2001 to 2005 the amount of equity extracted from the home averaged close to $1 trillion per year, which was more than three times the amount of equity extracted in the prior 10 years (Figure 9-1). These monies flowed throughout the U.S. economy and kept it buoyant, and in doing so it created an illusory appeal of the United States to foreign investors, who bought large quantities of U.S. Treasury and agency securities, as well as agency mortgage-backed securities (Figure 9-2).

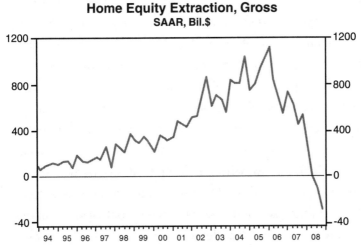

Figure 9-1 Who would've thought homes could be used as ATMs?

Source: Federal Reserve Board / Haver Analytics

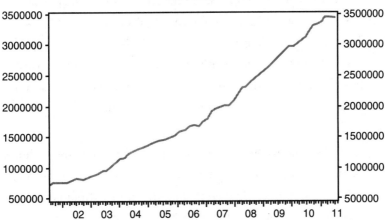

Figure 9-2 Foreign money added fuel to the housing market fire.

Source: Federal Reserve Board / Haver Analytics

When the housing ATM ran empty, cash flows worldwide were redirected, beginning first with a move toward assets deemed the least risky before eventually moving to a different set of opportunities. Housing is no longer a driver of global cash flows—sovereign debt is.

Investors in the age of deleveraging face a simple choice: to either invest in highly indebted nations where deleveraging is likely to result in a combination of lower-than-historical economic growth rates, financial repression, and weak foreign exchange values or invest in nations on the opposite end of the spectrum, where more stable public finances, favorable demographics, and high net national savings rates are facilitating relatively faster economic growth rates and appreciating currencies. Just like any good banker, investors are likely to increasingly shy away from indebted nations, particularly the United States, Japan, and those in Europe, preferring instead to cut off the left side of the distribution curve—the fat-tail, black swan risks that go with investing in highly indebted nations, by investing in other nations.

The basic question that investors will ask is this: In what part of the world will the return on capital be the highest? Will China answer "The United States," "Japan," or "Europe?" Figures 9-3 and 9-4 tell us why the United States won't be included in China's response nor that of any other global investor for that matter. Figure 9-3 speaks to the idea that economic growth will be held back by debt liquidation because at the Keynesian Endpoint nations can no longer turbocharge their economies through a finance-based economic system. Although the chart is of the United States, the same rule applies to Japan and Europe.

Figure 9-4 speaks to the same idea from a different angle. It shows the national savings rate for the United States. National savings are essential for any nation to finance its long-term investments and the amount of saving ultimately determines the amount of capital stock—plants, equipment, software, and machinery, for example—that exists in a nation, which is a major determinant of the potential growth rate for an economy. The capital stock is one of the three so-called factors of production that along with land and labor are vital foundations for economic growth.

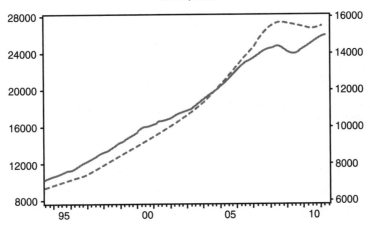

Figure 9-3 Debt turbocharged economic growth but the process is now in reverse.

Sources: Haver Analytics and Bureau of Economic Analysis

The national savings rate is thus calculated as follows:

National savings = private savings + public savings
where
private savings = disposable income—consumption
and
public savings = government receipts—government expenditures

Net Saving as Percentage of Gross National Income
SAAR, %

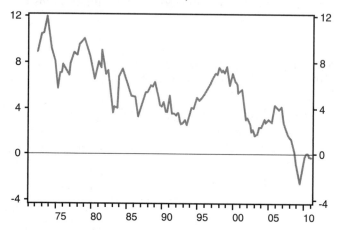

Figure 9-4 The huge U.S. trade and budget deficits give it a negative net national savings rate.

Sources: Haver Analytics and Bureau of Economic Analysis

The national savings numbers turn negative when the public balance sheet is levered up in response to a financial crisis. The releveraging causes the public deficit, or savings rate, to increase to a level that is greater than the private savings rate. Worsening this already difficult predicament is the constant depreciation of the existing capital stock. In other words, the aging of plants, equipment, buildings, and such represent a form of consumption that worsens an indebted nation's ability to grow its economy. This means that a nation must constantly invest in new capital stock in order to maintain its economic growth potential. Negative national savings rates hence threaten a nation's competitiveness from a growth perspective as well as cost because investing in new capital stock tends to boost productivity, which is a major element in the per unit cost of labor.

All of this technical mumbo jumbo means that highly indebted nations are disadvantaged by their debt burdens, and they will lose the race to the top of the economic heap. This is a point that has not been lost on China, which is increasingly deciding to invest its massive international reserves away from U.S. Treasuries into assets that appear less likely to decline in value and are denominated in currencies other than the U.S. dollar, which itself is poised to continue to decline in value just as it has for the past decade. China is instead investing in assets that fit its long-term needs, mining, mineral, agriculture, and energy companies, as well as commodities and other raw goods. China is also carving out shipping lanes and investing heavily in railroads in not just China but in foreign lands to ensure that it will have a capable infrastructure to support its massive international trading activity.

Did you know that China has a Ministry of Railways? They're serious about capital investing. China over the next decade plans to invest close to $300 billion in high-speed rail, according to China's Ministry of Railways and China.org, an amount absolutely gigantic in scale relative to the puny amounts planned by the United States and other nations investing in rail—roughly twenty times the amount that the United States will invest. The reasons for investing in rail from an economic perspective are obvious, including the realization of productivity gains from increasing the mobility of people and goods, and the promotion of energy efficiency and energy security.

In addition to rail, there are many other capital spending initiatives capable of bolstering economic activity, and we are likely to see capital increasingly moving away from developed countries toward investments likely to garner a greater return on capital. For nations that have both the wallet and the will, it is difficult to fathom any other outcome. At the Keyensian Endpoint, highly indebted nations unfortunately have neither the wallet nor the will to invest in their own economies in the way that developing countries do, making them relatively poor places to invest.

The relatively poor investment opportunities that exist in the real economies of highly indebted developed countries reduce the relative attractiveness of investment in financial assets in these countries. In addition to contributing to weakness in foreign exchange rates, the reduced cash flow will increase the cost of capital in indebted nations in two ways in particular. First, reduced economic growth rates will reduce returns on corporate equities and keep credit spreads wider than they would be if economic growth were strong. Second, nations such as Brazil, Russia, and China are likely to continue to reduce the proportion of reserve assets they hold in indebted nations, particularly the United States. This will boost real interest rates in these countries, chiefly for longer-term maturities, because longer rates bear the burdens of uncertainty with respect to inflation, volatility, and the future direction of short-term interest rates.

At the Keynesian Endpoint, sovereign debt burdens are likely to be the most important driver of global cash flows in economies and markets. Investors therefore should place substantial emphasis on the relative sovereign debt burdens they perceive for individual countries when formulating an investment strategy. Given the obvious debt burdens that developed countries have relative to developing countries, it is easy to see that developing countries will be preferred places to invest for the foreseeable future.

Financial Repression in the Age of Deleveraging

In 1914, Walter Bradford Cannon described in *The American Journal of Physiology* a condition called fight-or-flight, whereby animals, including humans, react to threats by priming them to either stay and fight or flee from danger. For example, wild animals sensing an immediate threat from a predator will respond vigorously with a degree of muscularity they do not normally show. The stress response is by nature temporary because the threat will either be pushed back or the animal will be mauled, perhaps to death.

The exact stress response that animals and people individually display when threatened differs dramatically. In some cases, doing nothing or standing still is the best response, just as in the movie *Jurassic Park* when the protagonist Dr. Grant, a paleontologist, tells a frightened young girl to stay perfectly still even as a menacing Tyrannosaurus Rex appeared to close in for the kill, putting is terrifying jaws and crushing body just inches from their trembling bodies.

We will never know just how frightening it feels to face death from the jaws of a dinosaur, or hopefully any of the dangerous creatures that still walk the earth and swim the seas (*Jaws!*), but we know exactly how our cavemen brethren must have felt because their reactions remain instilled in us. Put in modern vernacular, the caveman response to the threat of a T-Rex is hardwired in all of us and will be part of our nature until it isn't. It could be millions of years more until the flight-or-flight response is purged from us, if ever.

Highly indebted nations also display a flight-or-flight response to threats. The goals are the same as for individuals, which is to end the threat one way or another, either by responding vigorously through unconventional means or by fleeing, which you could say is a form of default, in order to exit the threat expeditiously.

Reinhart (2011) describes a subtle form of debt restructuring that occurs in the form of financial repression, a response by government to fight their plight using strong and unconventional remedies including: directed lending to government by captive domestic audiences (such as pension funds), explicit or implicit caps on interest rates, regulation of cross-border capital movements, and (generally) a tighter connection between government and banks. These actions have been applied in many instances since World War II, first by developed countries such as the United States and then by developing countries, primarily in the emerging markets in the 1980s and 1990s.

Reinhart describes five ways in which indebted nations historically have reduced their debt/GDP ratios:

1. Economic growth
2. A substantive fiscal adjustment/austerity plans
3. Explicit default or restructuring of private and/or public debt
4. A sudden surprise burst in inflation

5. A steady dosage of financial repression that is accompanied by an equally steady dosage of inflation

Reinhart emphasizes that options 4 and 5 are available only for domestic-currency debts. In other words, debts owed outside of the domestic currency cannot be liquidated through bouts of domestic inflation and or financial repression that are accompanied by inflation.

Resorting to Coinage and Inflation to Liquidate Sovereign Debts

Figure 9-5 shows the central government debt/GDP for the advanced economy and emerging market subgroups since 1900, using the Reinhart and Rogoff (2011) database for 70 countries. It is based on a simple arithmetic average; no weight is assigned to the sizes of countries. The chart highlights the five peaks in global indebtedness since 1900 as well as the resolutions for each episode.

One of these episodes was in the 1920s when Germany, Hungary, and other European nations liquidated their domestic-currency debts through hyper-inflation. Germany, for example, printed vast amounts of its currency, the Deutsche mark,[2] with the exchange rate reaching as many 4.2 million marks to the U.S. dollar and a single-denomination at 100 billion marks—you can buy these for a song on eBay. If you think that's a lot, consider that Hungary in 1946 printed the highest denomination for any currency ever, at 100,000,000,000,000,000,000 Hungarian pengo. The ravages of this excessive coinage led to hyper-inflation so massive that prices were doubling about twice per day. When Hungary scrapped the pengo for the forint (still in use today), the value of all pengo in circulation were worth less than a measly U.S. penny. How about that for debt liquidation?

Nations with the power to print money have for centuries held influence over the populace. This was true well before there were central banks, and it reminds us of the dangers of turning to coinage—or at least today's electronic version of it—as a means of shedding debt.

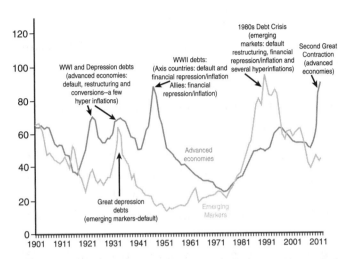

Figure 9-5 Increases in government indebtedness have tended to be followed by financial repression.

Sources: Reinhart (2010), Reinhart and Rogoff (2009 and 2011), sources cited therein and the authors, via Reinhart and Sbrancia (2011), "The Liquidation of Government Debt," National Bureau of Economic Research, *NBER Working Paper Series*, March 2011.

Notes: Listed in parentheses below each debt-surge episode are the main mechanisms for debt resolution besides fiscal austerity programs which were not implemented in any discernible synchronous pattern across countries in any given episode. Specific default/restructuring years by country are provided in the Reinhart-Rogoff database and a richer level of detail for 1920s-1950s (including various conversions listed in Table 1).

Figure 9-6 Hyperinflation: The 1923 German Deutsche mark

Numismatists understand well the relationship between supply and price because in their hobby of collecting coins, the quantity of a particular coin relative to demand affects its price a great deal. *Notaphilists* are the same, only their familiarity comes from the collection of paper currencies. *Scripophilists* understand the relationship, too, from their experience in collecting paper stock and bond certificates. *Philatelists*—stamp collectors—know a thing or two about the laws of supply and demand, too. An understanding of the basic relationship between supply and price is what prevents, say, a numismatist from being fooled by a novice who tries to sell him or her for a "song" a copper Chinese coin that was minted about 1,000 years ago during the Song Dynasty. The numismatist knows that literally billions of such coins were produced in the year 1085, for example, in factories across China.

The world can use a few more numismatists and notaphilists to warn against the ravages of coinage!

The Monetary Trilemma and Its Investment Implications

The consequences of the debasing of currencies have been readily transparent for ages. Yet in one form or another, nations in the developed world are resorting to their virtual printing presses to revive their economic fortunes. In the United States, the Federal Reserve has used its authority to engage in the purchase of more than $2.0 trillion of financial assets, an activity that increases the quantity of bank reserves, the money that banks use to expand the money supply—to increase coinage, in other words. This, in theory, puts at risk the purchasing power of the U.S. dollar. The hyperbole often heard in Washington over potentially stripping the Fed of its independence therefore is just that, leaving the Fed able to continue its efforts to reflate the U.S. economy, but also creating risk for the U.S. dollar.

In the U.S. and in the rest of the world, nations face a trilemma, where one objective must be sacrificed in order to achieve the other two. Here are their choices:

- Monetary policy independence
- Exchange rate stability
- Free flow of capital

Owing to its large budget deficit, the U.S. cannot sacrifice capital mobility, because it needs funding. As mentioned, no sacrifice of monetary policy independence is in the offing—certainly not to any foreign entity and not to the fiscal authority, either. This means the U.S. has chosen to sacrifice exchange rate stability.

The European Central Bank (ECB) is engaging in quasi-fiscal transfers by purchasing the sovereign debts of peripheral Europe. The purchases result in excess liquidity in Europe's banking system and at the same time contaminate the ECB's balance sheet, risking the purchasing power of the euro. Having selected monetary policy independence and capital mobility, Europe too is therefore sacrificing exchange rate stability. Internally, Europe's periphery has actually had to sacrifice two objectives: independent monetary policy and exchange rate stability. Europe faces a particularly daunting challenge trying to balance between its so-called fiscal and monetary corridors, representing the ECB's efforts to aid Europe's periphery on the one hand and control inflation on the other.

On the opposite end of the trilemma, nations with surplus funds—which in today's upside-down world include China, Brazil, South Korea and Russia, to name a few—wish to control the growth of their surpluses to keep economic activity from increasing too rapidly and inciting inflation. In other words, surplus nations are choosing to sacrifice capital mobility for the ability to keep monetary policy independence and exchange rate stability.

In game theory, in a noncooperative game such as the trilemma just described, each of the participants acts out of self-interest, resulting in big winners and losers, and this is what investors should expect because in today's multispeed world, central bankers are for the most part acting unilaterally, serving their own interests. For the foreign exchange markets, the investment implications are fairly obvious—indebted nations must sacrifice exchange rate stability if they are to correct the imbalances they have with the rest of the world. For the interest rate markets, efforts by indebted nations to reflate their economies will eventually erode the value of money, thus posing risk for holders of long-term government securities. In other words, the U.S. dollar and the euro are likely to fall in value against currencies that have surplus funds, and yield curves are likely to remain steeped in indebted nations.

Deflation Can't Cure a Debt Illness

If inflation is an elixir for curing the ills of excessive government debt, deflation is poison. Irving Fisher (1933) describes the quandary that transpires in indebted nations when deflation sets in, listing a sequence of nine factors that cause profligate debtors to experience severe stress, as occurred in the United States during the Great Depression:

> Assuming, accordingly, that, at some point of time, a state of over-indebtedness exists, this will tend to lead to liquidation, through the alarm either of debtors or creditors or both. Then we may deduce the following chain of consequences in nine links: (1) *Debt liquidation* leads to *distress selling* and to (2) *Contraction of deposit currency*, as bank loans are paid off, and to a slowing down of velocity of circulation. This contraction of deposits and of their velocity, precipitated by distress selling, causes (3) *A fall in the level of prices*, in other words, a swelling of the dollar. Assuming, as above stated, that this fall of prices is not interfered with by reflation or otherwise, there must be (4) *A still greater fall in the net worths of business*,

precipitating bankruptcies and (5) *A like fall in profits,* which in a capitalistic, that is, a private-profit society, leads the concerns which are running at a loss to make (6) *A reduction in output, in trade and in employment* of labor. These losses, bankruptcies, and unemployment, lead to (7) *Pessimism and loss of confidence,* which in turn lead to (8) *Hoarding and slowing down still more the velocity of circulation.*

The above eight changes cause (9) *Complicated disturbances in the rates of interest,* in particular, a fall in the nominal, or money, rates and a rise in the real, or commodity, rates of interest.

Evidently debt and deflation go far toward explaining a great mass of phenomena in a very simple logical way.[3]

Fisher describes how the combination of the two diseases—debt and deflation—"act and react on each other" in the same way that "a pair of diseases are sometimes worse than either or than the mere sum of both, so to speak." Fisher (1933) further notes the futility of debt liquidation:

> The very effort of individuals to lessen their burden of debts increases it, because of the mass effect of the stampede to liquidate in swelling each dollar owed. Then we have the great paradox, which, I submit, is the chief secret of most, if not all, great depressions: The more the debtors pay, the more they owe. The more the economic boat tips, the more it tends to tip. It is not tending to right itself, but is capsizing.

In other words, the liquidation of debts causes a decline in economic output, which reduces real incomes, thereby making it even more difficult for debtors to repay their debts. Hyman Minsky (1986) further notes that during such a state,

> market reactions to unemployment, which lead to falling wages and prices, are inefficient in raising employment because there are inherited private debts that can be validated only if money profits are sustained, and lower money wages and prices lead to lower profits. In other words, the cash flows

required to validate private debts would be forthcoming only if profits are sustained.[4]

To stop or prevent this depression-inducing spiral, Fisher notes, the level of prices must be reflated "up to the average level at which outstanding debts were contracted by existing debtors and assumed by existing creditors, and then maintain that level unchanged."

Minsky recognized the importance of monetary policy in preventing depressions, criticizing "the transformation of Keyne's economics from a serious critique of capitalism to a series of trivial policy manipulations," adding the notion that "Policy and mainstream economic thinking about our economy blithely ignore the need for and the effects of lender-of-last-resort interventions by the Federal Reserve."

Hence, the Federal Reserve's actions in the aftermath of the recent financial crisis are necessary medicine despite its many negative consequences because deflation and debts are a lethal mix.

Negative Real Interest Rates in the Age of Financial Repression

World War II left the world not only in ruins but also in debt. Figure 9-5 highlights the enormous debt explosion resulting from the War. Reinhart documents the resolution to these debts, which occurred over a 35-year period from 1945 to 1980 through a combination of financial repression and inflation. Figure 9-7 shows the history of real interest rates between 1945 and 2009 for advanced and emerging economies, with a marker dividing the financial repression era from the one that followed.

Negative real interest rates reduce government indebtedness in three ways by

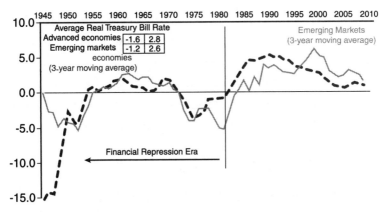

Figure 9-7 A history of ex-post real interest rates for advanced economies and emerging markets from 1945-2009 (3-year moving averages, in percent).

Sources: *International Financial Statistics,* International Monetary Fund, various sources listed in the Data Appendix, and authors' calculations, via Reinhart and Sbrancia (2011), "The Liquidation of Government Debt," National Bureau of Economic Research, *NBER Working Paper Series*, March 2011.

Notes: The advanced economy aggregate is comprised of: Australia, Belgium, Canada, Finland, France, Germany, Greece, Ireland, Italy, Japan, New Zealand, Sweden, the United States, and the United Kingdom. The emerging market group consists of: Argentina, Brazil, Chile, Colombia, Egypt, India, Korea, Malaysia, Mexico, Philippines, South Africa, Turkey and Venezuela. The average is unweighted and the country coverage is somewhat spotty prior for emerging markets to 1960, as detailed in the Data Appendix.

1. Reducing the interest expense of the debt

2. Transferring money from savers to borrowers

3. Enticing investors to move out the risk spectrum, thereby boosting asset prices and promoting economic growth

In perhaps the greatest warning to today's bond investors, in particular investors in government bonds, Reinhart cites work by Homer and Sylla (1963) who describe 1946–1981 as the second (and longest) bear market for bonds in U.S. history (Homer and Sylla identify the first bear market as 1899 to 1920).[5] Bond investors should take seriously the prospect that policymakers will keep real interest rates lower than they would otherwise be in order to reduce government indebtedness. In such an environment, the policy rate set by the central bank will be kept low, and the proclivity of the central bank to keep the policy rate low importantly will be communicated by the central bank in order to suppress forward rate expectations and thus induce a condition whereby interest rates are either low or negative in real terms. This sort of pocket-picking results in losses to savers and creditors in terms of the purchasing power of their money, especially for holders of shorter-dated interest-bearing assets, because these assets are closely linked to the policy rate set by the central bank, and it is the central bank that is likely to pursue negative real interest rates to promote conditions that aid the deleveraging process, which is likely to be longwinded—counted in many years, if not decades.

By enabling nominal GDP to increase at a rate that exceeds the interest rate on the existing stock of debt, a nation over time will liquidate its debt. In contrast, when the interest rate paid on the stock of debt exceeds the growth rate of nominal GDP, the stock of debt outstanding increases faster than the amount of nominal GDP, which means that the debt-to-GDP ratio for such a poorly plighted nation can't possibly stabilize.

The rate at which a nation can liquidate its debt therefore depends heavily on the differential between the nominal growth rate for GDP and the interest rate paid on the stock of debt. Reinhart calculates the annual amount of debt liquidation via negative real interest rates for the period 1945–1980 in the United States and United Kingdom at between 3 to 4 percent of GDP per year. For Italy and Australia, where inflation rates were relatively high, the liquidation rate was faster, at around 5 percent per year.

Investors in government bonds are thus behooved to prepare for a lengthy period of financial repression and its accompanying low to negative real interest rates. Investors should aim to avoid confiscation of their hard earned money by being leery of holding government bonds and seek alternatives by shopping in the many other segments of the $90 trillion global bond supermarket.

Bond investors in the aftermath of the financial crisis are already being subjected to financial repression. Figure 9-8 shows this quite dramatically. It shows the real interest rate for 5-year U.S. Treasury inflation-protected securities (TIPS). It has decreased substantially ever since the end of 2008 when the Federal Reserve began its long-term securities asset purchases and lowered its benchmark rate to between zero and 0.25 percent. The combination of the Fed's low policy rate and acceleration in the inflation rate, which by the middle of 2011 had reached 1.6 percent for all prices minus food and energy, are what resulted in the negative real interest rate for 5-year TIPS. This is a desirable outcome for the Federal Reserve as well as the U.S. Treasury because it will help the United States to achieve liquidation of its debt, but it is an undesirable outcome for savers and creditors. Why should investors tolerate this? They needn't if they recognize that an era of financial repression has begun. So bond investors unite! Just say no to negative real interest rates!

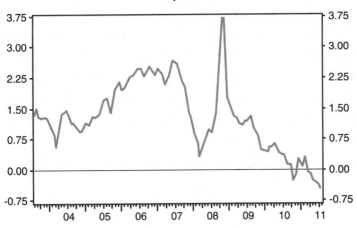

Figure 9-8 Treasury yields have fallen below the inflation rate.

Source: Federal Reserve Board / Haver Analytics

Detours and Lower Investment Returns Beyond the Keynesian Endpoint

In the years leading up to the financial crisis, much of the economic growth achieved in developed countries such as the United States was built on a false precept. We were fooled into believing that it was completely authentic. The fact is that much of the economic growth achieved was built on the expansion of credit rather than lasting drivers of economic activity, in particular investment in and the productive use of land, labor, and capital—the three primary factors of production.

More important, much of the debt built up in the United States in recent decades was household debt, and this sort of debt is as capable of boosting a nation's productive capacity as effectively as water makes a campfire grow faster. For example, when a household uses a credit card to purchase a new reclining chair, it does zilch to boost the productive capability of the nation. (In fact it probably decreases it if it makes Americans couch potatoes!) In contrast, a small business that borrows money for a faster Internet router or for computers with more computing power than their existing computers will more than likely achieve productivity gains. Unfortunately, debt use in the United States in recent decades has been concentrated more in the former than the latter. This is one of the reasons why the U.S. is at risk of losing competitiveness to the rest of the world and why it therefore must shift gears toward a less consumption-driven economic system.

Figure 9-9 highlights the increased dependency the U.S. has had on debt to boost its economy. The chart shows the increased amount of debt it took over to boost economic activity.

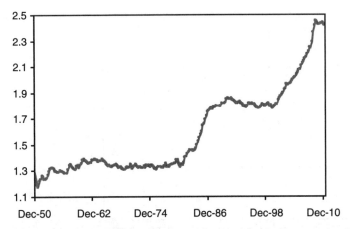

Figure 9-9 The total amount of U.S. nonfinancial private- and public-sector debts outstanding relative U.S. GDP.

Source: Federal Reserve, Bureau of Economic Analysis

Figure 9-10 highlights the decreased benefit that the debt use has had in boosting economic growth, which is to say that over the past 45 years each dollar of debt deployed has produced a smaller amount of economic activity compared to the past. The reason for this is as I discussed earlier, and it is critically important to investors: using debt for anything other than enhancing the productive use of the three primary factors of production decrease a nation's productive capability as well as its competitiveness.

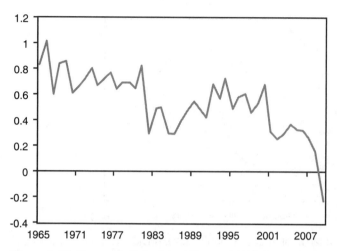

Figure 9-10 Change in U.S. debt / Change in U.S. nominal GDP

Source: Federal Reserve, Bureau of Economic Analysis

The major investment implication is that indebted nations are likely to experience relatively low economic growth rates compared to the less indebted. Indebted nations are hamstrung in several ways. First, they are hobbled by an inability to increase their debts and instead must reduce them. Consumption and hence overall economic activity therefore will be negatively affected. Second, the liquidation of debts on the aggregate will result in a slower growth in incomes, which itself will weaken consumption, creating a vicious feedback loop. Third, as Figure 9-10 showed, the marginal rate of return from debts decreases over time.

Relative growth rates are as a compass to investors; they tell investors where to go. This means that investors should look outside of the developed world for investment opportunities because it is saddled with debts that for many reasons weaken economic activity. This is hardly a prediction—it is already happening. Take a look at Figures 9-11 and 9-12. They show very starkly how consumption and investment is being hindered in indebted nations relative to nations less saddled by debt.

Automobile Sales

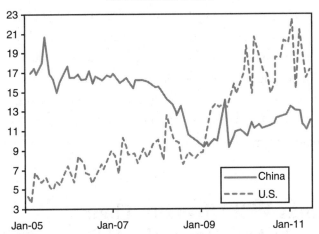

Figure 9-11 Debt burdens are driving car sales lower in the U.S. relative to nations with healthier balance sheets. Annualized monthly sales rates, in millions of units.

Source: U.S. Department of Commerce. China Automotive Information Net

The end result is rather bleak for national income, as shown in Figure 9-12, which shows the sharp differences in employment growth between the two classes of countries in the aftermath of the financial crisis.

Unemployment Rate

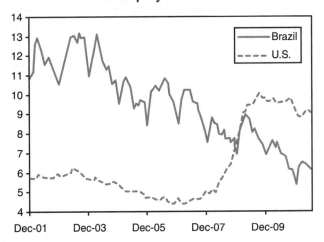

Figure 9-12 Creditor nations such as Brazil have better employment prospects than indebted nations such as the United States.

Source: Bureau of Labor Statistics, Instituto Brasileiro de Geographica e Estatistica (IBGE)

These charts speak clearly to the growth potential in developed countries compared to that of the rest of the world, where it is obvious the landscape has changed dramatically. Investors that stick to old maps will wind up investing in the wrong places, which is to say they will wind up investing in countries where investment returns are likely to lag other parts of the world, chiefly the emerging markets. This is another very strong case for investors to drop their home bias and scour the globe for opportunities.

Central Banks Will Diversify Their Reserve Assets Away from the U.S.

The old saying for diversification is as follows: Don't put your eggs in one basket. If the basket drops, you will lose more of your eggs than if you had kept them in separate baskets. This principle holds true on the international scene, where creditor nations must choose where to keep their eggs.

At the Keynesian Endpoint, a major force in the movement of global cash flows will be diversification of international reserve assets out of the U.S. dollar into other assets, including the euro, other currencies, gold, and alternative investments. This is a continuation of a trend, actually, because central banks have been diversifying their reserve assets out of the U.S. dollar for about a decade, as is shown in Figure 9-13.

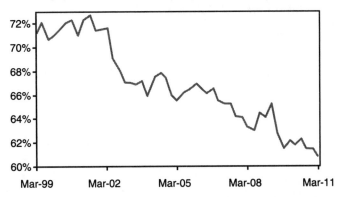

Figure 9-13 The U.S. dollar is slowly losing its reserve status.

Source: International Monetary Fund

Reserve assets are those assets held by (they are not necessarily owned) a central bank that are denominated in currencies other than the central bank's domestic currency. In a fiat, or paper currency system, nations build reserve assets basically by taking in more money than they transfer out, largely through their current account, which consists of international trade for both goods and services, income received on assets such corporate equities and bonds, and unilateral transfers, such as direct foreign aid, worker remittances, and gifts.

The expansion of global trade over the past decade or so has benefited all nations, but it has benefited some much more than others. China stands out. Its exports have grown dramatically, and as a result so have its holdings of international reserves, as shown in Figure 9-14. The growth of the world's reserve assets is shown in Figure 9-15, and Table 9-1 lists the world's ten largest holders of international reserves.

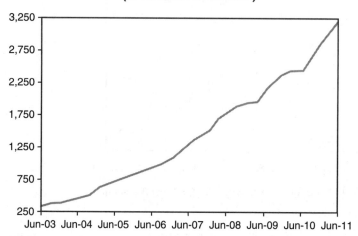

Figure 9-14 Ever wonder where your money goes when you buy goods that say "Made in China"?

Source: International Monetary Fund

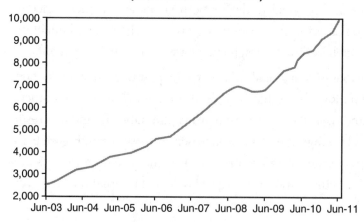

Figure 9-15 Nations are self-insuring against future crises, but this applies mostly to the emerging markets.

Source: International Monetary Fund

TABLE 9-1 Top-10 Holders of International Reserves—The United States and Europe Didn't Make the List

Country	Reserve Holdings (in Billions of Dollars)
China	3,197.5
Japan	1,071.5
Saudi Arabia	493.4
Russia	484.0
Taiwan	400.8
Brazil	348.3
South Korea	311.0
India	286.2
Hong Kong	272.5
Singapore	249.2

The question that arises from Figures 9-14 and 9-15 and the accompanying table is this: What is the world going to do with all of this money? The answer for many years has been to buy U.S. Treasuries. The answer from here on is likely to be to find alternatives to both U.S. Treasuries and the U.S. dollar because alternative investments are likely to earn a better rate of return. Whose decision is it? According to The Bank of England

> In most countries, the reserves are owned by the central bank; that is, they are on the central bank's balance sheet and the ultimate decisions on reserves management are taken within the central bank's management structure. But there are several counter-examples to this (the United States, the UK and Japan, to name three) where the reserves are formally owned by the government, and the ultimate decisions on their management are thus taken by the government (usually the Treasury or Finance Ministry).[6]

The Bank of England (BOE), which was founded in 1694, knows a thing or two about central banking, and the BOE highlights three objectives that central bankers have with respect to the reserve assets they manage: security, liquidity, and return. The BOE believes that of these,

Return is in most cases the third most important of the three. One rendition of the trilogy of objectives into a combined statement of official reserves management is that the objective of official reserves management should be to maximise return, subject to the maintenance of sufficient security of the assets and adequate liquidity for meeting the calls on the reserves.

In other words, return is first and foremost as long as the other objectives are also met.

The BOE's precept is an important one for investors to recognize because it suggests that central banks will invest their money with the objective of maximizing their rates of return. Increasingly this means investing in non-dollar assets. In China's case it means investing in assets that it knows it will need, as was discussed earlier in the chapter. It also means, both for China and the rest of the world, investing in currencies that are more closely aligned with its international trade. This is why China and other nations increasingly are signing bilateral agreements to transact in their respective currencies and bypass the dollar altogether. This makes complete sense; for example, China recently surpassed the United States as Brazil's biggest trading partner, so it is making less and less sense for transactions between China and Brazil to be denominated in dollars. Why can't the transactions between these countries be either the Chinese renminbi or the Brazilian real? Get the picture? The dollar is losing its reserve status slowly but surely.

No rapid loss of the dollar's reserve status is on the horizon; the reasons for this were discussed in Chapter 5, "How the Keynesian Endpoint is Changing the Global Political Landscape." Nevertheless, a gradual loss of the dollar's reserve status is underway. This means that more of the world reserve assets will be apportioned to non-dollar assets in the years ahead, just as has been the case over the past decade.

Keep in mind that the world's reserve assets are likely to continue to grow rapidly as a result of strong growth in global trade, particularly in the emerging markets. Many emerging nations in fact are pursuing growth in their reserve assets. They have two objectives in mind. First, they wish to "self-insure," which is to say they wish to guard against the potentially negative economic effects of either a sudden stop in economic growth or capital flight. These are possibilities for countries that are fully integrated in the global economic and financial system, which is to say that they are vulnerable to externalities. The Asian financial crisis in 1997 was a wakeup call to countries in the region. Many of them, especially South Korea, Indonesia, and Thailand, experienced substantial capital withdrawals that harmed their ability to service their large external debts. Reserve assets provide a buffer against such withdrawals.

The second objective of nations that pursue a strategy of building reserves is to promote domestic export growth. They do this by slowing or preventing appreciation of their domestic currencies, which they accomplish by accumulating foreign currencies, in particular, the U.S. dollar. This is the more controversial of the two objectives because when utilized it winds up harming exports in other nations, causing negative externalities. A case in point is China's manipulation of the value of its currency, which China keeps within a desired trading range by purchasing a sufficient amount of U.S. dollars to restrain the renminbi's rate of appreciation. This keeps the renminbi undervalued and thereby undercuts export growth in the rest of the world.

The accumulation of reserves by China and other export-oriented nations is thus seen as a modern form of mercantilism, sometimes called financial mercantilism, whereby a nation has an explicit industrial policy to promote economic growth through exports. Wypolsz (2007) describes a more elaborate version of mercantilism called monetary mercantilism whereby "monetary authorities wish to acquire assets that allow them to expand the money supply in order to target lending toward favored sectors or firms. In that sense monetary mercantilism is meant to serve the same growth purpose as financial mercantilism.[7]" The main risk to these strategies is that they eventually can destabilize a financial system because nations that have artificially suppressed currencies attract ever more capital, which at some point becomes too much of a good thing, either because it results in inflation or a bubble in financial or real assets.

The expansion of global trade and greater financial and economic integration thus appear to be the major underlying forces fueling the worldwide accumulation of reserves. Aizenman and Jaewoo summarize this idea by saying "growing trade openness and greater exposure to financial shocks by emerging markets go a long way towards accounting for the observed hoarding of international reserves.[8]"

To sum up, the world is for many reasons accumulating vast amounts of international reserves, and these reserves have enormous ability to influence both the financial markets and the global economy. In the past, these reserves were invested willy-nilly in the U.S. dollar, but this habit is slowly but surely being broken. Today, the world central banks, which manage the vast majority of the reserves, are seeking alternatives to the U.S. dollar, placing more significance than ever on maximizing their investment returns. Investors would be wise to follow their lead.

Benchmark Centricity Endangers Investment Portfolios

Who doesn't like to hug and be hugged? Many investors certainly do. They love the warm fuzzy feeling they get sticking with the consensus, and they do this by investing in instruments and funds that simply track indexes they are fond of, such as the S&P 500 for equities or any of the many bond indexes such as the Barclays Capital U.S. Aggregate Bond Index.

In today's changed world, investors aren't hugging teddy bears when they position their portfolios to mirror popular benchmark indexes; they're hugging grizzly bears, and they can get hurt. There are two reasons for this.

First, the indexes do not reflect the changed growth dynamic with respect to how indebted nations will perform relative to the rest of the world. This means the indexes will be suboptimal vehicles for capturing the significant investment opportunities that exist abroad. Moreover, popular benchmark indexes will fail to capture how the growth of the middle class in developing countries will affect the global output gap and hence the performance of a wide variety of asset classes, including commodities, for example. Popular benchmark indexes are also unlikely to adjust quickly enough to enable investors to adjust to the very major implications of financial repression discussed earlier in the chapter.

Second, the still-fragile economic and financial predicament that characterizes today's indebted nations increases the risks of investing in these countries, and many major indexes have not been adjusted to reflect these risks. This is a very important concept for bond investors in particular because one of the greatest risks they face is from the proliferation of government bond issuance.

Many major bond indexes such as the Barclays Capital U.S. Aggregate Bond Index are becoming increasingly exposed to government bonds, which is to say that government bonds are making up an increasing proportion of these indexes. The reason the exposure to government bonds is increasing is because many of these indexes are weighted by market capitalization. As a result, the increased issuance of U.S. Treasuries compared to other types of bonds will boost the proportion of Treasuries held by market-cap weighted indexes such as the Barclays Aggregate. Bond investors that invest to track the Barclays Aggregate therefore will find their portfolios increasingly exposed to Treasury securities. A better idea is for the indexes to be GDP weighted. In this way, investors are investing increasingly in countries that are grabbing an increasing share of the global economy, sort of like lending to people whose incomes are gaining relative to others. PIMCO's Global Advantage Index is an example of a GDP-weighted index.

Investors should also seek a more unconstrained style of investing by maximizing the flexibility of their portfolios. For bond investors, the unconstrained approach enables investors greater flexibility to toggle the many risk factors that, when managed correctly, can contribute alpha to a portfolio while minimizing risks. Flexibility should be sought to alter exposures in each of these five major risk factors:

1. Duration
2. Yield curve exposure
3. Volatility exposure
4. Credit selection
5. Country selection

To highlight the dangers of benchmark centricity, consider that the index-hugging, government-bond loving, constrained investor will have very little flexibility to navigate the very unstable and uncertain world that lies ahead. This could leave the investor with too much duration or interest rate exposure in countries where large deficits and low savings rates could eventually boost longer-term interest rates. Figure 9-16 shows the percentage allocation in the Barclays Aggregate to the various segments of the bond market. Is such a large (and growing) allocation to U.S. Treasuries the best idea for the twenty-first century? The constrained investor might also fail to capture the many opportunities that exist abroad. More than ever, investors need a "go anywhere" approach to successfully guard and grow their capital. Benchmark centricity is anything but "go anywhere." It's more like a straightjacket. Free yourself!

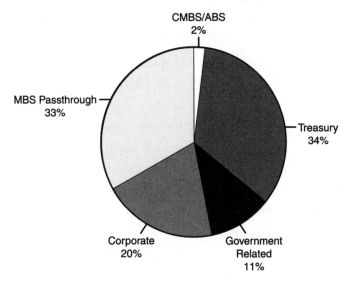

Figure 9-16 Benchmark centricity is a straightjacket for bond investors.

Source: Barclays Capital, Bloomberg

The World Has Been Turned Upside Down Financially and Economically: Find Your Inner Lewis and Clark

It is believed that before the advent of more modern means of transportation that people throughout their entire lives never ventured more than about 30 miles from where they lived. This is why when in May 1804 President Thomas Jefferson sent Meriwether Lewis and William Clark on a journey from St. Louis, Missouri, to the Pacific Ocean was called an "expedition" that became one of the most famous of all time. Twenty years earlier Jefferson had asked William Clark's brother and Revolutionary War hero George Rogers Clark to lead a cross-country expedition, but he declined. It wasn't the first or last example of a person exhibiting a home bias.

Lewis and Clark traveled about 7,000 miles during their journey, a pittance compared to how much people travel these days thanks to trains, planes, and automobiles. Yet, relative to everyone else, Lewis and Clark's expedition was a major leap forward. Sacagawea, a native American and the only woman on the expedition, was brought as an interpreter, providing great help to Lewis and Clark throughout their journey. She would wind up providing Lewis and Clark and the 29 other men who went on the journey with unexpected help when on the trip she have birth to a son, Jean Baptiste Charbonneau. She did this by softening the image the travelers cast when they confronted natives. The sight of Sacagawea and her baby quickly diffused tensions, and Sacagawea's presence facilitated communications with indigenous peoples, enabling the travelers a safer pass-through to their desired destinations, as well as the collection of "data" that helped make the journey possible.

Investors in today's upside-down world, which has seen by a titanic shift in the global balance of power economically and financially, are behooved to find their inner Lewis and Clark by dropping their home bias toward investments in their domestic markets and "exploring" investment opportunities in foreign countries. This home bias is well documented in a variety of research, including by Feldstein and Horika (1980), who find that the domestic savings and investment rates in individual countries within the OECD tends to be highly correlated despite the ability of savers to invest in foreign countries where investment returns could well exceed the returns they can achieve in their own country.[9] Other researchers, including Obstfeld and Rogoff (2000), cite the home bias in equity portfolios as one of the six major puzzles in international macroeconomics, finding very little satisfaction in the many theories that have been put forward to explain why investors are biased against investing abroad, despite convincing evidence that doing so provides a superior means of diversifying portfolios compared to concentrating investments in a single country.[10]

No longer can you, the investor, use the timeworn excuse of proclaiming you have insufficient information or roadmaps to guide you in making decisions about investing in foreign lands. Your Sacagawea is the Internet, and the plethora of information available to you to make informed judgments that will provide safe pass-through to help you on your journey to a destination that meets your investment objectives. Like Lewis and Clark you must travel to places you haven't been before. When you do this and thus subordinate fear, you will see the world as never before and thus expand your investment horizons.

Roadmap for Investing Beyond the Keynesian Endpoint

This book illuminates the major concepts that investors can use as a roadmap for investing at the Keynesian Endpoint. This chapter takes a more specific look at this roadmap, highlighting from 35,000 feet the six major investment themes to guide investors in these times. Table 9-3 describes a few additional ideas about what to expect and the rationale.

TABLE 9-3 Investing Beyond the Keynesian Endpoint

Investment Position to Take or What to Position For	Details and Rationale
Front-ends of developed-market yield curves	Policymakers will attempt to deflate their debts by promoting financial conditions that result in negative or low real interest rates, suppressing short-term interest rates at a minimum.
Steep yield curves in developed markets	Low policy rates will keep shorter-term interest rates low but boost inflation expectations, resulting in steep yield curves in high-debt developed countries. Position to benefit from maturities that have the maximum "roll down" on the yield curve. These are those securities that in a year's time (or other time frame) are likely to see their yields decline more than the yield decline realized on other maturities, resulting in price gains. For example, if a 6-year maturity yields 30 basis points more than a 5-year maturity, in a year, the 6-year maturity will age and become a 5-year maturity and its yield will approximate the yield on the 5-year, falling 30 basis points over a year's time, assuming the yield curve's shape does not change much. There might not be 30 basis points of spacing for other maturities; if there were, the 30-year bond would yield 9.0 percent (30 x 30). This is how to capture the maximum "roll down."
Floating-rate securities	When policy rates are near zero percent, there of course become more scope for rates to rise than to fall. This increases the attractiveness of floating rate instruments. Many have LIBOR-based floors, which keeps their yields up even as rates on other instruments falls.

Investment Position to Take or What to Position For	Details and Rationale
Emerging markets corporate credits	Ask yourself this question: What correlation is there between a corporate bond in a vibrant emerging economy and U.S. Treasuries? Not much is the correct answer. Emerging markets corporate credits therefore have the potential to provide significant diversification benefits as well as attractive real yields, or the yield achieved over and above inflation. Many emerging countries have both the wallet and the will to invest in their countries, and the cash flow provided by the healthiest of emerging countries is likely to be dependable, reducing the odds of default and increasing the odds of realizing the high real yields offered on many emerging corporate credits. An additional benefit for those that do not hedge their positions is the prospect of currency appreciation versus developed market currencies.
Foreign-exchange basket funded by the U.S. dollar, the euro, and the Japanese yen	Economic growth in highly indebted countries is likely to be relatively low compared to many developing markets with better initial conditions such as high savings rates, low indebtedness, current account surpluses, and favorable demographics. Use the funding currencies to purchase a basket of currencies that include the Mexican peso, the Brazilian real, the Singapore dollar, the Chinese renminbi, the Korean won, the Philippine peso, and the Indian rupiah. The objective is to achieve gains from "carry," or from holding currencies in countries whose policy rates are higher than for those achieved in the countries for the funding currencies and a gain from appreciation of the currencies against the funding currencies.

Investment Position to Take or What to Position For	Details and Rationale
Industrial commodities	Growth in exports is likely to be heavily concentrated in the export of goods. This will boost the demand for industrial materials, as will vibrant growth in the emerging markets, where the goods-producing sectors are more dominant than is the case in the developed world, where the service-producing sector grabs a large share of GDP. Industrial commodities include energy, metals, chemicals, tallow, cotton, print cloth, and rubber, among others.
Food	As the middle class grows in developing nations, they are likely to consume more food than they did when their incomes were lower, boosting the demand for agricultural products. In fact, more than half of the increase in demand for food products over the past decade can be attributed to the emerging markets. A continuation of this trend will benefit agricultural commodities directly, as well as exporters of food.
Water	Growth in the world's population, the increased consumption of food related to a growing middle class in developing countries, and increased use for electric power generation will along with other factors add to already high demands for the world's water supply.
Emerging markets equities	Relatively faster growth in emerging economies will propel earnings growth in these nations and feed gains in equities prices. The prospect of currency appreciation increases the attractiveness of emerging markets equities.
Global real estate investment trusts	Expansion of the world economy emanating from relatively rapid growth in developing countries will fuel demand for office space and boost household formation, boosting demand for shelter at a time when construction of new space in developed countries has weakened substantially. This will boost the ability of renters to increase their rates. Other forms of commercial demand will include storage and hospitality (hotels).

Investment Position to Take or What to Position For	Details and Rationale
Large-cap multinational equities	Large companies that have a large global presence are positioned well to capitalize on growth opportunities outside of the developed world. Investments in these companies therefore provide important diversification benefits not possible with smaller companies that have very little or no international presence nor any prospect for gaining one.
Alternative energy	Strains on the world's energy supply emanating from economic growth in developing countries will compel debt laden nations whose economic activity is already facing headwinds to shift to alternative forms of energy supply. Just as important, developing countries such as China will seek to preserve their economic growth stories by reducing their energy consumption per unit of GDP, driving investments in alternative energy.
Inflation-indexed securities	At the Keynesian Endpoint, many nations will use financial repression to inflate their way out of their debts. Negative real interest rates will promote acceleration in inflation in developed countries, while fast economic growth rates in developing economies will promote high rates of inflation in developing countries.
Prefer credit risk over duration from government bonds	Financial repression will pick the pockets of investors in government bonds by suppressing interest rates to levels that are either only slightly above the rate of inflation or, more likely, below it. Negative real rates of return reduce the attractiveness of government bonds compared to bonds in other segments of the $90 trillion global supermarket of bonds, which offer a yield spread over government bonds. Go shopping for safe spreads.

10

Conclusion:
The Transformation of a Century

As we contemplate our changed world and the challenges that lie ahead, consider these sentiments:

Adapt or perish, now as ever, is Nature's inexorable imperative.

—H.G. Wells

A mother's love is patient and forgiving when all others are forsaking, it never fails or falters, even though the heart is breaking.

—Helen Rice

We must never despair; our situation has been compromising before, and it has changed for the better; so I trust it will again. If difficulties arise, we must put forth new exertion and proportion our efforts to the exigencies of the times.

—George Washington

In February 1936, photographer Dorothea Lange sought to capture the desperate plight of the millions of migrant workers who sought to flee the Dust Bowl and the barren lands of the Great Plains, which were smitten by years of draught and dust storms at a time when there was already great suffering in the United States. On a pea farm in California, Lange sees a mother and her seven children sitting in a makeshift and torn open tent atop dried mud, their despondent faces covered with dust, their clothing soiled, their hands darkened with muck. As Lange draws yards nearer, two of the three children draped on their mother's shoulders turn their heads away from Lange to the back of the tent, as if shamed. Without prompting, the woman, Florence Owens Thompson, tells of her plight, seeming to hope her story will ease her family's suffering. The sad-faced woman tells Lange she and her children were living on vegetables from the fields upon which they labored, as well as on the meat of dead birds that the children had killed.

Figure 10-1 "Migrant Mother"

Source: Library of Congress; http://www.loc.gov/pictures/resource/fsa.8b29516/Source: Library of Congress

Lange snaps five photos in all, one of which becomes an iconic symbol of both the Great Depression and the Dust Bowl. Known as "Migrant Mother," the photo brings greater awareness to the plight of the 2.5 million who migrated from the drought-stricken midwest in what remains the largest migration ever to occur in the United States over the time in which it occurred.

Figure 10-2 Protestors at the Hellenic Parliament in Athens, Greece, June 2011

Source: bigstockphoto.com (http://www.bigstockphoto.com/image-20885534/stock-photo-greek-protests-at-parliament-square-in-athens)

In the same month, John Maynard Keynes publishes a book titled, *The General Theory of Employment, Interest, and Money*. It offers a policy prescription that Keynes believes will increase employment and ease the hardship that millions of people are suffering through the Great Depression. Hardship for mankind is nothing new, and people for ages have shown a remarkable ability to adapt to even the most trying of circumstance. This puts the suffering of the Great Depression in its proper context. Nevertheless, modern society endeavors to ensure the dignity of its citizens and to limit human suffering. This creates rationale for government programs as well as for deficit spending. The Keynesian philosophy is transformational, and it feeds the evolution of modern society, including the United States, which moves away from the fiscal prudence it had shown since it enacted the Sinking Fund Act of 1795 to establish piggybanks to repay the national debt.

Politicians and the beneficiaries of their fiscal illusions for the past 80 years abused the newfound economic philosophy, relentlessly and dangerously pursuing the use of debt for self-aggrandizement. Today, the citizens of indebted nations bear a heavy burden and must begin repaying the debts. It is a Herculean task because the debts are mountainous. Yet there is no choice because the Keynesian Endpoint means that indebted nations have tapped the last balance sheet and can no longer use debt to attempt to solve their problems.

The financial crisis has shown that the use of debt to ease the suffering of people went too far. Consumers also went too far in using debt to fulfill their primal needs and their desire to display status and power and to "keep up with the Joneses." Nevertheless, those who must now bear the burden of the solution to the world's debt problems are fighting to preserve the status quo, fearing that any rollback of government spending will cause them to suffer. The problem is that their definition of suffering is enormously different from the suffering that ignited the Keynesian philosophy in the first place.

No member of modern society should ever live as the Migrant Mother did, living in a tattered tent and eating dead birds killed by her children. Government, in other words, should indeed endeavor to maintain the dignity of people and provide for at least a minimal standard of living. The people of the world must nonetheless recognize that there are limits to what government can do and that what remains of a nation's tax receipts after it has done all it can to maintain the sanctity of human existence should be invested to help build a society that benefits all citizens.

This is the transformation that is now underway.

This is therefore not an endpoint but a beginning.

Endnotes

Introduction

1. Keynes, John Maynard, *The General Theory of Employment, Interest and Money* (New York: First Harvest/Harcourt Edition, 1964), 116.

2. Ibid., 117.

Chapter 1

1. Carmen Reinhart and Kenneth Rogoff, "A Decade of Debt," Centre for Economic Policy Research, *Discussion Paper No. 8310*, April 2011.

2. Charles Roxburgh and team, "Debt and deleveraging: The global credit bubble and its economic consequences," McKinsey Global Institute, January 2010.

3. National Population Projections, U.S. Census Bureau; http://www.census.gov/population/www/pop-profile/natproj.html.

4. R.D. Richards, *The Early History of Banking in England* (London: P.S. King), Chapter 3; and "Economic History: Supplement to the Economic Journal" II, 1930, 45–62.

5. John M. Keynes, "Economic Possibilities for Our Grandchildren," 1930. Reprinted in *Essays in Persuasion* (New York: W.W. Norton, 1963), 358–73.

6. John M. Keynes, *The General Theory of Employment* (New York: First Harvest/Harcourt Edition, 1964), 113.

7. Ibid, 118.

8. Alan Greenspan, "Activism," *International Finance* 14 (2011): 165–182.

9. Ibid.

10. Ibid.

11. Ibid.

12. Manmohan S. Kumar and team, "Fiscal Rules—Anchoring Expectations for Sustainable Public Finances," *IMF* December (2009).

Chapter 2

1. Abraham Maslow, "A Theory of Human Motivation," *Psychological Review* (1943): 370–396.

2. Ibid.

3. Thorstein Veblen, *The Theory of the Leisure Class* (New York: Macmillan, 1899).

4. Ibid.

5. James Duesenberry, "Income, Saving, and the Theory of Consumer Behaviors," *Harvard University Press* (1949).

6. Veblen, 1899.

7. Maslow, 370–396.

8. *Diagnostic and Statistical Manual of Mental Disorders* (American Psychiatric Association Pub, 2000).

9. Duesenberry, 1949.

10. Sigmund Freud, *New Introductory Lectures on Psychoanalysis* (New York: W.W. Norton, 1965).

11. Ibid.

12. Ibid.

13. Henry Murray, *Explorations in Personality* (New York: Oxford University Press, 1938).

14. Frederick Winslow Taylor, *The Principles of Scientific Management* (New York: Harper & Brothers, 1911).

15. Ibid.

16. Ibid.

17. Veblen, 1899.

18. Ibid.

19. Paul Nystrom, *Economics of Fashion* (New York: The Ronald Press Company, 1928).

20. Veblen, 1899.

21. Gordon Phillips, *Seven Centuries of Light: The Tallow Chandler Company* (Cambridge: Book Production Consultants, 1999).

22. Carolina Reid, "Sought or Sold? Social Embeddedness and Consumer Decisions in the Mortgage Market," Federal Reserve Bank of San Francisco, *Working Paper Series* (2010).

23. Mark Granovetter, "The Impact of Social Structure of Economic Outcomes," *The Journal of Economic Perspectives* (Volume 19, Number 1—Winter 2005).

24. Scott W. Frame and Lawrence White, "Technological Change, Financial Innovation, and Diffusion in Banking," Federal Reserve Bank of Atlanta, *Working Paper Series* (2009).

25. Karen Dynan and Donald Kohn, "The Rise in U.S. Household Indebtedness: Causes and Consequences," Federal Reserve Board, *Finance and Economic Discussion Series* (2007).

26. James W. Kolari, Donald R. Fraser, and Ali Anari, "The Effects of Securitization on Mortgage Market Yields: A Cointegration Analysis," *Real Estate Economics* December (1998).

27. Steven Todd, "The Effects of Securitization on Consumer Mortgage Costs," *Real Estate Economics* (2000).

28. Filipa Sa, Pascal Towbin, and Tomasz Wieladek, "Low Interest Rates and Housing Booms: The Role of Capital Inflows, Monetary Policy and Financial Innovation," Bank of England, *Working Papers* (2011).

29. Scott and White, 2009.

30. Emine Boz and Enrique Mendoza, "Financial Innovation, the Discovery of Risk, and the U.S. Credit Crisis," International Monetary Fund, *IMF Working Paper* (2010).

31. Enrique Mendoza and Marco Terrones, "An Anatomy of Credit Booms: Evidence from Macro Aggregates and Micro Data," NBER, *Working Paper* (2008).

32. John Muellbauer, "Wealth Effects: Housing, Credit and Consumer Expenditure," Federal Reserve Bank of Kansas City, *Proceedings* (2007).

33. John Benjamin, Peter Chinloy, and G. Donald Jud, "Real Estate Versus Financial Wealth in Consumption," *Journal of Real Estate Finance and Economics* (2004).

34. Alan Greenspan and James Kennedy, "Sources and Uses of Equity Extracted from Homes," Federal Reserve Board, *Finance and Economics Discussion Series* (2007).

35. Marques Benton, Stephan Meier, and Charles Sprener, "Overborrowing and Undersaving: Lessons and Policy Implications from Research in Behavioral Economics," Federal Reserve Bank of Boston, *Discussion Paper* (2007).

36. Ibid.

37. Sydney Ludvigson, "Consumption and Credit: A Model of Time-Varying Liquidity Constraints," *Review of Economics and Statistics* (1999).

38. Reuven Glick and Kevin Lansing, "Consumers and the Economy, Part I: Household Credit and Personal Saving," Federal Reserve Bank of San Francisco, *Economic Letter*, 2011

Chapter 3

1. Leo Troy, *The New Unionism* (Fairfax, VA: George Mason University Press, 2004).

2. Eileen Norcross, "Public Sector Unionism: A Review," George Mason University, *Working Paper*, 2011.

3. Troy, 80.

4. Wallace E. Oates, *On the Nature and Measurement of Fiscal Illusion: A Survey* (Canberra: Australian National University Press, 1988).

5. Amilcare Puviani, *"Teoria della illusione Finanziaria,"* Palermo, 1903.

6. James M. Buchanan, *Fiscal Theory and Political Economy* (Chapel Hill: The University of North Carolina Press, 1960).

7. Richard E. Wagner, "From the Politics of Illusion to the High Cost of Regulation," *Public Interest Institute at Iowa Wesleyan College* 3:8 (2001).

8. James M. Buchanan, *Public Finance in Democratic Process: Fiscal Institutions and Individual Choice* (Chapel Hill: The University of North Carolina Press, 1967).

9. Paulo Reis Mourao, "Sins of the Older: The Case of Fiscal Illusion in Democracies" University of Minho, Portugal, 2010.

10. Oates, Wallace E., "On the Nature and Measurement of Fiscal Illusion: A Survey," Australian National University Press, 1988.

11. Buchanan, 1967.

12. Milton Friedman, "The Limitations of Tax Limitation." *Policy Review* Summer (1978): 7–14.

13. Ronald Reagan, Presidential debate, September 21, 1980.

14. David Ricardo, "Essay on the Funding System" in *The Works of David Ricardo, with a Notice of the Life and Writings of the Author* by J.R. McCulloch (London: John Murray, 1888).

15. Robert J. Barro, "Are Government Bonds Net Wealth?" *Journal of Political Economy* Nov./Dec. (1974): 1095–1117.

16. Adam Smith, *An Inquiry into the Nature and Causes of the Wealth of Nations* (originally published 1776).

17. J. Tobin, "Essays in Economics," *Macroeconomics* Vol. 1. Amsterdam: North-Holland (1971).

18. Wallace Oates, "Lump-Sum Intergovernmental Grants Have Prices Effects," in *Fiscal Federalism and Grant-in-Aid*, eds. Peter Mieszkowski and William Oakland (Washington, D.C.: Urban Institute, 1979), 23–29.

19. Ibid.

20. J. Patrick O'Brien and Yeung-Nan Shieh, "Utility Functions and Fiscal Illusion from Grants," *National Tax Journal* 43:2 (1990): 201–205.

21. James M. Buchanan and Richard E. Wagner, *Democracy in Deficit: The Political Legacy of Lord Keynes* (New York: Academic Press, 1977).

22. The Center for Public Integrity, http://www.iwatchnews.org/2010/06/10/2654/white-house-visitor-log-too-big-some-spreadsheets, accessed June 11, 2010.

23. Ibid.

24. See http://www.nypost.com/p/news/opinion/opedcolumnists/item_cnW7XbCa9yS3ONgARv9gJL.

25. See http://articles.latimes.com/2009/may/11/local/me-cal-healthcare11.

26. See http://www.nytimes.com/roomfordebate/2011/02/18/the-first-blow-against-public-employees/fdr-warned-us-about-public-sector-unions.

27. Eileen Norcross, "Public Sector Unionism: A Review" (Working Paper, George Mason University, 2011).

28. Joseph D. Reid and Michael M. Kurth, "The Determinants of Public Sector Bargaining Legislation: Comment," *Public Choice* 66 (1990): 177–182.

29. Norcross, 2011.

30. Ibid.

31. Chris Edwards, "Public-Sector Unions," *Tax & Budget* No. 61 (March 2010).

32. Reynolds, M. "Making America Poorer: The Cost of Labor Law," Washington: Cato Institute, 1987.

33. Holcombe, Randall G. and Gwartney, James D., "Unions, Economic Freedom, and Growth," Cato Institute, *Cato Journal*, 30:1, 2010.

34. Norcross, Eileen, page 13.

35. Troy, Leo, "The New Unionism," George Mason University Press, 2004.

36. Norcross, Eileen, page 15.

37. Edwards, Chris, "Public-Sector Unions," Cato Institute, *Tax & Budget*, No. 61, March 2010.

38. Holcombe and Gwartney, 2010.

39. See http://www.nytimes.com/2009/11/04/us/04transit.html.

40. See www.kasiseredu.org.

41. See http://www.standardandpoors.com/ratings/articles/en/us/?assetID=1245302232522.

42. Joseph A. Narens and Christian Stracke, "Muni Market Bargains? A Closer Look at Municipal Debt, Deficits, and Pensions," PIMCO, February 2011 (see http://www.pimco.com/EN/Insights/Pages/MuniMarketBargainsACloserLookatMunicipalDebtDeficitsandPensions.aspx).

43. Ibid.

44. See http://www.agingstats.gov/agingstatsdotnet/Main_Site/Data/2010_Documents/Docs/OA_2010.pdf.

45. See http://www.standardandpoors.com/ratings/articles/en/us/?assetID=1245302232522.

46. Buchanan and Wagner, 1977.

47. Ibid.

48. Ibid.

49. Ibid.

50. See http://www.nytimes.com/2011/06/24/nyregion/nj-legislature-moves-to-cut-benefits-for-public-workers.html?pagewanted=1&_r=1&ref=christopherjchristie.

51. Ibid.

52. Ibid.

53. Ibid.

Chapter 4

1. Joseph Gagnon, Matthew Raskin, Julie Remache, and Brian Sack, "Large-Scale Asset Purchases by the Federal Reserve: Did they Work?" *Federal Reserve Bank of New York Economic Policy Review* (April 2011).

2. J. Tobin, "Liquidity Preference as Behavior Towards Risk," *Review of Economic Studies* 25, No. 2 (February1958): 65–86.

3. J. Tobin, "A General Equilibrium Approach to Monetary Theory," *Journal of Money, Credit, and Banking* 1, No. 1 (February 1969): 15–29.

Chapter 5

1. See http://www.buffalonews.com/topics/chris-lee/special-election/article432808.ece.

2. Ibid.

3. Ibid.

4. Congressional Budget Office.

5. International Monetary Fund, report on the Currency Composition of Official Foreign Exchange Reserves (COFER): http://www.imf.org/external/np/sta/cofer/eng/index.htm.

6. CIA World Factbook; www.cia.gov.

7. See the OECD report, "Social Assistance in OECD Countries," 1996, http://research.dwp.gov.uk/asd/asd5/rrep047.pdf.

8. www.g20.org and International Monetary Fund at http://www.imf.org/external/np/sec/memdir/members.aspx.

Chapter 6

1. U.S. Census Bureau.

2. See http://www.ssa.gov/oact/progdata/fundFAQ.html.

3. Social Security Administration, "Annual Report on the Financial Status of the Social Security Program," August 2010.

4. Mary Meeker, "USA Inc., a Basic Summary of America's Financial Statements," February 2011.

5. Ibid.

6. John Maynard Keynes, *The General Theory of Employment, Interest and Money* (New York: Harcourt, Brace & World, 1936).

7. Ethan Ilzetzki, Enrique G. Mendoza, and Carlos A. Végh, "How Big (Small) are Fiscal Multipliers?" (Working Paper, IMF, March 2011).

8. Ibid.

9. Congressional Budget Office, "The Economic Effects of Federal Spending on Infrastructure and Other Investments" (June 1998).

10. Adam Smith, An Inquiry Into The Nature and Causes of The Wealth of Nations, (New York: Modern Library, 2000).

11. Daniel J. Wilson, "Fiscal Spending Jobs Multipliers: Evidence from the 2009 American Recovery and Reinvestment Act" (Working Paper Series, Federal Reserve Bank of San Francisco, February 2011).

12. Ibid.

13. See: http://mobility.tamu.edu/ums/report/congestion_cost.pdf.

14. American Society of Civil Engineers, "2009 Report Card for America's Infrastructure," (March 25, 2009): www.asce.org/reportcard.

15. Organisation for Economic Co-operation and Development "Main Science and Technology Indicators," OECD Science, Technology, and R&D Statistics database (2010): http://dx.doi.org/10.1787/data-00182-en.

16. Ben Bernanke, "Promoting Research and Development: The Government's Role," delivered at Georgetown University at a conference titled "New Building Blocks for Jobs and Economic Growth," May 2011.

17. Joseph Schumpeter, *Capitalism, Socialism, and Democracy* (New York: Harper Perennial Modern Classics, 2008 reprint).

18. Theodore W. Schultz, "Investment in Human Capital," *The American Economic Review* 51, No. 1 (March 1961): 1–17.

19. Named after Joseph Schumpeter (1883–1950) who was the originator of the theory that economic growth was strongly influenced by cycles of innovation. Northwestern economist Joel Mokyr devised the phrase in honor of Schumpeter, seeking to give a title to economic growth that is attributable to innovations and increased knowledge. Joel Mokyr, *The Lever of Riches* (New York, NY: Oxford University Press, 1990), 6.

20. Edward F. Denison, *Trends in American Economic Growth, 1929–1982* (Washington, DC: Brookings Institution, 1985).

21. Nicolo Machiavelli, "Il Principe," written c. 1505.

Chapter 7

1. Milton Friedman, "The Permanent Income Hypothesis: Comment," *American Economic Review* 48 (1957): 990–991.

2. James Duesenberry, "Income, Saving and the Theory of Consumer Behavior" (Cambridge, MA: Harvard University Press, 1949).

3. Francisco Alvarez-Cuadrado and Ngo Van Long, "The Relative Income Hypothesis" (Department of Economics, McGill University, March 2009).

4. David Neumark and Andrew Postlewaite, "Relative Income Concerns and the Rise in Married Women's Employment," *Journal of Public Economics* 70 (1998): 157–183.

5. Matthew 19:23–24.

6. Richard Easterlin, "Does Economic Growth Improve the Human Lot? Some Empirical Evidence," in *Nations and Households in Economic Growth: Essays in Honor of Moses Abramowitz,* eds. Paul A. David and Melvin W. Reder (University of Pennsylvania: Academic Press, 1974).

7. Easterlin, 1974 (http://graphics8.nytimes.com/images/2008/04/16/business/Easterlin1974.pdf.)

8. H. Cantril, *The Pattern of Human Concerns* (Rutgers University Press, 1965).

9. James Braid, *Neurypnology* (London: John Churchill, 1843).

10. Bernheim Hippolyte, *Hypnosis & Suggestion in Psychotherapy* (1884): 15–16.

11. J. Karremans, W. Stroebe, and J. Claus, "Beyond Vicary's Fantasies: The Impact of Subliminal Priming and Brand Choice,". *Journal of Experimental Social Psychology* 42:6 (2006): 792–798.

12. Karremans, Stroebe, and Claus, 2006.

13. Luciano Fadiga, Leonardo Fogassi, Vittorio Gallese, Giuseppe di Pellegrino, and Giacomo Rizzolatti, "Understanding Motor Events: A Neurophysiological Study," *Experimental Brain Research* 91 (1992): 176–180.

14. S. McClure, D. Laibson, G. Lowenstein, and J. Cohen, "Separate Neural Systems Value Immediate and Delayed Monetary Rewards," *Science* 306:5695 (October 2004).

15. McClure, Laibson, Lowenstein, and Cohen, 2004.

16. Baba Shiv, and Alexander Fedorikhan, "Heart and Mind in Conflict: The Interplay of Affect and Cognition in Consumer Decision Making," *Journal of Consumer Research* (1999).

17. Board of Governors of the Federal Reserve, "Report to the Congress on Practices of the Consumer Credit Industry in Soliciting and Extending Credit and their Effects on Consumer Debt and Insolvency," June 2006.

18. John Rae, *Statement of Some New Principles on the Subject of Political Economy, Exposing the Fallacies of the System of Free Trade, and of Some Other Doctrines Maintained in the "Wealth of Nations"* (New York: A.M. Kelley, 1834/1964).

19. Marco Battaglini, Roland Benabou, and Jean Tirole, "Self-Control in Peer Groups" (Princeton University, October 2001).

20. David Laibson, Andrea Repetto, and Jeremy Tobacman, "A Debt Puzzle" (NBER Working Paper Series, 2001).

21. R.H. Thaler and S. Benartzi, "Save More Tomorrow: Using Behavioral Economics to Increase Employee Savings," *Journal of Political Economy* 112:1 (2004): 164–187.

Chapter 8

1. Franco Modigliani and Richard H. Brumberg, "Utility Analysis and the Consumption Function: An Interpretation of Cross-Section Data," in *Post-Keynesian Economics*, ed. Kenneth K. Kurihara (New Brunswick, NJ: Rutgers University Press, 1954), 388–436.

2. James S. Duesenberry, *Income, Saving and the Theory of Consumer Behaviour* (Cambridge: Harvard University Press, 1949).

3. John Maynard Keynes, *The General Theory of Employment, Interest and Money* (New York: Harcourt, Brace & World, 1936).

4. Franco Modigliani, "Life Cycle, Individual Thrift, and the Wealth of Nations," *The American Economic Review* 76: 3 (1986).

5. Robert Barro, "Are Government Bonds Net Wealth?" *Journal of Political Economy* 82 (1974).

6. See www.recovery.gov.

7. Milton Friedman, "A Theory of the Consumption Function" (Princeton University Press, 1957).

8. Alan Greenspan, "Activism," *International Finance* 14:1 (2011): 165–182.

9. James M. Buchanan, "Public Debt and Capital Formation," in *Taxation and the Deficit Economy: Fiscal Policy and Capital Formation in the United States*, ed. Dwight Lee (San Francisco: Pacific Research Institute for Public Policy, 1986), 177–94. Reprinted in *Debt and Taxes*, Vol. 14 of "The Collected Works of James M. Buchanan," (Indianapolis, IN: Liberty Fund, 2000): 365–382.

10. James M. Buchanan, "Budgetary Bias in Post-Keynesian Politics: The Erosion and Potential Replacement of Fiscal Norms." In "Deficits," eds. James M. Buchanan, Charles K. Rowley, and Robert D. Tollison (New York: Blackwell, 1987), 180–98. Reprinted in *Debt and Taxes*, Vol. 14 of "The Collected Works of James M. Buchanan," (Indianapolis, IN: Liberty Fund, 2000), 455–472.

11. James M. Buchanan, "Clarifying Confusion About the Balanced Budget Amendment," *National Tax Journal* 48: 3 (1995).

12. James M. Buchanan and Richard E. Wagner, *Democracy in Deficit: The Political Legacy of Lord Keynes* (New York: Academic Press, 1977).

13. Ibid.

14. Jerry H. Tempelman, "James M. Buchanan on Public Debt Finance," *The Independent Review* 11:23 (2007).

15. James M. Buchanan, "Public Principles of Public Debt: A Defense and Restatement" Vol. 2 (1958) of "The Collected Works of James M. Buchanan," (Indianapolis, IN: Liberty Fund, 1999).

16. Jerry H. Tempelman, "James M. Buchanan on Public Debt Finance," *The Independent Review* 11:23 (2007).

17. James M. Buchanan, "Public Debt and Capital Formation," in *Taxation and the Deficit Economy: Fiscal Policy and Capital Formation in the United States*, ed. Dwight Lee (San Francisco: Pacific Research Institute for Public Policy, 1986), 177–94. Reprinted in *Debt and Taxes*, Vol. 14 of "The Collected Works of James M. Buchanan," (Indianapolis, IN: Liberty Fund, 2000): 365–382.

Chapter 9

1. Alan Greenspan and James Kennedy, "Sources and Uses of Equity Extracted from Homes," Federal Reserve Board, *Finance and Economics Discussion Series* (2007).

2. Constantino Bresciani-Turroni, *The Economics of Inflation, a Study of Currency Depreciation in Post-War Germany* (Great Britain: Unwin Brothers Ltd, 1937), 335.

3. Irving Fisher, "The Debt-Deflation Theory of Great Depressions," *Econometrica* (1933): 337–357.

4. Hyman Minsky, "Stabilizing an Unstable Economy" (Yale University Press, 1986).

5. Sydney Homer and Richard Sylla, *A History of Interest Rates* (Hoboken: John Wiley & Sons, Inc., 2005).

6. John Nugee, "Foreign Exchange Reserves Management," The Bank of England, *Handbooks Central Banking* 19, 2011).

7. Charles Wyplosz, "The Foreign Exchange Reserves: Business as Usual?" *Workshop on Debt, Finance and Emerging Issues in Financial Integration*, United Nations Department of Economic and Social Affairs and Commonwealth Secretariat (March 2007).

8. Joshua Aizenman and Jaewoo Lee, "International Reserves: Precautionary versus Mercantilist Views, Theory and Evidence" (Working Paper, IMF, 2005).

9. Martin Feldstein and Charles Horioka, "Domestic Saving and International Capital Flows," *Economic Journal* 90 (358) (1980): 314–329.

10. Maurice Obstfeld and Kenneth Rogoff, "The Six Major Puzzles in International Macroeconomics: Is There a Common Cause?" from Ben Bernanke and Kenneth Rogoff, *NBER Macroeconomics Annual 2000*, 15 (The MIT Press, 2000): 339–390.

INDEX